D0930530

ELOQUENT ZEN

ELOQUENT ZEN

DAITŌ AND
EARLY JAPANESE ZEN

Kenneth Kraft

UNIVERSITY OF HAWAII PRESS · HONOLULU

© 1992 by Kenneth Kraft
All rights reserved
Printed in the United States of America

97 96 95 94 93 92   5 4 3 2 1

Library of Congress Cataloging-in-Publication Data
Kraft, Kenneth, 1949–
Eloquent Zen : Daitō and early Japanese Zen / Kenneth Kraft.
p.   cm.
Includes bibliographical references and index.
ISBN 0-8248-1383-9 (alk. paper)
1. Myōchō, 1282-1337.   2. Priests, Zen—Japan—Biography.
I. Title.
BQ972.Y587K7   1992
294.3'927'092—dc20
[B]   91-44864
CIP

University of Hawaii Press books are printed
on acid-free paper and meet the guidelines for
permanence and durability of the Council on
Library Resources

Designed by Ken Miyamoto

LIBRARY
ALMA COLLEGE
ALMA, MICHIGAN

CONTENTS

ILLUSTRATIONS

ACKNOWLEDGMENTS

I AM deeply grateful to the many people who contributed to this book. Yanagida Seizan patiently guided my initial work on primary texts. Hirano Sōjō suggested new directions through his own research. Kobori Nanrei, Ozeki Sōen, Matsunaga Gozan, and other abbots of Daitokuji temple graciously provided access to Daitokuji's archives. Martin Collcutt and Marius Jansen contributed scholarly expertise and enthusiasm to every phase of the project. Stephen Berg assisted with translations of poetry, and Alan Sponberg helped to focus my attention on issues of interpretation. Sōhō Machida generously shared his first-hand knowledge of monastic Zen. Sōgen Hori commented astutely and at length on several versions of the manuscript. Trudy Kraft offered steady encouragement and sound advice, as always.

I am indebted to the Japan Foundation for providing two opportunities to conduct extended research in Kyoto. A fellowship from the Edwin O. Reischauer Institute for Japanese Studies, Harvard University, supported further work on the manuscript.

Grateful acknowledgment is made to Daitokuji for permission to reproduce two portraits and three calligraphic works from the temple archives; and to the Eisei Bunko Foundation for permission to reproduce a portrait of Daitō by Zen master Hakuin.

1

ENTERING THE WORLD
OF DAITŌ

A great man of the past is hard to know,
because his legend, which is a sort of friendly
caricature, hides him like a disguise. . . .
And when a man is so great that not one but
half a dozen legends are familiar to all who
recognize his name, he becomes once more a
mystery, almost as if he were an unknown.

JACQUES BARZUN*

His eyes glare angrily. His mouth turns
down in scowling wrath. He is an enemy of
buddhas and patriarchs, an arch-enemy of
Zen monks. If you face him, he delivers a
blow. If you turn from him, he emits an
angry roar. Bah! Who can tell whether the
blind old monk painted here is host or guest?
But never mind that, Inzen. Just bow to the
floor before your mind begins to turn.

DAITŌ, ON HIS OWN PORTRAIT**

ACCORDING TO the Zen lore of medieval Japan, when a young monk named Myōchō attained enlightenment, he was told by his teacher to ripen his understanding in obscurity for twenty years. Myōchō went to the capital, Kyoto, and joined the crowd of beggars living along the banks of the Kamo River, near the Gojō Bridge. Barefoot and unshaven, wearing only a tattered robe and a cloak of rough straw, he endured the cold and hunger of twenty winters as his insight deepened. Rumors about an uncommon mendicant began to circulate, even within the walls of the imperial compound. One day the Emperor himself went down to the riverbank to investigate. When he challenged the assembled beggars with a paradoxical command, one of them boldly rephrased the paradox and tossed it back to the Emperor. Myōchō's identity was thereby revealed. The Emperor became the monk's patron and personal disciple, and together they proceeded to build a great Zen temple.

1

Remarkably, many elements of this tale have a historical basis. Myōchō (1282–1337), better known by his honorary title Daitō, is one of the most important figures in Japanese Zen. The exhortation to pursue twenty years of postenlightenment cultivation survives on a scroll written by his teacher. Daitō did train in relative seclusion for at least ten years at a small Kyoto temple in the vicinity of the Gojō Bridge, and several contemporary scholars continue to believe that he spent at least some of his time among the beggars in the area.[1] Not just one but two emperors, Hanazono (1297–1348) and Go-Daigo (1288–1339), actively supported Daitō, and Hanazono became a serious student of Zen. Daitokuji, the temple that Daitō founded with his patrons' assistance, remains influential today.

Daitō appeared at a critical point in the development of Japanese Zen, as leadership was passing into the hands of native Japanese monks. During the preceding hundred years, Ch'an (Chinese Zen) had been brought to Japan by Japanese pilgrims and émigré Chinese masters. Daitō's own teacher Nanpo Jōmyō (Daiō Kokushi, 1235–1308) trained in China for eight years, yet Daitō never attempted the trip himself. Like others of his generation, he believed that authentic Zen could also be found in Japan. This newfound confidence was expressed in a fellow monk's pronouncement that sending Japanese pilgrims to China for spiritual guidance was like "trading Japanese gold for Chinese gravel."[2]

Daitō not only reflected the cultural and spiritual ethos of his era; he also had a lasting impact on the development of Zen. Among the Zen monks who did not travel to China, he was the first to establish a major monastery. In his teachings he clarified the essential components of an assimilated Japanese Zen. He took the lead in applying an unfamiliar commentarial genre, capping phrases, to the classic texts of Ch'an. Daitō also came to be seen as a paradigmatic embodiment of the Zen life. His insistence on the primacy of enlightenment, his severity in the training of monks, his own period of postenlightenment cultivation, and his exemplary death have long been equated with the highest ideals of the Rinzai Zen tradition. The great Zen master Hakuin (1686–1769) confirmed posterity's assessment when he praised Daitō in the Zen manner as "Japan's most poisonous flower."[3]

Daitō's lineage eventually became the dominant branch of Japanese Rinzai Zen; most (if not all) of today's Rinzai masters regard themselves as his spiritual descendants. Monks continue to undergo rigorous training at Daitokuji, and Daitō's "Final Admonitions" are chanted daily in Rinzai monasteries throughout the country. The capping-phrase exercise that Daitō helped to bring to fulfillment now plays a central role in the koan training of Rinzai monks. When Daitō's 650th death anniversary was commemorated at Daitokuji in 1983, Emperor Shōwa granted the master a new title, and over three thousand guests attended a week of solemn ceremonies.[4]

Contemporary commentators reaffirm Daitō's prominence. Isshū Miura and Ruth Sasaki single out the *Record of Daitō* as the "most important" of the early Japanese Zen discourse records.[5] Yanagida Seizan believes that Daitō "marks the beginning of koan Zen in Japan."[6] D. T. Suzuki accords "an important place in the history of Zen thought and literature" to one of Daitō's capping-phrase commentaries.[7] Ogisu Jundō exalts the master as "the highest peak of the Zen world in our country."[8] Heinrich Dumoulin places Daitō alongside the great Ch'an masters: "With Daitō, the process of transplanting Zen from China is complete; the Japanese masters have themselves equaled the heights of their Chinese prototypes."[9] Despite such lofty estimates of Daitō's significance, an inclusive study of Daitō's life and teachings has yet to appear in Japanese, and he remains virtually unknown in the West.[10]

Zen's Transmission to Japan

The period during which Zen took root in Japan lasted nearly two hundred years, from the late twelfth century through the mid-fourteenth century. Monks from Japan braved the perils of sea travel and endured the hardships of life in a foreign country to seek Ch'an in China, while Chinese masters made similar sacrifices to emigrate to Japan. Kakua (1143–1182), the first Japanese monk to encounter a Ch'an master in China, returned home in 1175. The last Japanese pilgrim to transmit Ch'an teachings, Daisetsu Sonō (1313–1377), completed his travels in 1358. The two endpoints delineate an eventful era of religious and cultural transmission that has decisively influenced the development of Japanese civilization.

Daitō qualifies as a pioneer of Japanese Zen even though he lived during the latter part of this period. He pursued a public career as a Zen master when that role was still relatively undefined, he grappled with Ch'an texts that remained alien to most of his peers, and he made his mark on an institution that had previously been dominated by émigré Chinese masters. Though Zen scholars have not adopted precise periodization, early Japanese Zen roughly parallels the Kamakura era (1185–1333), and medieval Japanese Zen is associated with the Muromachi period (1338–1573). Daitō died in 1337, at the point of transition between these two eras.

Originally, Zen was quite foreign to the Japanese—it began as an imported sect with unfamiliar practices, doctrines, language, architecture, and monastic organization. The monks who struggled to master and promulgate this new tradition were compelled to identify its essential features, for themselves as well as others. The primary criterion of authenticity in Ch'an/Zen, regardless of cultural setting, is enlightenment. Yet the discourse of early Japanese Zen reveals that the matter did not end there: in many cases, neither enlightenment nor authenticity was self-evident. For example, if an "enlightened" teacher violated moral precepts or lacked a formal certificate, could he nonetheless be a real Zen master? Those who tackled such questions also recognized that the more they spoke of "enlightenment," the more they tended to reify and obscure it (a caveat we too must bear in mind). Daitō's style of teaching and practice reflects an emerging consensus in regard to these and other central issues, a refinement forged from the ambiguities and fissures that had characterized earlier phases of Japanese Zen.

Like the concept of enlightenment, the word "Zen" may begin to imply something monolithic and unchanging, but the term is best regarded as a shorthand for a continuously evolving spiritual and historical tradition that varies considerably from one context to another. The same written character is pronounced *ch'an* in Chinese and *zen* in Japanese. Although certain continuities justify the use of "Zen" or "Ch'an/Zen" to refer inclusively to both cultural variants, from a historical standpoint it is advantageous to distinguish between Ch'an and Zen. This terminological point did not concern the Japanese pioneers, however. Not only did the same character refer equally to Ch'an and Zen, but the monks believed they were being faithful to the tradition they inherited. Gaps in our knowledge of Ch'an in the Southern Sung (1127–1279) and Yüan (1260–1368) periods make it difficult to contrast Chinese precedents with Japanese reformulations, but it is clear that new interpretations were part of the transmission process. For example, some elements that the Japanese identified with authentic Ch'an were common forms of Sung Buddhism.[11] Rather than attempting comparisons with these Chinese antecedents, this study focuses on the ways that Ch'an/Zen was conceived and experienced by the Japanese. Daitō's avoidance of a trip to China extended his distance from anterior Chinese models. Whether or not he was conscious of his role, he represents an important step in the indigenization of Japanese Zen.

Daitō and Capping Phrases

The pioneers of Zen in Japan were compelled to respond to a vast corpus of texts inherited from China and India. Buddhist sutras, treatises, and commentaries introduced during earlier periods were already familiar, but the koan collections, discourse records, and biographies of Ch'an were new. Avidly sought by the early Japanese pilgrims, these novel Ch'an texts were rapidly incorporated into Japanese Zen. An apt symbol of the transmission process is the traditional claim that the Zen monk Dōgen Kigen (1200–1253) spent his last night in China making a complete copy of the *Blue Cliff Record (Pi-yen lu)*, a seminal koan collection.

Whether or not Dōgen accomplished such a task in one night, many more nights were surely devoted to the problems associated with the interpretation of Ch'an/Zen texts. Though enlightenment was not to be found in the words of any text, even a Ch'an or Zen one, a text could still be infused with enlightenment. Someone with the "Dharma eye" was supposed to have the ability to ascertain the depth of insight represented by a sermon, a dialogue, a poem, or even a single phrase. Here the Japanese practitioners confronted knotty hermeneutical issues close to the heart of Zen. For example, what constitutes an authentic reading of a Ch'an/Zen text? Is enlightenment the final arbiter of validity, or do other factors come into play? What is the proper role of an exegete who attempts to interpret a Ch'an/Zen work within the tradition? How does one respond in a manner that does not undermine the spirit of the original?

The answers to these and similar questions were not always clear. As precious records of the "transmission of the lamp" from a different time and culture, Ch'an texts were comparable in some ways to the Buddhist sutras, yet they deliberately departed from standard sutra formats. In addition, some of the Ch'an genres were uniquely textual and untextual at the same time. A koan collection such as the *Blue Cliff Record*, for example, had a fixed and complex structure; like other texts it could be copied, printed, glossed, and even burned. Yet koan practice was more of an oral tradition than a written one. The textual form of a koan, in isolation, rarely sufficed as a tool for meditative practice. Koans acquired their spiritual and interpretive context through their actual use in the monastic community, especially in the interaction between master and disciple.

Among the early Japanese masters, Daitō was one of the few to confront important interpretive challenges and work out solutions that endured. The most distinctive feature of his Zen was his gifted use of capping phrases *(agyo, jakugo)* to express his own understanding and spark insight in others. Capping phrases and verses had played a role in the literary history of East Asia independent of Ch'an/Zen; their use in Ch'an and Zen coincided with the development of koan practice. A Zen capping phrase is something of a cross between a koan and a footnote. Applied to live situations as well as written texts, a capping phrase is supposed to be able to make a comment, resolve a specific conundrum, convey a Zen insight, transform another's awareness, resonate like a line of poetry, or perform several of these functions simultaneously.

Novices and adepts are equally entitled to compose or quote capping phrases, as long as the conventions of the genre are observed. The shortest examples are just one word, such as "Who?" or "Blind!" The longest rarely exceed twenty-five words. Most are quotations from other sources: Buddhist sutras, Ch'an/Zen discourse records, classic koans, Chinese poetry, Confucian texts, popular proverbs, and so on.

Daitō's involvement with capping phrases began early in his Zen training, when he used them to answer koans orally. Achieving enlightenment through a Chinese koan, he rushed to his master and expressed his understanding with a capping phrase: "Almost the same path!" When asked about Zen in a public religious debate, he replied with a capping phrase that baffled his opponent: "An octagonal millstone flies through the air." Capping phrases abound in the *Record of Daitō,* because the master used them constantly in his formal dialogues with his monks. In his teaching and his written commentaries, Daitō sought to respond to the Ch'an corpus without sanctifying it, to interpret koans and discourse records without explaining them. Capping phrases seemed to answer these needs. The written commentaries preserved in the *Record of Daitō* and other sources include over two thousand different phrases. The inclusion of a capping-phrase commentary in Daitō's discourse record is itself an indication of the importance attached to Daitō's interpretation of Ch'an. One looks in vain for similar texts among the writings of other masters from the Kamakura or Muromachi eras. Daitō's consummate handling of this ingenious interpretive device puts him in a league with two other luminaries noted for their devotion to the genre—Ch'an master Yüan-wu K'o-ch'in (1063–1135) and Zen master Hakuin in eighteenth-century Japan.

After Daitō's death a century passed before the oral capping phrases used in training began to be recorded in Japan. The earliest records of capping-phrase practice are anonymous semisecret accounts of encounters between masters and their disciples. By the time Tōyō Eichō (1429–1504) compiled his [Zen] *Phrase Book (Kuzōshi)* in the late fifteenth century, the capping of koans had become a recognized and indispensable part of Zen practice for monks of the Rinzai sect. Tōyō culled roughly five thousand quotations from diverse sources, arranging them on the basis of length. His work was the progenitor of the two capping-phrase collections used by Rinzai Zen monks today: *Zen Phrase Anthology (Zenrin kushū)* and *Poison-painted Drum (Zudokko).* [12]

Little has been written about capping phrases, in Japan or elsewhere, because of their difficulty and the confidential nature of their use in Zen practice. [13] Since World War II, however, Japanese scholars have affirmed the significance of the capping-phrase exercise in past and present Japanese Zen, and they have acknowledged Daitō's exceptional mastery of the genre. The initial publication of one of Daitō's capping-phrase commentaries in 1944 was facilitated by D. T. Suzuki.[14] In 1967 Yanagida Seizan drew attention to the capping-phrase text in Daitō's discourse record: "Daitō's capping phrases on the *Record of Hsüeh-tou* are exceedingly well-wrought, and they reflect the highest level of Zen experience. The beauty of Zen literature lies in the suggestiveness of these phrases and the depth of mind which permeates them."[15] In 1968 the abbot of a Daitokuji branch temple brought to light a valuable recension of Daitō's capping-phrase commentary on the *Blue Cliff Record.* Hirano Sōjō edited and published this work in 1971.[16] In 1983 curators of the Kyoto National Museum discovered an aged and partial manuscript listing about 550 capping phrases, with a colophon by a later monk who attested that the calligraphy was by Daitō. A year later the remaining segment was found and identified.[17] This text attributed to Daitō is the earliest known capping-phrase anthology in Japan.

It is well known that Zen is skeptical of language and distrustful of texts. Claiming that the deepest insights cannot be verbalized or even conceptualized, Zen defines itself as a "mind-to-mind transmission" that is "not dependent on words." Masters are often portrayed as transcending the constraints of conventional discourse through shouts, blows, gestures, silence, and other nonverbal forms of expression. However, the actual use of language in Zen is far more diverse than these depictions suggest. In a formal encounter a master like Daitō might tell a monk, "Swallow the Kamo River in one gulp"; then half an hour later he might say to the monk, "Join me for a cup of tea." That same day Daitō might employ various kinds of language in composing a richly allusive verse, in writing some cryptic lines of commentary, or in posting some rules for newcomers to the monastery. He might also express himself through different flavors of silence—sitting in meditation, communicating something to a disciple with a glance, or refusing to offer an oral explanation to a novice. Taking Zen's antilanguage rhetoric too literally not only obscures the complex role that language and texts played in the lives of monks; it also overlooks the tradition's sophisticated hermeneutical awareness.

During the Sung period, Ch'an monks participated prominently in literati culture, and masters such as Chüeh-fan Hui-hung (1071–1128) promoted "literary Ch'an" *(wen-tzu Ch'an).* In Japan, a typical Zen adherent of Daitō's day frequently wrote poetry on such topics as meditation, religious doctrine, travel, weather, illness, holidays, tea, and so on. Masters were also expected to compose appropriate verses right after enlightenment and right before death. These stanzas typically consisted of only a few lines, yet they were supposed to reveal the depth of the writer's realization. In such contexts, "not dependent on words" also indicated the ability to use language freely to convey or generate insight. The minimum measure of eloquence in Zen was the skillful use of words in the service of enlightenment. Language that was conducive to awakening and also beautiful in a literary sense was prized by some masters as the paramount form of Zen expression. Daitō's significance is enhanced by his prowess in this realm, still evident in his discourse record, his capping-phrase commentaries, and his poetry.

"Half Open, Half Closed"

The kernel of the koan that precipitated Daitō's enlightenment experience was the single word "barrier" *(kan)*, used in the sense of a tollgate placed across a road. We too confront a number of barriers in a study of this nature, beginning with language itself. Ch'an and Zen texts are full of apparent non sequiturs, obscure allusions, and specialized technical terms. The formal language of Japanese Zen for over six centuries has been an unusual hybrid called *kanbun*—Chinese as read and written by the Japanese. In Daitō's era the Ch'an classics were not translated into Japanese, nor were they read in Chinese. Rather, the Chinese characters were given a Japanese approximation of the Chinese pronunciation, supplied with Japanese declensions, and read out of sequence according to Japanese syntax. Just as medieval European monks attempted to write in Latin, the Japanese monks composed most of their principal works in a "Chinese" that differed from classical and vernacular forms of the original language. For example, when Daitō wrote poems in *kanbun,* he usually observed the rules of Chinese rhyme even though these "rhymes" were based on ancient Chinese pronunciations inaccessible to the Japanese. Daitō also composed his formal lectures in *kanbun,* which is difficult to comprehend aurally unless the listeners also have copies of the text. There must have been many occasions when even Daitō's own monks were baffled by what they heard.

A second barrier we face concerns gaps in the surviving records. Though a considerable number of Daitō's original texts and other valuable documents have been preserved over the centuries, certain details about his life and his era can never be recovered historically. The first biography of the master did not appear until eighty-nine years after his death, and the information it contains is not always reliable: the author attributes to one emperor documents that were written by another, and subsequent biographers give several different dates for Daitō's move to the site of Daitokuji. Furthermore, none of Daitō's capping-phrase commentaries survive in his own hand, and the oldest extant version of his "Final Admonitions" is found in a 1617 text. When an original manuscript is missing, recensions of it may have been transmitted from generation to generation through handwritten copies. Influential texts are sometimes revealed to be completely spurious: the "Admonitions" of Daitō's heir Kanzan (1277–1360) appeared 373 years after Kanzan's death, created to fulfill sectarian needs at the time.[18]

Given the limitations of the available sources, we will find that no single image of Daitō captures him fully. He appears variously as the consummate outsider and the consummate insider, a beggar under a bridge who founded a major monastery. Described by his contemporaries as austere and unapproachable, he seems in his correspondence to have been a caring and dedicated teacher. At times he was a clever innovator, at times a conservative guardian of tradition. An erudite and sensitive poet, he allegedly had the grit to break his own leg so he could assume the meditation posture at his death.

Many of Daitō's descendants struggled to reconcile these disparate perceptions. In the late fifteenth century, when Daitō was being exalted as a successful founder patronized by two emperors, one outspoken Daitokuji monk argued that a more authentic depiction of the master would stress his years of hardship and obscurity. In the eighteenth century, Hakuin embraced almost every possible view of Daitō without any sense of contradiction. While commenting extensively on Daitō's formal lectures, Hakuin revered his predecessor's detachment from the monastic system. While exalting Daitō's refined Chinese poetry as unmatched in the history of Zen, Hakuin painted portraits of the master as a ragged beggar near the Gojō Bridge. In Zen terms, all such images are like multiple reflections of the moon in pools along a path. As long as one does not confuse the reflections with the moon, the real Daitō continues to swing his sleeves as he sweeps the leaves in the garden.

2

JAPAN IN THE EARLY
FOURTEENTH CENTURY

DAITŌ LIVED during a colorful and tumultuous period of Japanese history. The year before his birth in 1282 the Mongol leader Kubilai Khan sent an armada to invade Japan, and the year before his death in 1337 the rebellious general Ashikaga Takauji established a new national government, displacing a defeated emperor. In this era bracketed by clashes of arms, the warriors confirmed their status as Japan's ruling elite, and Zen rose to prominence in the religious and cultural life of the country.

When Kubilai Khan sent his first message to the "King of Japan" in 1268, the Japanese were already aware that Kubilai's army had dethroned the Sung dynasty on the Chinese mainland and that his ambitions had not been sated. Nonetheless, the proud shogun Hōjō Tokimune (1251–1284) forsook diplomacy and readied his military defenses. In the eleventh month of 1274, 30,000 Mongols and Koreans invaded Kyushu in southwestern Japan. After weeks of bloody but inconclusive fighting, a fierce typhoon decimated the Mongols' ships, and the armada was repulsed. In a mood of national crisis, the Japanese mobilized fresh troops and began to construct defensive walls along the Kyushu coast. When Kubilai sent two more embassies, the shogunate responded by beheading the hapless envoys.

Then, in the sixth month of 1281, a massive force of over 150,000 Mongol, Chinese, and Korean soldiers and sailors reached Kyushu. As battles raged on land and at sea, the besieged nation prayed for deliverance. The retired emperor Kameyama appealed to the sun goddess Amaterasu, Shinto priests petitioned other native gods, and Buddhist monks invoked the aid of buddhas and bodhisattvas. About two months after the second attack, another typhoon struck the coast of Kyushu. The invaders' ships foundered in the narrow harbors and on the open sea. Many thousands of sailors drowned, and the soldiers caught on land were killed or captured. Again the Mongols had been thwarted.

Popular sentiment in Japan attributed the dramatic victory to the *kamikaze,* or "divine wind," that seemed to have arisen in response to the nation's prayers. More credit was given to the native gods *(kami)* than to the figures of the Buddhist pantheon. As Kitabatake Chikafusa (1293–1354) wrote a few decades later,

> In the fourth year of Kōan [1281] the Mongol army assembled many ships and attacked our country. There was fierce fighting in Kyushu, but the gods, revealing their awesome authority and manifesting their form, drove the invaders away. Thus a great wind suddenly arose and the several hundreds of thousands of enemy ships were all blown over and demolished. Although people speak of this as a degenerate later age, the righteous power displayed by the gods at this time was truly beyond human comprehension.[1]

Divine intervention or not, it was Japan's good fortune to be attacked at a time when it possessed an active warrior class and capable leaders.

Daitō was born the year after the second invasion in the province of Harima, a strategically important region between Kyushu (the first line of defense) and Kyoto (the home of the emperor). In his youth Daitō witnessed local preparations for an expected third invasion amidst reports of persistent Mongol hostility. Then in 1294 Kubilai died, the Mongol threat abated, and the informed members of Japanese society began to savor a new sense of national pride. Since Japan's earliest days of nation building in the sixth century, China had loomed large in realms of politics, culture, and imagination, alternately alien and familiar; now another dimension had been added to this complex relationship. The venerable Sung dynasty had fallen to the Mongols, and Japan —never before invaded—had "defeated China." Reaffirmations of Japan's uniqueness and occasional assertions of its superiority invigorated artistic, religious, and intellectual circles. The Mongol threat had prompted one Zen monk to vow, "Until the end of the end of the world our country will be superior to all other countries,"[2] a sentiment that events of the period seemed to validate.

The Ascendant Warrior Class

Three groups dominated Japan during Daitō's life—warriors, nobles, and Buddhist priests. The warrior class, which ruled on both national and local levels, had its roots in the Heian era (794–1185), when the nobility first commissioned *samurai* ("retainers") to police provincial estates. That era ended with the establishment of a military government that was still exercising power at the time of Daitō's birth a century later. The ensuing Kamakura period (1185–1333) takes its name from the city that served as the shogun's headquarters.

Though wars attended the beginning and end of the Kamakura period, battles were often small-scale affairs. A fighting unit might consist of a leader and a few loyal vassals from the extended clan; even when larger armies were raised, commanders rarely committed all their forces to a single engagement. As in other realms of Japanese culture, appearances mattered: the correct attire of a warrior included an undergarment of brocade or damask, heavy armor made of cowhide, leggings and armbands, a silk cape, and a helmet with fierce-looking ornaments. If all went according to form, a battle opened with an exchange of arrows, led to confrontations between individual horsemen, and climaxed in hand-to-hand combat. The foremost military history of the period, the *Taiheiki (Chronicle of Grand Pacification),* describes a deadly encounter between two warriors, Shidara and Saitō, who engage each other only after they have properly introduced themselves:

> These two galloped forward, and with clashing armor-sleeves grappled together furiously until they fell down. Being the stronger, Shidara got on top of Saitō and set about to cut off his head, but Saitō, nimble of limb, thrust upward and stabbed Shidara three times. Truly these were mighty men, that even in death did not relax their gripping hands, but pierced each one the other with their swords, and laid themselves down on the same pillow.[3]

Though such violent scenes may seem far removed from the cloistered routine of the Zen monasteries where Daitō trained, political and religious realms were intimately linked in medieval Japan. Daitō's uncle, Akamatsu Norimura (1277–1350), was a leading general and an ardent patron of Zen.[4] As military governor of Harima, Akamatsu supported Emperor Go-Daigo in the Emperor's attempt to topple the Kamakura-based shogunate. But when Go-Daigo failed to reward Akamatsu adequately, the disgruntled commander threw in his lot with Ashikaga Takauji (1305–1358), another former supporter who proceeded to oust Go-Daigo and establish a new shogunate of his own. Akamatsu exemplifies a success story repeated throughout medieval Japanese history: a ruthless provincial chieftain steadily gains in strength until his ambitions affect national events. Once when Akamatsu was defending a fortress against a superior force, he maneuvered the attackers into a trap: "Soon for three leagues men and horses lay dead in heaps, from the foot of the castle to the west bank of the Muko

River, nor could travelers make their way past them"; on another occasion he ordered the decapitation of several hundred prisoners, whose heads were then displayed on poles.[5] Along with his martial pursuits, Akamatsu took religious vows as a "lay monk" *(nyūdō)* and facilitated the establishment of Daitō's new Zen monastery.

It is well known that Japanese warriors subscribed to a demanding code of loyalty. In principle, a retainer owed unqualified allegiance to his lord, though by the end of the Kamakura period most vassals expected rewards for their service. A true warrior was prepared to give up his life for his lord or his honor: in 1247 five hundred trapped fighters committed *hara-kiri* rather than endure the shame of surrender. Although some allegiance was paid to the throne, the ideology of absolute sovereignty was not well developed, and the emperor was not the focus of the kind of national loyalty he attracted later in Japanese history. Matters were complicated by the existence of rival imperial branches and "cloistered" (retired) emperors, an unstable arrangement that Daitō had to accommodate in dealing with his patrons.

However brutal a typical vassal's existence may have been, the more privileged warriors enjoyed interludes of repose and refinement. Higher-ranking figures hosted tea ceremonies, patronized artists and craftsmen, consulted advisors on cultural matters, and discussed philosophy with learned monks. One of Takauji's generals, forced to abandon his mansion after losing a battle, made sure it was fit for the rival general who would occupy it:

> [He] spread rush matting with boldly emblazoned crests on the floor of the six-bay banquet chamber and arranged everything in its proper place, from the triptych of hanging scrolls to the flower vase, incense burner, tea kettle, and server. In the study he placed a Buddhist verse in grass-writing by Wang Hsi-chih and an anthology by Han Yü, while in the sleeping chamber he laid silken night-garments beside a pillow of scented aloe wood. He provisioned the twelve-bay guardhouse with three poles bearing chickens, rabbits, pheasants, and swans and with a three-*koku* cask brimming with sake.[6]

When the occupying general was himself forced to withdraw a few weeks later, he reciprocated with comparable provisions and gifts.

During Daitō's lifetime one shogunate collapsed in Kamakura and another was established in Kyoto, a doubly momentous change of ruling clan and capital city. The Kamakura regime had been weakened by changes in provincial landholding patterns and the burden of defending the country from the Mongols; its decline was accelerated by its inability to satisfy all the warriors and clerics who demanded rewards for their (alleged) contributions to the Mongols' defeat. The last of the Hōjō rulers, Takatoki (1303–1333), was little more than a figurehead when he assumed power in 1316 at the age of thirteen. Two years later Go-Daigo gained the throne in Kyoto at the relatively mature age of thirty, and in 1331 he launched his campaign to restore full authority to the emperor. Within seven years another warrior clan—the Ashikaga—had triumphed, confirming the centrality of the warrior class in Japanese society. Ashikaga Takauji made Kyoto his capital, and vassals from the provinces seemed to overrun the city in the final years of Daitō's life. In one notorious incident a band of rowdy retainers ripped branches from a tree in the cloistered emperor's garden and attempted to set fire to a palace building; when they were expelled from the city, they impudently staged a festive parade. Soon the warriors in Kyoto were skillfully taking advantage of their enhanced status, "increasing their wealth a hundredfold day by day."[7]

The Aristocracy and the City of Kyoto

The second group in the triad that shaped medieval Japan—the nobles —remained vigorous and influential even after a century of warrior rule. In 1300 a reigning emperor and no fewer than five former emperors lived in Kyoto, dispensing the titles and ranks coveted by nobles and warriors alike. A politically astute aristocrat might begin his career as a captain of the palace guard, rise to become middle counselor, then minister of the right, and eventually chancellor of the court. Emperor Go-Daigo's attempt to claim hegemony for the throne, a vision that would also have signified a return to aristocratic dominance, may appear anachronistic to later observers, yet at the time the triumph of his warrior opponents was far from assured.

Whatever their political prospects, the nobles saw themselves as the principal guardians of Japan's rich cultural heritage. Not only did they patronize and participate in traditional arts, they also tried to keep abreast of philosophical and aesthetic developments in China. Because Zen monks were often the most knowledgeable informants on such matters, the nobles welcomed them at poetry sessions and tea ceremonies. While the warriors grappled with Chinese soldiers on Kyushu beaches, the nobles grappled with Chinese manuals on rhyme and meter. One popular new genre ingeniously combined Chinese and Japanese poetry: by taking turns and linking verses, participants adroitly alternated between the two languages.

Though countless nobles held titles empty of real authority, some participated prominently in the political struggles of the age. After Emperor Go-Daigo, perhaps the most important representative of the aristocracy during Daitō's mature years was Kitabatake Chikafusa. Equally adept in civil and military arts, he was an effective commander of Go-Daigo's forces and the author of an influential history of Japan's imperial succession, *A Chronicle of Gods and Sovereigns (Jinnō shōtōki)*. Kitabatake believed that the nobles were Japan's rightful rulers and that Go-Daigo represented the legitimate branch of the divided imperial family, yet his arguments were rendered moot by the march of events.

Another contemporary of Daitō, Yoshida Kenkō (1283–1350), lamented the impending loss of the aristocrats' rarefied subculture. A middle-ranking court officer, Kenkō was nostalgic for the days before the Kamakura shogunate: "In all things I yearn for the past."[8] The tone of his classic work *Essays in Idleness (Tsurezuregusa)* is wistful, ironic, and conflicted. Describing the transfer of the imperial regalia from a retiring emperor to the imperial successor, Kenkō focuses on the loneliness of the man stepping down:

> The moment during the ceremony of abdication of the throne when the Sword, Jewels, and Mirror are offered to the new emperor is heartbreaking in the extreme. When the newly retired emperor abdicated in the spring he wrote this poem, I understand:
>
> > Even menials
> > of the palace staff treat me
> > as a stranger now;
> > in my unswept garden lie
> > the scattered cherry blossoms.
>
> What a lonely feeling the poem seems to convey—people are too distracted by all the festivities of the new reign for anyone to wait on the retired emperor. This is precisely the kind of occasion when a man's true feelings are apt to be revealed.[9]

The newly retired emperor in this passage is Hanazono, Daitō's influential patron and disciple.

In Japan the aristocracy was associated with one particular city, Kyoto, which had been the country's capital from 794 to 1185. Kyoto was also the setting for most of Daitō's Zen career—he sought his first Zen teachers there and later returned to build his own monastery. Originally called Heian, the city was centrally located on Japan's main island, Honshu, midway between Kamakura in the east and Kyushu in the west. Surrounded by hills on three sides and without exposure to the sea, Kyoto is known for its distinct seasons: a long, temperate fall; a cold, clear winter; a flower-filled spring; then weeks of "plum rain" followed by a hot, muggy summer. Kyoto's initial reign as the center of national affairs effectively ended in 1221, when the Kamakura regime installed its deputy in a section of the city called Rokuhara. For the next century the shogunate firmly controlled the city and the court, at times manipulating the succession of emperors. The imperial family, reduced to near poverty, was forced to abandon the palace, which fell to ruin. Gradually the city reoriented itself along an east-west axis—warriors, nobles, and priests became dominant in the upper half, while merchants flourished in the lower half.

Daitō's Kyoto was a thriving religious center. The two most powerful Buddhist sects of the Heian period, Tendai and Shingon, continued to exert considerable influence; Tendai's presence was especially visible because its headquarters towered over the city from atop Mt. Hiei in the northeast. Countless other temples were affiliated with the popular Buddhist faiths that had arisen during the Kamakura period, principally the Pure Land, True Pure Land, and Nichiren sects. By the mid-fourteenth century, major Zen monasteries could also be found in all quadrants of the city: Kenninji in the east along the Kamo River, Tōfu-kuji in the south, Nanzenji in the southeast, Daitō's Daitokuji in the north, and Rinsenji at the foot of the western hills.

In tandem with the port city of Sakai (near present-day Osaka), Kyoto was also the hub of medieval Japan's most prosperous region, a crossroads for well-traveled trade routes to and from the surrounding provinces. Commercial activity grew steadily during the Kamakura period, survived the disruptions of the shogunate's collapse, and reached new heights under the Ashikaga regime. As the merchants of Kyoto welcomed the warriors flocking to the capital, more goods were produced and agricultural output rose. Some of the larger Zen monasteries sponsored markets and guilds; others took an active role in international trade.

In 1336, the year before Daitō's death, the Ashikaga leaders selected a site in Kyoto for a new imperial residence, and there they installed a compliant emperor from the "northern" court, Kōmyō (1321–1380). Though the founding of the Ashikaga shogunate brought down the curtain on the aristocracy, it marked the rebirth of Kyoto as the political, cultural, and commercial center of the country.

The Priesthood and the Buddhist Worldview

Buddhist monks and priests constituted the third element of the triad that dominated medieval Japan. The warriors may have controlled politics, and the nobility may have preserved aesthetic refinement, but the priests were specialists in a realm antecedent to the activities of all classes. Buddhism's ascendancy in Japan began about five centuries before Daitō's birth and endured for at least 250 years after his death. The prevailing Buddhist worldview affected all the named and unnamed actors in Daitō's life, from illiterate peasants to courtier poets; it shaped their perceptions of the physical world, their notions of birth and death, their language, and their dreams.

Foremost among the era's shared assumptions were the concepts of karma and rebirth. Intimately linked, they were used to explain the differing fortunes of men, the relation between humans and animals, the process of salvation, and a host of other phenomena. Karma was a morally sensitive law of causation, its operation constant and orderly: just as past behavior fashioned one's present circumstances, current behavior shaped one's future existence. Classic Buddhist texts distinguished karma from determinism or fatalism, yet popular conceptions were less subtle. A chronicle of Daitō's era claimed, "Even when people take shelter together under the same tree or dip water from a single stream, it is because strong karmic ties from many lives bind them together."[10] A warrior about to kill a captured noble tried to calm his victim (and justify his act) by invoking karma: "Please console yourself by remembering that all things are the result of the deeds of previous lives."[11]

The succession of lifetimes was depicted graphically in the popular imagination as a spoked wheel with six realms or courses: gods, humans, fighting titans, animals, hungry ghosts, and denizens of hell. Created in India, this scheme was modified in China and then transmitted to Japan, where it gained wide acceptance. A work completed the year after Daitō's birth gave a dramatic illustration of an upward passage from the animal realm to the human realm; it told of a beached clam that became the priest of a prestigious temple:

> Kakukai, steward of Nanshōbō on Mount Kōya, had a reputation as a prominent contemporary scholar of the Shingon sect. Wishing to know about his earlier existence, he prayed to the Great Teacher [Kūkai] and was shown the circumstances of seven of his former lives. "First of all you were a small clam in the sea west of Tennōji temple, tossed ashore by the waves. While you were lying on the beach, a small child picked you up and brought you to the front of the Golden Hall, where you heard the chanting of the *Hymn in Praise of Relics (Sharisandan)*. By virtue of this you were reborn as a dog living at Tennōji who constantly heard the sutras and mystic formulas being chanted. Then you were reborn as an ox, and because of having carried paper used for the copying of the *Great Wisdom Sutra* you were reborn as a horse. The horse carried pilgrims to Kumano and was reborn as a votive-fire attendant, who lit the way for people by always keeping the fires bright. Having gradually become suffused by the karmic activity of wisdom, you were reborn as caretaker of the Inner Chapel, where constantly your ears were moved and your eyes exposed to the practice of the Three Mysteries. And now you are living as the steward Kakukai."[12]

Though favorable rebirths were desirable, the ultimate aim was to get off the wheel of transmigration altogether. If enlightenment or salvation was not attained in this life, it might be attained in the intermediate state between death and rebirth, in a future life, or through rebirth in the Pure Land of Amida Buddha. In Amida's paradise, surrounded by wish-fulfilling trees and spiritually advanced companions, one had an unparalleled opportunity to hear the Dharma—the truth of the universe and the teachings of the Buddha. The conditions for an easy enlightenment were thereby fulfilled. A warrior parting from his wife promised her wistfully, "If I am born in the Pure Land, I shall await you, making a seat for two on a single lotus calyx."¹³ The alternative to emancipation was continuous suffering through repeated human rebirths or, worse yet, descent into one of the subhuman realms.

Faith in deities, spirits, spells, and the transcendent power of faith itself was a basic element in the prevailing worldview. As a young boy, Daitō was initiated into this mysterious realm at Enkyōji, a major Tendai temple near his home. There he learned that Enkyōji's Buddha figures had been made by a heavenly artisan, that the temple's tenth-century founder Shōkū had taken a daily walk to and from Mt. Hiei (about sixty-five miles away), and that Shōkū's scarf had been washed in an Indian lake "because the water of Japan was not fittingly pure."¹⁴ The year that Daitō founded Daitokuji in northern Kyoto, high-ranking Shingon clerics were attracting attention elsewhere in the city, performing esoteric rituals to facilitate the conception of a royal heir. When they invoked various healing buddhas, male-producing gods, and bodhisattvas associated with longevity, "smoke from their sacred fires filled the Inner Princess's garden, and the sound of their hand bells reverberated through the women's apartments."¹⁵ Warriors were equally convinced of faith's miraculous power. The loyalist general Kusunoki Masashige (1294–1336), shot by an archer at close range, reportedly survived because the arrow "struck an amulet wherein was preserved the *Kannon Sutra,* which Masashige had trusted and read for many years." Furthermore, "Its arrowhead had stopped in the two-line poem 'wholeheartedly praising the name [of Kannon].' "¹⁶

In this milieu dreams were taken seriously as a means of clarifying the past, foretelling the future, and communicating with the deceased. In Daitō's biography, revelatory dreams precede his birth, enlightenment, and emergence as a public figure. The era's best-known dream is credited to Emperor Go-Daigo: at a low point in his political fortunes, he dreamt about a giant evergreen tree that was especially luxuriant on its south-facing side. Interpreting the dream himself, Go-Daigo noted that the characters for "tree" and "south" could be combined to create the word *kusunoki* (camphor tree). Soon thereafter he was pleased to encounter Kusunoki Masashige, his most stalwart supporter. Dreams were also associated with the Buddhist doctrine of impermanence:

everything that arises must perish, everything that is born must die. Whereas Buddhist monks in India had deepened their awareness of transience by meditating on decomposing corpses, the Japanese preferred aesthetic images such as morning dew, falling cherry blossoms, or flowing water. "The world is as unstable as the pools and shallows of the Asuka River," wrote Yoshida Kenkō in his *Essays*.[17]

Daitō's contemporaries believed that human history was coming to the end of a long downward cycle. They pointed to scriptural passages in which Shakyamuni himself had predicted that the Dharma would eventually perish. Three phases of decline were identified: true Dharma, counterfeit Dharma, and degenerate Dharma. Though the length of these periods was variously calculated in India and China, the Japanese focused on the year 1052 (supposedly two thousand years after the Buddha's passing) as the onset of the third epoch. Accordingly, they thought of themselves as living in the Dharma-ending or Final Age *(mappō, matsudai)*. The aristocratic priest Jien (1155–1225) wrote a work depicting Japanese history as a steady decline, and popular religious leaders such as Hōnen (1133–1212) asserted that because the Buddha's teachings were beyond ordinary comprehension, believers could no longer attain salvation through their own efforts.

Still, dissenting voices were heard in various quarters. In the following verse by the poet-monk Saigyō (1118–1190), Vulture Peak alludes to a site where the Buddha had preached:

> Those who view the moon over Vulture Peak
>   as sunk below the horizon
> are men whose minds, confused,
>   hold the real darkness.[18]

Among the medieval Buddhist sects, Zen and Shingon were less affected by Final Age assumptions. Zen master Bassui Tokushō, born a decade before Daitō's death, expressed a characteristic attitude when he vowed: "During this period when authentic Buddhism has declined to the point where it is about to expire, may my desire for Self-realization be strong enough to save all sentient beings in this Buddha-less world."[19] For Kitabatake Chikafusa, the *kamikaze* typhoon that had driven off the Mongols signaled a shift in the wind sufficient to reverse the Final Age's downward trend: "We should not automatically despise ourselves simply because we are said to have arrived at a 'later age.' It is a principle that the beginning of heaven and earth starts today."[20]

In Buddhism the monks found not only a worldview and a spiritual path, but also a career that offered a better chance for upward mobility than most other occupations. Any number of motivations and circumstances could impel entrance into a monastery. A six-year-old boy might be enrolled because his father had too many mouths to feed, a youth might be inspired by a sincere religious aspiration, an older man might seek release from burdensome social obligations, and so on. The activities of monks included meditation, chanting, rituals (including funerals), scriptural study, pilgrimage, religious dancing, public works, political affairs, and financial matters. In most sects priests took vows of celibacy, but some of the Pure Land schools broke with tradition and began to allow their priests to marry.

Becoming a Buddhist monk meant "leaving home" *(shukke)*. In religious terms, *shukke* signified departure from the phenomenal world of ceaseless change and entrance into an unchanging realm of perfect repose. In social terms, it meant severing all (or most) ties to one's family and forsaking all (or most) worldly pursuits. Yet complexities inevitably arose, because monks were not required to spend their entire lives in a monastery and because the Buddhist institution also played a vital role in society. The Tendai abbot Gen'e (1279–1350), "renowned for learning beyond all men of the age,"[21] was an early proponent of Neo-Confucianism in Japan and a contributor to the *Taiheiki*. In 1324 he was invited to instruct a group of Emperor Go-Daigo's supporters, and a year later he debated Daitō in a contest that pitted the established sects against their newest challenger, Zen. Other monks struggled to find the proper balance between withdrawal and involvement. Daitō's peer Musō Soseki (1275–1351) served as abbot of eight successive temples and participated in national politics, yet his writings reveal an unfulfilled yearning for a life of seclusion and calm.

Another type of priestly status, usually distinguished from the regular priesthood, was acquired when someone took Buddhist vows but did not enter a monastery for a prolonged period of training. Such a person was called a *tonseisha*, "one who has escaped the world." Motives ranged from the religious to the ridiculous: one warrior who performed poorly during a hunting expedition assuaged his shame by shaving his head and donning monastic robes. The most prominent *tonseisha* were the emperors who took Buddhist vows after abdicating their thrones, a practice inaugurated by Emperor Shōmu in the eighth century. Go-Daigo's father, Go-Uda, considered exceptional among this group for the depth of his devotion, was honored in his own day as a "great holy teacher."[22] The best-known renunciant in Daitō's milieu was Kenkō, author of *Essays in Idleness*. Though Kenkō depicted himself as a recluse, other sources indicate that he joined courtly poetry gatherings and mingled with the leaders of the new Ashikaga regime. Like Kenkō, most *tonseisha* continued to pursue at least some of their customary activities, and the contradictory aspects of the role did not go unnoticed. The Buddhist priest Mujū Ichien (1226–1312) bluntly commented:

They only bear the name of "recluse" but do not know its reality. Year after year we can see an increasing number of people who "escape the world" simply to get ahead in life and in spite of the fact that they have no religious aspiration at all. . . .

> Let us change
> the character *ton* in *tonsei*
> to accord with the times:
> of old it meant "to escape,"
> and now it means "to covet."[23]

Other Roles in Medieval Society

Sometimes the boundaries between warriors, nobles, and priests became blurred. When Kamakura served as Japan's capital, courtiers from Kyoto mingled freely with the nation's military rulers, who in turn appointed an imperial prince as shogun. After the capital shifted to Kyoto in 1336, marriages between members of warrior and aristocratic families became more frequent. Distinctions were shaded in another way by those who combined the roles of warrior and priest, or noble and priest, or noble and warrior. Not only did warriors like Akamatsu call themselves lay monks *(nyūdō)*, but the monks of several temples actually bore arms and affected the military balance. Emperors who took Buddhist vows and other aristocratic renunciants exemplified the noble-priest combination; noble and warrior roles fused in the lives of courtiers who took up arms on Go-Daigo's behalf. As Kenkō commented: "Everybody enjoys doing something quite unrelated to his normal way of life. The priest devotes himself to the arts of the soldier; the soldier (apparently unfamiliar with the art of drawing a bow) pretends to know the Buddhist Law and amuses himself with linked verse and music. . . . Not only priests, but nobles, courtiers, and even men of the highest rank are fond of arms."[24]

One prominent figure who combined all three roles was Prince Morinaga (1308–1335), a son of Emperor Go-Daigo. At the age of twenty, after only a year in a monastery, Morinaga was appointed abbot of the Tendai sect (a politically strategic post), and when hostilities broke out, he became one of Go-Daigo's most effective generals. He was also an early patron of Daitō. In an unusual letter to his father, Morinaga attempted to justify his military aims in Buddhist terms:

> If I should return to the priesthood, casting aside the power I command as a great general, who would defend the court militarily? There are two methods by which the buddhas and bodhisattvas seek to aid living beings: through force and through persuasion. . . . Which course on my part would be better for the country—to live in obscurity on Mt. Hiei guarding but one temple, or as a great general to pacify the country to its farthest extent?[25]

The aspirations expressed in this passage were cut short when Morinaga was killed in prison at the age of twenty-seven.

The majority of the population, greatly outnumbering the visible minority at the top of society, of course had nothing to do with swordsmanship, linked verse, or Buddhist exegesis. In the background of all the remembered events of the period were the anonymous peasants—laboring in muddy rice paddies, transporting goods along the highways, scheming to avoid oppressive taxes, and cleaning up after bloody battles. Periodic natural disasters intensified their suffering. In the mid-thirteenth century a series of earthquakes and floods caused widespread famine and plague; the starving peasants ate roots and grass, and streets were clogged with corpses.

Women in Japan had long been subordinate to men, though opportunities for women of the warrior class expanded briefly during the early Kamakura period, when they could inherit and even administer provincial estates. At the national level, Hōjō Masako (1157–1225) initiated the regent system by ruling first through her son and later through her great-grandnephew. However, the status of women declined as feudalism reshaped society; their subjugation was justified by a mix of indigenous beliefs, assimilated Chinese precedents, and Buddhist doctrines. Because blood was an ancient taboo in Japan, menstruation and childbirth were treated as pollutants. Confucianism contributed its male-dominated hierarchies and its traditional justifications for divorcing a wife: failure to produce a son, gossiping, lewdness, jealousy, stealing from one's husband, disrespect toward his parents, or disease. Many Buddhists believed that a woman had little chance for enlightenment unless she was reborn as a man. Kenkō again expressed attitudes typical of Daitō's era: "In fact, women are all perverse by nature. They are deeply self-centered, grasping in the extreme, devoid of all susceptibility to reason, quick to indulge in superstitious practices. . . . Only when a man enslaved by his infatuation is courting a woman does she seem charming and amusing."[26]

The one realm besides the family in which women enjoyed some degree of autonomy was religion. In Buddhism they were active as lay parishioners, nuns, and patrons; for example, many of Daitō's letters were addressed to female disciples. One woman who entered the lore of Japanese Zen was a Zen nun named Shōtaku, widow of a prominent vassal slain in 1331. She is said to have thwarted a rapist who was armed with a sword: "The nun took out a piece of paper and rolled it up, then thrust it like a sword at the man's eyes. He became unable to strike and was completely overawed by her spiritual strength. He turned to run and the nun gave a 'Katsu!' shout, hitting him with the paper sword. He fell and then fled."[27] Whatever their individual accomplishments, nuns were not permitted to ordain disciples, hold high ecclesiastical posts, or visit holy sites such as Mt. Hiei and Mt. Kōya.

Emperor Go-Daigo's Kenmu Restoration

Emperor Go-Daigo's short-lived Kenmu Restoration, a major turning point of Japanese history, provided the backdrop for the final years of Daitō's life. Go-Daigo assumed the throne in 1318 as an adult (child emperors had been the custom), and his father, Go-Uda, soon dissolved the office of the cloistered emperor, unifying the authority of the throne for the first time in over two hundred years. In 1324 Go-Daigo was implicated in an abortive antishogunal plot, and in 1331 he was forced to flee to the hills west of Nara. The following year he went into exile on the Oki islands. Despite these reversals, the generals who had taken up the Emperor's cause were victorious in the field: Ashikaga Takauji captured Kyoto, and Nitta Yoshisada seized Kamakura. Go-Daigo's triumphant reentry into Kyoto in 1333 signaled the end of the Kamakura shogunate that had ruled Japan for over a century.

For the next three years Go-Daigo sought to create a new government based on unconditional imperial hegemony. Some of his most dramatic policies involved the religious establishment, over which he had already established a measure of control. As part of his plan to shift the country's center of gravity from Kamakura to Kyoto, he reorganized the rankings in the official Gozan, or "Five Mountains," network of Zen monasteries. Go-Daigo singled out Daitō's new monastery as "the nation's peerless Zen temple," ranking it at the top of the system and praising it as "a grand and auspicious site for the enhancement of the Emperor's destiny."[28] Go-Daigo also patronized other Zen masters, including the Chinese émigré Ming-chi Ch'u-chün (1262–1336) and the politically agile Musō Soseki, who was summoned to Kyoto within months of the Emperor's return to power. Even though many of Go-Daigo's initiatives were later reversed, the Kenmu Restoration marks the entry of the Zen institution into the religious and political mainstream of medieval Japan, a development that Daitō witnessed and facilitated.

Political difficulties soon plagued Go-Daigo, who rewarded supporters capriciously and delegated authority clumsily. Prince Morinaga and Ashikaga Takauji began to feud, and turmoil persisted in the provinces. The case of Daitō's uncle Akamatsu was indicative: though instrumental in Go-Daigo's success, he was rewarded with only one estate, and his appointment as governor of Harima was revoked. "It is said that it was because of this that Enshin [Akamatsu] quickly changed his heart and became an enemy of the court," the *Taiheiki* reported.[29]

The Kenmu Restoration was soon over. Takauji turned against Go-Daigo, captured Kyoto in 1336, and enthroned Kōmyō as the new emperor. In contrast to Go-Daigo, Takauji efficiently satisfied his warrior allies' hunger for land; this time Akamatsu was confirmed as lord of Harima. In the first month of 1337 Go-Daigo escaped to a lonely exile in the hills of Yoshino, south of Kyoto. That year Daitō's strength was also waning, and during the winter he died sitting upright in the meditation posture. In 1338 Takauji was declared shogun, and Go-Daigo died the next year, at the age of fifty-two. After the failure of the Kenmu Restoration, the court was excluded from national leadership for five hundred years.

Modern scholars acknowledge Go-Daigo's independent spirit and lively mind, yet most of them also fault his lack of political acumen and his callous treatment of his own supporters. In the view of historian Ivan Morris, "He was a proud, arrogant ruler who would let nothing stand in his way, yet who, for all his intelligence and learning, pursued his ambitions with a remarkable lack of realism."[30] Because the Kenmu Restoration lasted only a few years, it is difficult to assess. More than a coercive redistribution of power, it arose in response to a complex mix of political, social, and intellectual forces. Though the Restoration is generally seen as a reactionary attempt to reverse the inexorable rise of the warrior class, some scholars now challenge the thesis of the inevitability of warrior domination. Rather, they credit Go-Daigo with a workable vision of feudal monarchy, comparable to the autocratic centralization achieved sixty years later by the shogun Ashikaga Yoshimitsu.[31]

Contemporary observers, Daitō among them, also struggled to interpret these dramatic events, which raised fundamental and unsettling questions of legitimacy. Who was entitled to rule—emperor or shogun, nobles or warriors? Within the divided imperial family, which line represented the true succession—Go-Daigo's defeated southern branch or the northern branch forcibly enthroned by Takauji? What criteria should be used to resolve these dilemmas? Out of this milieu came Kitabatake's *Chronicle of Gods and Sovereigns,* a sustained investigation of imperial legitimacy. As we will see, parallel issues of religious authenticity occupied Daitō and other pioneers of Japanese Zen.

For someone who deliberately remained in the background of public affairs, Daitō was personally involved with a surprising number of the era's leading figures. Three of his key patrons were the principal representatives of the imperial family: Emperor Go-Daigo, Emperor Hanazono, and Prince Morinaga. Another powerful patron (and a relative) was the influential general Akamatsu Norimura. Daitō had a celebrated encounter with the highly respected Tendai abbot Gen'e, who allegedly asked to become Daitō's disciple.[32] One other name might be added to the list of the luminaries whose lives touched Daitō's—Yoshida Kenkō, author of *Essays in Idleness*. Born a year apart, both men were active in Kyoto at the same time, and both had been students of Zen master Nanpo Jōmyō. Though Kenkō does not mention his religious affiliations in his writings, his name appears in early Daitokuji documents.[33] It is possible to imagine Kenkō paying a visit to Daitō in the abbot's quarters on a cold winter day—the courtier poet and the Zen master discussing a Chinese text or a recent battle as they warm their hands over a charcoal brazier.

3

DAITŌ'S EARLY ZEN TRAINING

THE EARLIEST accounts of Daitō's life are a creative blend of history and hagiography. The biographers sought to express the character and spirit of their subject, exalt him as the founder of their religious lineage, and direct attention to a paradigm—a life committed to Zen practice. Whether or not they were conscious of their adherence to a genre, they structured their texts according to the conventions of Buddhist biography. Their task was facilitated to a considerable degree by Daitō's own inclination to model himself after his eminent predecessors. Accordingly, an auspicious birth and a precocious response to Buddhism are followed by the highlights of the spiritual path: an initial encounter with a master, a deep enlightenment experience, a period of seclusion, and eventual success as a teacher. The master's final admonitions and his exceptional death complete the traditional pattern. Most of the writers and readers of these accounts were monks who regarded themselves as Daitō's spiritual descendants, and they were not overly concerned about questions of historical accuracy. Those who may have recognized elements of hagiography would have contended nonetheless that Daitō's life was infused with an extraordinary significance that transcended literal truth.

The sectarian sources are augmented and clarified by many documents that have survived from Daitō's era. Remarkably, we can still inspect a considerable body of calligraphy in Daitō's own hand: two satori verses, a final testament, a death poem, letters, and transcriptions of various religious and secular classics. Numerous imperial proclamations addressed to the master, written by the emperors themselves,

26

have also been preserved. Other valuable materials include the diary of Emperor Hanazono and the records kept by Tettō Gikō (1295–1369), a senior disciple. The first biography of Daitō appeared in 1426, nearly a century after the master's death, written by a monk in Daitō's lineage named Shunsaku Zenkō. Little is known about Shunsaku except that he was a disciple of the seventeenth abbot of Daitokuji and served as head priest of Tokuzenji, the oldest Daitokuji subtemple. His text, the *Exploits of National Master Daitō (Daitō Kokushi gyōjō)*, is brief and sporadically dated, yet it became the basis for all subsequent biographies of the master.[1]

The second known biography of Daitō, written in 1617, is called the *Chronicle of National Master Kōzen Daitō Kōshō Shōtō, Founder of Daitokuji (Daitoku Kaisan Kōzen Daitō Kōshō Shōtō Kokushi nenpu)*.[2] The writer was Takuan Sōhō (1573–1645), an eminent Zen master in his own right. Takuan trained at Daitokuji and was the 154th abbot there briefly in 1608. He also founded temples in other parts of the country, instructed a retired emperor, and had many prominent samurai disciples. At the age of seventy-one he wrote the single character for "dream" and passed away. Takuan's writings include a well-known treatise on the unity of Zen and swordsmanship, and his name has been given to a pickled radish that remains part of the Japanese diet. In his *Chronicle* Takuan incorporated the bulk of Shunsaku's *Exploits* and added an equal amount of new material, some of it drawn from historical documents and the rest unverifiable. In order to create a "chronicle," he appended dates to every incident and alleged incident in Daitō's life. Takuan's original manuscript remains in excellent condition, housed in the Daitokuji subtemple Daisen-in. One can catch glimpses of the writer energetically revising his own work: lines are crossed out, characters are squeezed into margins, and the calligraphy flows more freely as the story nears its end.

In the late seventeenth century a spate of brief Daitō biographies appeared, most of them written for collections of the lives of famous Japanese monks.[3] They are derivative of Shunsaku's *Exploits* and omit some material found in Takuan's account, suggesting that the latter had not circulated widely. In 1767 Takuan's *Chronicle* was edited and reissued by Kokai Sōnyo (1695–1770), the 349th abbot of Daitokuji.[4]

Daitō's Youth

Daitō was born sometime in 1282. Though the actual day was not recorded, one late biography claims that the birth occurred on the seventh day of the twelfth month, the eve of the traditional date of the Buddha's enlightenment. Daitō's parents lived in the small farming village of Oyake, about seventy miles west of Kyoto. At the time the region,

called Isei, was part of Harima province; today it is the town of Tatsuno, near the city of Himeji in Hyōgo prefecture. In the Tenmon era
(1532–1555) Daitō's birthplace was honored by the construction of a
modest temple, now called Hōrinji. An old well on the temple grounds
is said to have been used by Daitō's family.

Daitō's father, Urakami Kamon, was a descendant of the ancient Ki
clan, which had exercised influence in the Harima region for centuries.
Though the Urakami family belonged to the warrior class, the specific
occupation of Daitō's father is not known. Daitō's mother was of the
Suga clan. His uncle on his mother's side was the leading general Akamatsu Norimura, later confirmed as the governor of Harima. Only five
years older than Daitō, Akamatsu entered the Zen sect as a youth,
shaved his head, and took the Buddhist name Enshin. He is said to have
trained for some time at Shōrinji temple in Niwase.[5]

Shunsaku's description of Daitō's birth in the *Exploits* is unabashedly
hagiographic:

> The mother had a dream in which a monk held a white flower; it blos-
> somed with five petals, and he gave it to her. She became pregnant.
> After conception she remained in a sleeplike state without waking.
> When the time of birth arrived, she was sleeping deeply, unaware.
> Suddenly the midwife heard the single cry of a baby. She went and
> looked. The infant's skin had a lustrous glow even before he was
> bathed. He was remarkably precocious. The top of his head bulged
> upward, and there was a protuberance on his forehead. His eyes
> emitted a light that pierced other people, and he was able to turn his
> head to watch the movements of those around him.[6]

The allusions in this passage boldly place Daitō in the highest spiritual
rank: according to tradition, Shakyamuni Buddha's mother also conceived through a dream, and the infant Shakyamuni exhibited similar
attributes.

Shunsaku recounts just one incident from Daitō's childhood, in
which the sharp-tongued youth uses a paradoxical question to outwit an
adult. Takuan's *Chronicle* adds three more tales and arbitrarily dates all
four. Though these accounts are surely apocryphal, they introduce Zen
teachings and convey the authors' sense of Daitō's character. For example, Takuan tells the following story about the six-year-old Daitō:

> One day the Master [Daitō] was playing around a Buddhist temple
> with a group of children. He pointed to the Buddha inside the hall
> and asked one of the children, "What's this?" The child said, "Bud-
> dha." The Master said, "No it's not." "If it's not Buddha, then what
> is it?" the child said. The Master replied, "If it were Buddha, it
> would not have a human face like yours." He then climbed onto the

Buddha's shoulders. All the other children ran off in fear, yet the Master's expression did not change.[7]

When Daitō was about ten, his parents sent him to Enkyōji, the Tendai Buddhist temple less than twenty miles from their home. Commanding a magnificent view of the surrounding area from its perch on wooded Mt. Shosha, Enkyōji had a distinguished history that spanned three centuries, and it flourished in Daitō's day as a regional center for Buddhist studies and devotional activities. The *Taiheiki* describes Enkyōji's principal image, the bodhisattva Kannon, as "carved from a tree that was a buddha,"[8] and Shunsaku states that Daitō's parents had directed their prayers for a son to this figure.

For about nine years Daitō lived and studied on Mt. Shosha. One of his teachers, Kaishin, specialized in the *Vinaya* texts that contained the ancient rules of conduct for the Buddhist priesthood. During this period Daitō was initiated into the scriptures, monastic regulations, and meditation techniques of Tendai, which represented the Buddhist mainstream at the time. Most of the major religious figures of the Kamakura period received their initial Buddhist training from the Tendai sect, yet the Zen monks who followed Daitō typically spent their entire careers within the Zen institution. Daitō thus stands at a point of transition between two eras. The Tendai training that he acquired on Mt. Shosha continued to nourish him throughout his subsequent involvement in Zen. Years later, one of his regulations for Daitokuji stated: "Novices, postulants, and young trainees . . . should devote themselves to study."[9]

In his own writings Daitō offers no information about his youth or his early religious experiences. Though the circumstances surrounding his departure from Enkyōji are not known, Takuan depicts the sixteen-year-old Daitō turning away from Tendai in favor of Zen. He allegedly reflected:

Even if I were to study exhaustively the *Tripiṭaka* [Buddhist canon], I would only be a person whose learning is based on the words of others. Though such people may be called wise, there must be another way to live [spiritually]. If I construe famous phrases to be the Buddha-Dharma, I will never be able to resolve the great matter. It would be far better to enter the [Zen] sect that "does not depend on words, points straight [at a person's mind], and is singly transmitted."[10]

These words are a standard Zen criticism of Tendai and the other Buddhist schools labeled by Zen as "doctrinal." The final sentence alludes to a well-known stanza ascribed to the Ch'an/Zen patriarch Bodhidharma. Whatever Daitō's actual sentiments, the above account echoes the biography of the Ch'an master Lin-chi (d. 866), who alluded to another line of Bodhidharma's verse: "Suddenly Lin-chi said with a sigh: 'These are prescriptions for the salvation of the world, not the principle of "a separate transmission outside the teachings." ' Then he changed his robe and traveled on a pilgrimage."[11]

Zen Training under Masters Kōhō and Nanpo

After leaving Enkyōji, Daitō went first to Kyoto and then farther east to Kamakura. The centers of Japanese Zen at the time were Kyushu (Hakata) and Kamakura, with Kyoto a distant third. According to Shunsaku, Daitō had a dialogical encounter *(mondō)* with an unnamed abbot of Kenchōji temple in Kamakura. Takuan dates the meeting 1301, when Sōden Dōkai (d. 1309) was serving as abbot; two years later the famous Chinese master I-shan I-ning (1247–1317) assumed the post. Daitō reportedly challenged the abbot with a koan: "When you encounter a dying snake in the road, don't beat it to death. Carry it home in a bottomless basket."[12] At the end of their brief dialogue the senior figure hesitated, and Daitō gave a shout. The nineteen-year-old Daitō is thus portrayed by his biographers as already conversant with Zen texts and adept at *mondō,* though he had not yet trained under a Zen master or even been ordained as a monk.

Soon thereafter, in 1303 or 1304, Daitō presented himself to his first Zen teacher, Kōhō Kennichi (1241–1316), also known by his title Bukkoku Kokushi. An emperor's son who studied in Japan under two émigré Ch'an masters, Kōhō was one of the leading Zen figures of the day. At the time he was abbot of Manjuji temple in Kamakura. The first interview between Daitō and Kōhō stretches over three days, according to the version offered by Shunsaku. For a dialogue of this nature there was no one present to make a careful transcription; either participant might have reported the exchange to his students, and there may also have been a period of oral transmission within the lineage before an account was recorded. Some encounters were undoubtedly recreated at a later date by those who composed and compiled texts. That such dialogues have long been given credence within Zen is reason enough to take them seriously, even if we choose to regard them more as literature than as history.

The language of the first Daitō-Kōhō encounter is terse, difficult to follow, and full of references to Buddhist and Zen writings. Daitō demonstrated a mastery of the Ch'an corpus, alluding to such classics as the *Record of Lin-chi (Lin-chi lu),* the *Transmission of the Lamp (Ching-te ch'uan-teng lu),* and the *Blue Cliff Record (Pi-yen lu).* His later style of teaching and writing—direct, self-assured, almost brusque—is already apparent. For example, he gave replies such as "With each step I trample on Vairocana's head" or "I alone am holy throughout heaven and earth" (Vairocana is the cosmic Buddha of the Shingon sect; "I alone am holy . . ." is attributed to the infant Shakyamuni).[13] Following the second day of dialogue, Kōhō accompanied the newcomer to the temple gate and said to him: "I have seen many Zen practitioners, but none have been as brilliant as you. I invite you to shave your head and become a monk here. You will be a pillar upholding my Way."[14]

The decisive moment of the *mondō* reportedly occurred on the third day, as follows:

> The Master [Daitō] visited Bukkoku [Kōhō] again the next day. When Bukkoku saw him coming, he quoted an ancient master and asked, "When the Great Function manifests, unbound by restrictions, what then?" The Master replied, "It is already manifest, long before you asked the question." "Where?" Bukkoku countered. "Last night a wild wind broke a pine tree in front of the gate," the Master answered. Bukkoku said, "What is this wild wind?" The Master fanned himself with his fan. Bukkoku paused. The Master demanded, "Isn't the wild wind coming from this fan?" Bukkoku laughed and said, "You nearly saw it but went right past."[15]

In encounters of this kind, the participants are striving to use language in a manner that undercuts and transcends the recognized limits of language. The most valued responses make their point through demonstration rather than argument, and the ideal is to sustain a lively pace that does not tolerate self-conscious reflection or calculation. Too long a hesitation signifies some kind of shortcoming and can result in "defeat" (though in other cases a deliberate pause is a proper response). Even in Daitō's initial exposure to Zen, the importance of words is already evident. Far from rejecting verbal discourse, *mondō* acknowledge language's potential ability to express insight, stimulate awareness, and transform a given situation.

These encounter dialogues tend to resist customary forms of interpretation; even the simplest gloss raises a number of challenging hermeneutical issues. Perilous as the enterprise may be, we must nonetheless make some attempt to unpack the cryptic language handed down by Zen tradition. A master may ask a Zen monk to demonstrate the essence *(tai)* and the function *(yū)* of a particular koan or of Buddha-nature itself. In the dialogue quoted above, not only does wind manifest the wondrous functioning of Buddha-nature, but a wind wild enough to topple a tree also expresses the primordial, "unbound" quality of Buddha-nature, beyond the grasp of the discursive mind. Daitō's final response is to fan himself. While the "Great Function" manifests spontaneously, at the same time each person is also its creator; though it is here already, one still has to prove or demonstrate it. The wind cited by

Daitō, besides illustrating the Great Function, may also allude to his interaction with the master—in that case, the pine tree in front of the temple gate symbolizes Kōhō, who has been "blown away" by the bold young Daitō. Kōhō catches on and asks, "All right, show me this wild wind," and Daitō silently indicates himself through the use of his fan. Kōhō's pause is a further test, and this time he apparently catches Daitō, whose attempt to verbalize his meaning betrays a lack of certainty. Daitō was close, but not close enough: "You nearly saw it but went right past."

Soon after his arrival at Kōhō's temple, Daitō was ordained as a monk. The biographers pass over the meaning of this event for Daitō or for his role in the Zen community. At the least, "taking the tonsure" involves a ritual shaving of the head, a formal declaration of monastic vows, and the acceptance of a new Buddhist name. Daitō's full monastic name was Shūhō Myōchō, though the records do not indicate how or when it was acquired. Myōchō ("Wondrous Transcendence") is Daitō's *imina,* usually the first name that a monk receives from his teacher, and it is likely that he was given this name when he became a monk under Kōhō. Shūhō ("Peak of the [Zen] School") is Daitō's *go,* sometimes chosen by the monk himself; he was using it by 1326. The name Daitō ("Great Lamp") is part of an honorary title bestowed by Emperor Hanazono late in the master's career.[16]

During this same period, Kōhō was also visited by the person who went on to become Daitō's most illustrious contemporary, Musō Soseki. The comparison between Kōhō's initial meetings with the two young practitioners is revealing. Unlike Daitō, Musō had already experienced several years of formal Zen training in a major metropolitan monastery, but he was frustrated by his teacher I-shan I-ning, and he had been trying for some time to meet Kōhō. According to the earliest *Chronicle* of Musō's life, Kōhō greeted the new arrival with a challenge: "Show me what Master I-shan has taught you." In reply, Musō quoted his teacher: "In my school there are no words, no Dharma, to give people." Kōhō raised his voice and demanded, "Why didn't you answer that such a teaching already reveals a lot?" Upon hearing this response, Musō immediately had an insight. He vowed to himself, "I won't come to see the Master again until I have attained deep enlightenment!" and thereupon left.[17] Whereas Daitō's *mondō* with Kōhō lasted for three days, Musō's ended in five minutes. Daitō gave many creative replies, but Musō offered only one quote from his former teacher. Yet Musō had some kind of insight and Daitō did not. The outcomes of these encounters also varied: Musō departed promptly, whereas Daitō stayed for a year or two as one of Kōhō's monks. In the end, however, it was Musō, not Daitō, who became Kōhō's Dharma heir. One further comparison is of interest—the *Chronicle* of Kōhō confirms this exchange between Kōhō and Musō, but there is no mention in Kōhō's biographies of any meeting with Daitō.

One night Daitō was practicing zazen meditation in the Manjuji monks' hall when he overheard someone in another room reciting a verse by the Chinese master Pai-chang Huai-hai (720–814):

> Truth's naked radiance,
> cut off from the senses and the world,
> shines by itself—
> no words for it.[18]

When Daitō heard this stanza, he had a sudden insight, and that same night he went to Kōhō to present his understanding. No *mondō* is recorded, and no satori poem emerged from the incident, but Kōhō was unstinting in his praise. He allegedly told Daitō: "This is true insight. You must raise aloft the banner of the Dharma and fortify the teachings of our sect."[19]

Though enlightenment is sometimes depicted as an all-or-nothing experience, insights may vary considerably in depth, clarity, and intensity. The biographers' phrase for Daitō's (and Musō's) first insight under Kōhō is *sei ari,* which usually indicates an initial glimpse or taste of self-realization. Kōhō's more emphatic expression "true insight" *(shinshō no kenge)* echoes a famous phrase in the *Record of Lin-chi,*[20] and his reference to the banner of Dharma is a Zen response to high attainment, an idiom that often signifies recognition of a Dharma heir.

Pai-chang's deft poem and Daitō's electric response to it demonstrate one of the ways in which Zen language and Zen practice can converge. The stimulus that precipitated Daitō's first awakening experience was not only verbal; it also happened to be a sixteen-character verse. For Daitō, the entire stanza or one of its phrases apparently functioned as a "turning word" *(ittengo):* a word or expression, delivered at just the right moment, that powerfully transforms the experience of the listener or reader. In this case, the pivotal utterance was not even aimed specifically at Daitō. Later, as a mature master, Daitō freely used poetry and poetic capping phrases to create his own turning words. It is in a sense ironic that Pai-chang's highly regarded poem concludes with a statement about the ultimate ineffability of truth. And yet for practitioners of eloquent Zen, declarations like "there are no words for it" paradoxically function as an effective type of religious language.

As Kōhō and Daitō seemed to be developing a fruitful rapport, another distinguished master attracted Daitō's attention: Nanpo Jōmyō, known also by his title Daiō Kokushi.[21] Nanpo had trained in China for eight years under a leading Ch'an master, Hsü-t'ang Chih-yü (1185–1269). Upon his return to Japan, Nanpo settled in Hakata, Kyushu, where he taught for thirty years. In his seventies he was invited to assume the abbacy of monasteries in Kyoto and Kamakura. Shunsaku credibly states that Daitō was motivated by Nanpo's excellent reputation, and Takuan even depicts Kōhō as encouraging the move to another teacher, in response to a question by Daitō about a koan:

> The Master [Daitō] had previously asked Bukkoku [Kōhō] about the koan "An Ox Passes Through the Window." Bukkoku said, "Old Nanpo has intimately inherited Hsü-t'ang's teaching. Someday go to Nanpo and question him."²²

The practice of working with more than one Zen master was well established in China, where students traveled on pilgrimages in order to seek their true teacher or test their understanding through "Dharma combat." Some of the Chinese monks chronicled in such texts as the *Transmission of the Lamp* seemed to be continuously en route from one temple to another, traversing vast distances mostly on foot. During the early phases of Japanese Zen, similar patterns were followed. Nanpo trained for ten years in Japan under the émigré Ch'an master Lan-ch'i Tao-lung (1213–1278), for eight years in China under Hsü-t'ang of the same line, and then again under Lan-ch'i for three years after returning to Japan. Musō began his career under I-shan I-ning, left for a while to seek another master, returned, and then left again to work under Kōhō Kennichi. Kanzan Egen, one of Daitō's two principal disciples, was fifty years old and an experienced monk when he first met Daitō; he received Daitō's sanction as a Dharma heir after only three years. At the same time, the independence of students was limited by propriety and lineage affiliations. In one extreme case, Chūgan Engetsu (1300–1375) suffered ostracism and even threats on his life because he changed Zen masters in a manner that was considered improper.

In 1304 Daitō left Kōhō's temple in Kamakura and traveled west to Kyoto, where he found Nanpo at Tōkō-an temple. The first Nanpo-Daitō interview, which was relatively brief, began as follows:

> The Master [Daitō] said, "I have come a long way to receive your guidance—please grant me a brief interview." Nanpo replied, "I am getting old, and my strength has waned. Sit down for a while and have some tea." The Master said, "If that is how you deal with this, I'm afraid I cannot accept it." Nanpo said, "You are just a new arrival. How can you know about this matter?" The Master responded, "For gentlemen, isn't the wind the same over a thousand-mile distance?"²³

This exchange follows a classic pattern of Zen *mondō*. When Nanpo humbly parries the newcomer's request for guidance, he expresses the

Zen tenet that fundamentally there is nothing to teach and nothing a student can acquire that he does not already have. His reply also functions as a kind of test, a way of probing Daitō's understanding. Daitō's reaction is bold: "Don't kid me!" Then Nanpo challenges him more directly. Again Daitō demands to be taken seriously, by alluding to a Confucian maxim about the essential equality of "gentlemen." His response also recalls a famous answer given by the Sixth Patriarch of Ch'an, Hui-neng, upon meeting his teacher: "Although my barbarian's body and your body are not the same, what difference is there in our Buddha-nature?"[24] The newly ordained Daitō is characteristically fearless and quick-witted even in the presence of a venerable Zen master like Nanpo.

Sometime after this encounter Nanpo assigned Daitō the koan "An Ox Passes Through the Window," perhaps at Daitō's request. The koan appears in a number of Ch'an texts, including the thirteenth-century koan collection called the *Gateless Barrier (Wu-men-kuan):*

> Wu-tsu Fa-yen said, "An ox passes through the window. His head, horns, and four legs all go through. But why can't the tail pass too?"[25]

This koan is considered to be one of the most difficult in Zen. According to a standard interpretation, it deals with the traces of delusion or pride (the tail) that remain after enlightenment (the ox going through), though sometimes the tail itself is taken as a symbol of enlightenment or Buddha-nature. Others insist that the koan does not involve symbols at all. We do not know how long Daitō worked on this koan or how much interaction he had with Nanpo during this phase of his training. The records merely state that Daitō eventually expressed his understanding of the koan to his teacher in two capping phrases, those cryptic comments that later characterized his Zen style. According to Shunsaku, Daitō first replied, "Crooked mind is apparent." He may have been saying to Nanpo, "I see your intention to entrap me with that question, but the tail has already passed for me." The comment could also be directed at Wu-tsu Fa-yen, who originally formulated the koan. This response did not satisfy Nanpo, who urged Daitō to probe more deeply. Three days later Daitō gave his second reply: "To listen to the empty words of the fortune-teller." Here the words of a soothsayer suggest something illusory or delusional, so Daitō may be asserting that those who are still troubled by the tail are deluded by something nonexistent, by a self-created problem. Nanpo still was not satisfied, but he spurred Daitō on with a single comment, "You have gotten close."[26] His language recalls Kōhō's remark to Daitō at the end of their *mondō* about the wild wind and the fan: "You nearly saw it but went right past."

The specific nature of Daitō's koan practice remains obscure, because the material provided by his biographers is so fragmentary. Capping phrases appear to have played a key role in his early training, though it never becomes clear whether he succeeded in answering the "Ox Passes Through the Window" koan. The eighteenth-century biographer Kokai, perhaps sensing this gap, asserts that Daitō "investigated and solved nearly two hundred koans" during the next year.[27] In any case, the bond between master and disciple intensified and deepened. Nanpo reportedly told Daitō: "You are a natural monk. Surely you are someone who has been practicing the Way for longer than one or two lifetimes."[28] When Nanpo fell ill for ten days, he closed his door to all of his students except Daitō. In 1305, when Nanpo moved from Tōkō-an to another Kyoto temple, Manjuji, he took Daitō with him as his personal attendant.

Sometime during the two-year period at Manjuji, Daitō was given the koan "Barrier," the full version of which is called "Ts'ui-yen's Eyebrows" or "Ts'ui-yen Instructs the Assembly at Summer's End." A seminal rendering of this koan is found in the *Blue Cliff Record:*

> At the end of the summer retreat, Ts'ui-yen said to the assembly, "All summer long I've been talking to you. Look and see if my eyebrows are still there." Pao-fu said, "In his heart the thief is afraid." Ch'ang-ch'ing said, "They've grown." Yün-men said, "Barrier."[29]

Ts'ui-yen Ling-ts'an, an influential tenth-century Ch'an master, alludes to an adage that one's eyebrows will fall out if one talks too much or teaches erroneously. Having just finished a series of sermons during the summer training session, he seems to be asking, "Did I violate the ineffable Dharma when I spoke about it?" In the traditional Zen interpretation, Ts'ui-yen was not particularly concerned about having erred; his primary intention was to set up a test for his disciples. Using something as concrete and familiar as "eyebrows," he frames the problem in terms of existence and nonexistence. The first disciple suggests (indirectly) that the eyebrows are not there, the second says that they are; but either answer, by itself, is one-sided. Then Yün-men Wen-yen (862?–949) says, "Barrier" (Ch. *kuan;* Jp. *kan*), as in a tollgate or a frontier pass. Yün-men's one word also has the force of a command: "Stop!" or "Shut up!" In Zen practice this "Barrier" is regarded as an expression of the realm that transcends duality—by refusing to get caught in an either/or formulation, Yün-men escapes Ts'ui-yen's trap.

According to Shunsaku, Daitō first answered the koan with the capping phrase "To add error to error." This response implies that Ts'ui-yen's question erred, but so did Yün-men's reply, which somehow made matters worse. Zen language, because of its multifaceted nature, can express censure and praise simultaneously; in that case, Yün-men's "error" (deft response) also rectified Ts'ui-yen's "error" (penetrating question), thereby resolving the whole situation. Nanpo told Daitō that he must go even deeper into the koan: "That is all right, but you still must grasp the essence of 'Barrier.' Then one day your whole life will be different."[30]

Satori at Kenchōji

At the end of 1307, Daitō and Nanpo left Manjuji in Kyoto and went to Kamakura. Daitō was twenty-five, Nanpo seventy-two. Nanpo became abbot of Kamakura's prestigious Kenchōji temple on the twenty-ninth day of the twelfth month. Two or three years had passed since Daitō was first assigned the koan "Barrier," and he still had not resolved it. Biographer Shunsaku does not attempt to describe Daitō's practice or suggest the vicissitudes of Daitō's inner life; he simply reports on the climax of the process:

> Less than ten days had passed [at Kenchōji] when the Master [Daitō] tossed a key onto a desk. In that instant he broke through "Barrier." He attained a boundless satori of complete interpenetration in which the great Dharma was fully manifest. Sweat covered his body.[31]

A profound awakening experience resists verbal expression, though Shunsaku attempts to convey its impact by resorting to conventional phrases. The one time Daitō spoke directly of the event, at the inauguration of Daitokuji, he used metaphoric language. Offering incense, he said:

> This incense is within Master Yün-men's "Barrier," an inexplicable koan that I could not resolve for the longest time. When I was at Kenchōji near Kamakura, I grasped this incense, and since that time its fragrance has filled the air.[32]

Once a practitioner has reached the requisite state of ripeness, usually after years of intense inner questioning, a seemingly insignificant event can trigger awakening. Given this state of readiness, enlightenment can also be generated from within, independent of any noticeable external stimulus. In Daitō's case, there may have been something about the tossing of the key that precipitated the experience: the sharp sound of metal striking wood, the sight of an object falling, or simply the act of releasing something—he had been holding tightly to "Barrier" for years without resolving it. The numerous associations between a "key" and a "barrier" are suggestive: perhaps Daitō had just finished unlocking a gate or a door, and something about the act suddenly showed him the way through his own barrier. It is also possible that there was no inherent connection between the two events (beyond their simultaneity). In that case, the breakthrough could just as easily have come when Daitō was washing his face the next morning.

Even within the Zen tradition, accounts of enlightenment experiences vary widely in setting, narrative detail, and emotional intensity. Chronologically, the closest point of comparison to Daitō is Musō, who came to awakening about three years earlier, at the age of thirty-one. Though Musō had trained formally in major monasteries, he was living alone in a secluded hermitage in the town of Usuba, Hitachi province (present Ibaraki prefecture). One evening at the end of the fifth month, Musō did zazen outdoors until after midnight and then went inside to go to bed. In the darkness he reached out to support himself against a wall, but he misjudged its location and stumbled to the floor. In that instant of surprise he experienced enlightenment. Musō's *Chronicle* does not explicitly state that Musō awakened, nor does it attempt to describe the experience; it merely reports that Musō composed his satori poems.[33]

Daitō, certain that he had penetrated Yün-men's "Barrier," rushed to his teacher and exclaimed, "Almost the same path!" He thereby affirmed the essential oneness of his own spiritual path with the path of Yün-men and, by extension, the entire lineage of Ch'an/Zen masters. It must have been as evident to Nanpo as it was to his disciple that the koan had been resolved, because this time Nanpo did not test Daitō or evaluate his verbal response. Instead he related an experience of his own:

> Nanpo was greatly surprised. "Last night," he exclaimed, "I dreamt that Master Yün-men entered my room. Today you penetrated 'Barrier.' You must be a second Yün-men!" The Master [Daitō] covered his ears and left.[34]

Nanpo's intuition that Daitō was spiritually bonded to Yün-men (prompting Daitō to cover his ears in a gesture of humility) eventually gained wide acceptance in Rinzai Zen. Yün-men Wen-yen, one of the leading lights of T'ang dynasty Ch'an, founded a lineage that flourished under his name for three hundred years before it was absorbed into the Lin-chi school. Renowned for his incisive one-word answers, Yün-men is credited with the creation of hundreds of koans, including eight in the *Blue Cliff Record* and five in the *Gateless Barrier.* Whether or not Nanpo actually had such a timely dream, it appears that Daitō himself felt a close affinity with Yün-men after struggling for years with Yün-men's "Barrier." Daitō greatly admired the masterful use of language by Yün-men and his religious heirs; he was especially drawn to the writings of Hsüeh-tou Ch'ung-hsien (980–1052), a third-generation descendant in Yün-men's line. Yün-men did not allow his disciples to build the customary memorial hall, and Daitō gave a similar order at the time of his death. One further connection may be coincidental. Because of the manner in which Yün-men attained satori (tradition claims that a gate was slammed on his leg), his leg was injured. Daitō also had an injured leg by the end of his life, yet both men nonetheless insisted on dying in the full-lotus posture. The apparent link between Yün-men and Daitō was made into a felicitous koan that is still used by the monks of Daitokuji:

> Daitō Kokushi is called the reincarnation of Yün-men, but they were separated by several hundred years. What was he doing all that time?[35]

Daitō was the first native Japanese Zen master to be identified in this way with a seminal Ch'an master, a pairing that symbolizes his exceptional mastery of Ch'an. One hundred years after Daitō, the Japanese Zen master Ikkyū Sōjun (1394–1481) identified himself with the Chinese master Hsü-t'ang (Nanpo's teacher). As James Sanford has noted,

> [Ikkyū] came to consider himself not simply a spiritual descendant of the Chinese monk [Hsü-t'ang] but his veritable reincarnation. This more than half-seriously held conviction found repeated expression not only in Ikkyū's poems, but even more interestingly in two paintings done by members of his circle. Though nominally likenesses of Ikkyū, these pieces each have the beard and moustache of a famous depiction of Hsü-t'ang added over Ikkyū's features so as to bring both men into a single portrait.[36]

Such developments show how ardently the Japanese Zen monks sought to embrace and internalize Ch'an.

On the day following his enlightenment, Daitō presented two written verses to his teacher. The rare document duplicated in Figure 1 is the earliest extant record in Daitō's own hand:

> I've broken through Cloud Barrier—
>   the living way is north south east and west.
> Evenings I rest, mornings I play,
>   no other no self.
> With each step a pure breeze rises.
>
> Cloud Barrier pierced, the old path's gone—
>   clear sky bright sun my true home.
> Activity's wheel turns freely beyond men.
> Golden Kāśyapa departs,
>   hands clasped on his chest.

Following the poems, Daitō wrote to Nanpo:

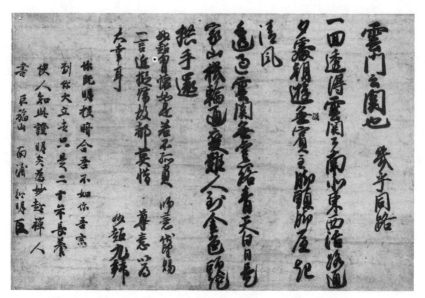

FIGURE I. DAITŌ'S TWO ENLIGHTENMENT VERSES, WITH A RESPONSE BY HIS
MASTER. COURTESY OF DAITOKUJI.

This is my inner state. If it is acceptable to you, Master, I bow down
and humbly request a word from you. I am planning to return soon
to the old capital [Kyoto]; your kind permission would please me
greatly.[37]

In the two poems Daitō expresses his profound joy and his sense of
freedom through a variety of colorful metaphors and allusions. Cloud
Barrier is a contracted form of Yün-men (literally, "Cloud-gate") and
"Barrier," the koan that precipitated Daitō's awakening. Penetrating
the Cloud Barrier, Daitō simultaneously plumbed the koan, the former
master, and the deluded aspect of his own mind; the vanishing of clouds
to reveal a clear sky (or a full moon) is a well-known Buddhist metaphor
for enlightenment. Other images in the poems reinforce the sensation
that all obstructions have disappeared. The absence of self and other
(more literally, "host" and "guest") points to a transcendental awareness beyond ordinary subjectivity. In the first line of the second verse,
"the old path's gone" indicates the radical nature of Daitō's experience
—his old self is gone, and he even forgets what brought him to his
present wonderful state. At the same time he has forged his own new
path, no longer relying on buddhas or patriarchs. Activity's wheel is the
mysterious functioning of his own satori, incomprehensible to others.
Kāśyapa, the Buddha's disciple who is said to have received a wordless

transmission of Dharma, came to be honored as the second Indian patriarch of Zen. In Daitō's verse Kāśyapa departs deferentially because he is no longer needed—such is Daitō's confidence that *he* is now an authentic recipient of the Buddha's Dharma.

These two verses attest to the central role of poetry in Ch'an/Zen and in Daitō's own development. Upon attaining enlightenment, a Zen monk was not expected to preach a sermon, write a treatise, observe silence, or do as he pleased; he was supposed to write a poem that expressed his Zen understanding. Simply on the basis of an enlightenment poem or two, masters were thought to be able to assess the depth of the writer's realization, even across considerable gaps of time or culture. Originally, enlightenment poems were also presented as calligraphy, a practice that intensified the link between religious experience and aesthetic expression.

Nanpo wrote his response to the poems directly on the scroll submitted by Daitō, so his words have also been preserved:

> You have already cast away brightness and united with darkness. I am not equal to you. Because of you, my school will become firmly established. Before making this sanction public, you must continue your spiritual cultivation for twenty years.[38]

Nanpo's prediction that Daitō would assure the survival of his lineage echoes traditional language, yet it was confirmed by later developments. The early biographies, having established Daitō's spiritual credentials, provide no further information on the interaction between Daitō and his teacher. Kokai's edition of the *Chronicle* merely notes that Nanpo gave Daitō a purple robe as an emblem of Dharma transmission.

The Making of a Zen Master

When Nanpo told Daitō, "Before making this sanction public, you must continue your spiritual cultivation for twenty years," he was standing within an ancient Buddhist tradition. The canonical term for the spiritual practice that comes *after* enlightenment is *shōtaichōyō:* "sustained nurturing of the sacred embryo [of insight or truth]." One of the earliest uses of this expression is found in a fifth-century Chinese translation of the *Prajñāpāramitā Sutra on Benevolent Kings Protecting Their Countries.*[39] In Ch'an texts the phrase first appears in the writings of the Chinese master Ma-tsu Tao-i (709–788),[40] and in the Sung period the Japanese pilgrim Dōgen Kigen learned it from his teacher T'ien-t'ung Ju-ching (1163–1228).[41]

During the T'ang era in China, the notion of postenlightenment cultivation became closely associated with another ideal, that of the recluse. Ch'an master Fen-chou Wu-yeh (762–823), for example, claimed that the ancient sages "erased their traces and completely forgot the world" for twenty or thirty years.[42] The figure of twenty years itself acquired special status in conjunction with notions of cultivation and seclusion. For most Buddhists, "twenty years" evoked the *Lotus Sutra* parable of the prodigal son, who wandered in poverty for two decades before returning home. Other references are found in Ch'an: Lin-chi reportedly trained under Huang-po for twenty years, and a verse by Hsüeh-tou laments, "For twenty years I have suffered bitterly."[43]

In most religions one finds figures of speech that are later interpreted literally (often with serious repercussions). Daitō, his biographers, and his religious heirs all took pride in what they considered to be Daitō's scrupulous fulfillment of his teacher's injunction. When Daitō became the founding abbot of Daitokuji in 1326, he compared his enlightenment at Kenchōji to the fragrance of incense and then stated, "Though I stored this fragrance in a bag for twenty years, the more it was hidden, the more it became manifest."[44] Kokai emphatically makes the same point:

> From the time the Master received Nanpo's sanction in the second year of Tokuji [1307] until the time of this ceremony, exactly twenty years had elapsed. Earlier, in the Shōchū era [1324–1326], the abbot's seat at Nanzenji had become vacant, and Emperor Go-Daigo had invited the Master three times to take the position, but he had declined. The Master's period of spiritual cultivation accorded with his master's instructions exactly, like the two matching pieces of a tally.[45]

Daitō's period of postenlightenment cultivation spawned a number of legendary and semilegendary accounts that significantly affected his image and his Zen legacy. For those who have a passing familiarity with the leading figures of Japanese Zen, the first picture of Daitō that may come to mind is a beggar under a bridge, based on the traditional account of the master's years of seclusion:

> It is said that he really spent them living among the beggars under the Gojō Bridge in Kyoto, quite indistinguishable from his ragged associates. Eventually, so the story has it, Emperor Hanazono heard of him, and wished to invite him to preach at his palace. Having also heard that this unusual beggar was fond of a certain melon known as *makuwa-uri*, the Emperor went to the Gojō Bridge in disguise carrying a large basket of the fruit. There he handed the melons to the beggars one by one, carefully scanning each face as he did so. Noticing one with unusually brilliant eyes, the Emperor said, as he offered the melon, "Take this without using your hands." The immediate response was, "Give it to me without using your hands."[46]

One of the earliest references to Daitō's alleged twenty years of begging near the Gojō Bridge is a poem by Ikkyū, composed on an anniversary of Daitō's death. Ikkyū had just read Shunsaku's *Exploits*, and he felt that the biographer had glossed over the hardships endured by Daitō during these years. The first line of Ikkyū's poem plays on the literal meaning of Daitō's name, "Great Lamp":

> After Reading the *Exploits of National Master Daitō*
>
> Holding aloft this Great Lamp would illuminate heaven.
> Imperial carriages jostled before the Dharma hall
> but no one recorded his life of wind and water
> for twenty years at the Gojō Bridge.[47]

Another influential proponent of this depiction of Daitō was Zen master Hakuin. A Hakuin text of 1750 may be the first published version of the melon story,[48] and Hakuin painted many expressive portraits of Daitō as a bearded and barefoot beggar, alms bowl in hand, his tattered robe covered by a straw cloak. On one of these portraits (figure 2), Hakuin wrote the following poem:

> Wearing a straw mat among the beggars,
> through his greed for sweet melons
> he's been taken alive.
> "If you give me the fruit without using your hands
> I'll enter your presence without using my feet."[49]

Ikkyū and Hakuin both turned to poetry when they sought to appraise or mold Daitō's story. Ikkyū was commenting on a text, and Hakuin was inscribing a portrait, yet poetry satisfied their needs in both cases. Hakuin's colorful stanza may even be seen as an answer to Ikkyū's call for a more intimate depiction of Daitō's life as a beggar. Nearly three centuries after Ikkyū composed his versified memo, it received a suitably poetic reply.

Casting Daitō in the role of a mendicant has rich mythic nuances. In many cultures, gods or sages have disguised themselves as beggars when they entered the world to test or assist ordinary mortals. Mendicancy carries additional meaning in Buddhism: Shakyamuni himself lived on the alms collected daily in his bowl, and a ritualized form of begging was retained in most schools of Asian Buddhism. Chinese pilgrims who encountered an old beggar in the vicinity of the sacred Mt. Wu-t'ai wondered if they had seen the bodhisattva Mañjuśrī in one of his favorite guises. A twelfth-century Japanese text, *Tales of Times Now Past (Konjaku monogatari)*, reaffirmed: "Among beggars, in the present as well as the past, there are incarnations of buddhas and bodhisattvas."[50]

FIGURE 2. DAITŌ AS A BEGGAR, BY ZEN MASTER HAKUIN.
COURTESY OF EISEI BUNKO FOUNDATION.

Although Daitō did not refer specifically to begging in his written works, he did exalt poverty as a reflection of spiritual integrity.

If we move from hagiography to history, it is possible to reconstruct several of Daitō's activities during the years preceding the inauguration of Daitokuji. On the twenty-ninth day of the twelfth month, 1308, Nanpo Jōmyō died at the age of seventy-three. Daitō had resolved the koan "Barrier" at the beginning of that year and had remained at Ken-chōji to continue his training. After Nanpo's funeral service and an appropriate period of mourning, Daitō left Kamakura and returned to Kyoto in 1309. Rather than seek another teacher or attempt a pilgrimage to China, he moved into a small temple called Ungo-an in eastern Kyoto. Though none of Ungo-an's buildings remain, it was located in the area where the Yasaka pagoda and Kōdaiji temple stand today. Only a few blocks away is the prominent Rinzai Zen temple Kenninji, founded in 1202 by Myōan Eisai (1141–1215).[51] A few more short blocks to the west is the Kamo River, which runs north-to-south through Kyoto. Of the many bridges that cross this river, the one closest to the probable site of Ungo-an is the Gojō Bridge, where the local beggars are said to have congregated.

This entire section of Kyoto had the qualities of a sacred space in the religious minds of the medieval age. Mt. Hiei, the dominant peak in the Higashiyama hills, was considered a sacred mountain, responsible for protecting the city from any malevolent influences emanating from the northeast. When Eisai built Kenninji, he compared the Kamo River to the Ganges, India's holy river. And he likened his new temple to India's Jetavana Grove *(vihāra)*, where Shakyamuni taught his assembled disciples. The present name of this area, Gion, is a contraction of *Giju Gikko-doku-on*, the Japanese transliteration for Jetavana Vihāra.

So little is known about Daitō's activities during the Ungo-an period that we cannot even assess the begging stories with any degree of confidence. Some modern commentators accept them at face value; others dismiss them entirely. D. T. Suzuki writes, "Daitō Kokushi lived the life of a beggar for more than twenty years and tasted the lowest levels of human life."[52] Jon Covell claims that "Daitō actually spent only about five years begging at the Gojō Bridge," though Covell offers no evidence to support this estimate.[53] Several Japanese scholars believe that Daitō joined the beggars under the Gojō Bridge by day and returned to Ungo-an in the evening.[54] Shunsaku merely states (in the passage that disappointed Ikkyū): "The Master returned to the capital and resided east of the river. Only six or seven monks joined him. He threw himself so completely into the hard work that he was oblivious to cold and hunger."[55]

Had Daitō actually spent twenty years as a beggar near the Gojō

Bridge, it is highly unlikely that he could have achieved the mastery of Ch'an literature that he later exhibits in his Dharma lectures, his poems, and his commentaries.[56] Only one dated manuscript survives from Ungo-an, yet it suggests that Daitō became more of a scholar than a beggar during his years of *shōtaichōyō*. The extant document is a complete transcription of the *Transmission of the Lamp (Ching-te ch'uan-teng lu)* in Daitō's own hand, with a postscript. Originally compiled by Tao-yüan in the tenth century and later edited by Yang I (968–1024), the *Transmission of the Lamp* presents biographies of nearly a thousand Ch'an monks and lists the names of another seven hundred. In Japanese Zen of the Muromachi period it was the most revered of the Ch'an classics. By his own testimony, Daitō made his copy in forty days, a short time for such a painstaking task and a clear indication of the intensity of his exertion. His postscript states:

> This is indeed the spiritual activity of a thousand sages, the life-artery of the heroic patriarchs. It goes beyond even the "elusive" and the "rarefied" [of Lao-tzu]. It exceeds by far the land of ultimate truths and principles. Broad and vast, deep and profound, it cannot be fathomed, it cannot ever be known. Much less could anyone hope to be capable of tracing its vestiges in ink. It would be like gouging out wounds on a healthy body. And yet for forty days my brush never left my hand. There are thirty chapters, filled with great and varied circumstances. It would take a craftsmanship altogether beyond my small ability even to begin to do justice to them.
>
> Copied in the second year of Shōwa [1313], on the twenty-third day of the fifth month, by the rustic monk Myōchō.[57]

Two other transcriptions by Daitō, both undated, are also thought to come from his Ungo-an period. In one, he recorded some verses from the *White Cloud Collection (Po-yün chi)*, a compilation of about 150 poems by the celebrated Yüan dynasty poet Shih-ying Shih-ts'un.[58] The fact that one of the first texts in Daitō's hand is a copybook of poems implies an early absorption in the genre, and it is worth noting that the poetry he chose to reproduce came from outside the Ch'an/Zen tradition. In the second document, Daitō copied the discourse record of Ta-ch'uan P'u-chi (1179–1253), author of a comprehensive history of Ch'an called *A Compendium of the Five Lamps (Wu-teng hui-yüan)*.[59] As Daitō transcribed this respected Ch'an text, he parenthetically added his own glosses, beginning a lifelong activity that came to fruition in his capping-phrase commentaries.

During this period Daitō probably immersed himself in a wide variety of texts: the discourse records of eminent Ch'an masters such as Lin-chi, Chao-chou, and Hsü-t'ang; koan collections such as the *Blue*

Cliff Record and perhaps the *Gateless Barrier;* biographies of Ch'an monks; Confucian classics; and secular works of prose and poetry. It is safe to assume that his practice of zazen also continued without remission. When Nanpo died, Daitō ended his formal training under a living master, yet he used texts such as the *Transmission of the Lamp* as a means of continuing his training under the greatest masters of Ch'an, testing himself with their koans and *mondō*. At this level of *shōtaichōyō*, the scholarly "study" of Zen and the disciplined "practice" of Zen are no longer discrete. As Daitō quietly prepared himself for the more public phase to follow, Zen was also on the verge of a new and influential role in Japanese society, culminating nearly a century and a half of steady growth.

4

THE FOUNDATIONS OF JAPANESE ZEN

WHEN DAITŌ spent forty days copying the *Transmission of the Lamp* at Ungo-an, he must have been aware that he was not only transcribing the history of Zen but participating in it as well. Recently sanctioned by an eminent Japanese master who had trained in China, he found himself in a position to affect the tradition at a decisive juncture in its history. It was becoming apparent to the monks of Daitō's generation that Zen would be successful in its new home. Amidst this personal and historical transition, he turned to the past for bearings, for inspiration, and for confirmation of the authenticity of his spiritual heritage. A brief review of Zen's development in Japan will illuminate the Zen milieu that nurtured Daitō and that Daitō was about to influence in turn.

Early Phases

The first phase of Japanese Zen began in the late twelfth century.[1] Tendai monks traveled to China, found that Ch'an was the dominant school of Sung Buddhism, and brought its teachings back to Japan. Such pilgrimages were made possible by the resumption of contact between China and Japan after a lapse of nearly three hundred years. For both countries the lure of trade could no longer be resisted: the Chinese sought swords, fans, and screens from their island neighbor; the Japanese valued brocades, incense, and tea found only on the mainland. With the renewal of official relations, the Japanese struggled to master the advanced techniques used by the Chinese to build and sail seaworthy ships.

Japan was as eager to import Chinese culture as it was to sample Chinese goods. The monks who accompanied the trading vogages also served as the leading transmitters of the latest developments in Chinese government, technology, art, and religion. Interest in China's religious resources was heightened by discontent with the domestic Buddhist establishment of twelfth-century Japan. Critics accused the entrenched Tendai and Shingon sects of worldliness, elitism, and laxity in monastic life. One response to these perceived flaws was the spread of radical new doctrines that claimed that salvation was open to all, especially through the grace of Amida or the potency of the *Lotus Sutra*. A second response, demanding a return to monastic purity, reaffirmed the more traditional stance that salvation was achieved through one's own spiritual exertions, however arduous. The pioneers of Japanese Zen belonged to this second movement, which attempted to recover its Buddhist roots in China or even in India.

The first Japanese figure to go to China in quest of Ch'an teachings was Kakua, the Tendai monk from Mt. Hiei. Hearing from a merchant that Ch'an was ascendant on the mainland, Kakua and a fellow monk left Japan in 1171. At Ling-yin-ssu temple in Hangchow, Kakua encountered Hsia-t'ang Hui-yüan, a disciple of the famous Ch'an master Yüan-wu K'o-ch'in (1063–1135). Unable to speak Chinese, Kakua was forced to converse with Hsia-t'ang through an exchange of written notes. Before his return in 1175 he achieved enlightenment and received his master's formal certification. The *Genkō [Era] Record of Buddhism (Genkō Shakusho)*, composed in 1322, describes Kakua's reception in Japan: "In the Kaō era [1169–1175] the Emperor heard of Kakua's Ch'an practice. He invited the monk to court and asked him about the essentials of Ch'an. In reply Kakua played a flute. . . . The Emperor and his retainers did not understand."[2]

Even if this story is apocryphal, it illustrates how strange Ch'an must initially have appeared to most Japanese. Kakua had little impact on the Buddhist world of his day, and he failed to produce any religious heirs. Yet he was the first Japanese monk to be included in Chinese histories of Ch'an, recognized as the earliest transmitter of Sung dynasty Ch'an to his native country.

The early phase of Japanese Zen has been labeled "syncretic" because Ch'an teachings and practices were initially combined with familiar Tendai and Shingon forms.[3] For example, monks at a given temple might become ordained and study sutras in the Tendai manner, yet follow a Zen style of meditation. This tendency was in part a response to political realities—Zen provoked considerable opposition from the established sects and the emerging popular faiths. At the same time, just as Chinese Ch'an embraced elements common to Sung Buddhism, areas of fundamental congruence between Zen and older schools of Japanese Buddhism were recognized in Japan. Tendai especially had incorporated certain Ch'an/Zen elements earlier in its development, because its Japanese founder, Saichō, had brought Ch'an texts from China in the early ninth century. Zen's coexistence with the established sects was centered on Kyoto and lasted about half a century, roughly from 1200 to 1250.

An anomaly during this early period was the short-lived Daruma school, established by the monk Dainichi Nōnin (d. 1196?). A self-proclaimed Zen master who never went to China, Nōnin taught a brand of Zen that challenged the value of many customary Buddhist practices. He claimed that his teachings were based on the Ch'an texts that had been in Japan since Saichō's era, such as three treatises attributed to Bodhidharma. The considerable impact of Nōnin's Zen in the Kyoto area is known from the intensity of the opposition it aroused at the time. One early account, by an author partial to Myōan Eisai's lineage, asserted that Eisai "debated several times with Nōnin on doctrinal matters and eventually defeated him."[4] After Nōnin's death, a number of his heirs joined the community of monks led by Dōgen. Scholars have recently concluded that the Daruma school had discernible influence on Dōgen's teachings and the subsequent development of Sōtō Zen.[5]

Zen itself might have been absorbed into Tendai or Shingon, without achieving an independent identity, had it not been for two factors: powerful patrons began to support the fledgling sect, and several distinguished Ch'an masters arrived from China. These developments engendered a period of growth and consolidation that lasted nearly a century, from about 1250 to 1340, during which Kamakura displaced Kyoto as the hub of the Zen world. The patrons attracted to Zen included nobles, provincial governors, members of the imperial family, and—most critically—the Hōjō regents of the Kamakura shogunate. Following a pattern set by the fifth regent, Hōjō Tokiyori (1227–1263), several of the Hōjō leaders became disciples of émigré Chinese masters, built and endowed Zen monasteries, and enforced monastic regulations. The Hōjō were sincerely impressed by the Zen masters they met, and they saw that association with Zen bolstered their cultural credentials. Alert to new ways of exercising influence over the country's religious institutions, they inaugurated the system of officially ranked Zen monasteries known as the Five Mountains (*Gozan*). In 1299 Jōchiji was designated the first Gozan temple, and three other Kamakura temples were added in 1310. Within the next half-century (under the Ashikaga) three hundred Zen monasteries would eventually be brought into the Gozan network.[6]

In Zen circles it was a source of pride that the Hōjō rulers who repulsed the Mongols were among the first Zen students in Japan.

Musō lauded Hōjō Tokiyori and his son Hōjō Tokimune in the following manner:

> In the Kamakura period the Zen disciple Hōjō Tokiyori revered the Zen Dharma and built Kenchōji. . . . In the Kōan period [1278–1287] the world was in an uproar because the Mongols were invading. The lay disciple Hōjō Tokimune, however, remained composed, and every day he summoned Zen master Wu-hsüeh Tsu-yüan, then head of Kenchōji, or various experienced Zen monks, and they would speak about matters of Dharma. This attitude was so praiseworthy that it was noted in Wu-hsüeh's *Record.* Later, Tokimune built Engakuji, continuing to foster the prosperity of the Zen school. Isn't this the reason why the Mongols did not destroy our country? The world was kept secure during the two generations of father and son, and both men are reported to have died in an exemplary manner.[7]

During this period of growth and consolidation, interaction between the worlds of Chinese Ch'an and Japanese Zen increased. Japanese monks went to China hoping to return with Chinese masters, and Chinese masters urged Japanese students to carry Ch'an teachings back to Japan. Some Chinese masters in Japan arranged for promising Japanese disciples to acquire further training on the continent, as in the case of Nanpo. A number of Japanese pilgrims remained in China for decades, and several ended their lives there. Of course, the relationship was not always harmonious—a few of the émigré Ch'an monks were accused of spying for the Mongols, and at least one Ch'an master, unhappy with what he found in Japan, abruptly went back to China.

Though Japan and China were again in contact, they were still separated by enormous cultural gaps, nowhere more evident than in the world of Zen. The first Zen monasteries in Japan, constructed and administered in accord with Chinese precedents, seemed strangely foreign in their new setting. The design and placement of their buildings differed from the architecture of existing Buddhist temples. Zen monks used unfamiliar forms of dress, etiquette, and speech; in some temples Chinese could still be heard. Martin Collcutt has described these new Zen monasteries as "outposts of Chinese religion and culture in medieval Japanese society,"[8] an assessment that is apt for the first Kamakura monasteries though perhaps less appropriate for the monasteries of Daitō's time.

Language was one of the most serious obstacles faced by the Japanese who aspired to understand Zen. The classics of Ch'an were of course written in Chinese, and the peculiar style of Ch'an texts differed from the vernacular Chinese then in use. Moreover, the Japanese did not read or pronounce this Chinese as Chinese. Instead they marked the Chinese text so that it could be read in Japanese, a complex process that involved inversions of word order and additional verb conjugations. At the outset there were no dictionaries of Zen terms, and most texts were copied by hand (with varying degrees of accuracy). Woodblock printing did not begin in Japan until the late Kamakura period, and its diffusion was gradual. Consequently, many individuals who expended great energy to master the language of Zen never achieved satisfying results. It was ironic that those wishing to enter the sect "not dependent on words" first had to grapple with a foreign language; yet the process may also have served positive functions consistent with Zen principles (for example, reducing attachment to the most literal dimensions of language). In spite of these difficulties, Japanese monks were expected to use Chinese *(kanbun)* for their serious written works, and *kanbun* remained prominent in Japanese Zen for over five hundred years.

The arrival in Japan of Ch'an masters who could not speak Japanese presented challenges to hosts and guests alike. Ming-chi Ch'u-chün reached Japan in 1330 and informed his Japanese patron in verse:

> I came ten thousand leagues over the seas to these shores,
> knowing nothing of the language that people here spoke:
> all I could make out was a babble of "ba ba ba,"
> couldn't catch more than something like "li li li."[9]

If no interpreter was present, Japanese scribes attempted to record the Chinese master's words phonetically in the Japanese *kana* syllabary, though they often did not understand what they were hearing. When possible, these transcriptions were later translated into Japanese. It is recorded that Lan-ch'i, in an interview with Toyama, lord of Tango, said, "Maku-maa-sun, maku-maa-sun, nyuzu kunrii fuya." A native of Szechuan, Lan-ch'i spoke a dialect that was not the standard Chinese of the time, and his utterance was then put into Chinese characters by another Szechuan native living in Kamakura. The characters were then translated into Japanese as "No delusive thoughts, no delusive thoughts! It is you who are from the very beginning Buddha."[10] A remark by master Wu-hsüeh, transcribed in a similar fashion, was long assumed to be a koan, but it could not be deciphered. Centuries after Wu-hsüeh's death, a later master realized that what Wu-hsüeh had said was "Come in, come in! I have something to say to you."[11]

Inevitably, the language barrier also hampered the Japanese monks who went to China. Eisai still could not speak Chinese on his second pilgrimage to the mainland, nineteen years after his first trip. Well-financed pilgrims customarily hired interpreters, many of whom were merchants. The Japanese monks seemed to be less adept linguistically than students from other nations, and few among them achieved genuine competence. One of the more able Japanese students was Betsugen

Enshi (1295–1364), whose fluent Chinese earned him the distinction of being "often mistaken for a Korean."[12]

The biographies of monks such as Betsugen reveal a tendency in both Japan and China to regard skill in the composition of Chinese prose and poetry as an indication of an advanced state of Zen understanding. A well-known example in Japan is the examination administered by the émigré master I-shan I-ning after his arrival in Kamakura. To select disciples from those petitioning him for instruction, I-shan tested their ability to compose Zen-style verse in Chinese. The young Musō Soseki was one of the monks ranked in the highest category. It would not be long before Japanese monks began to make explicit assertions about the connection between Zen and poetry, as will be seen below.

The language barrier gave rise to a practice called *hitsudan*, literally, "brush-conversation." Though the Japanese and the Chinese could not understand each other's spoken language, they could all *write* Chinese characters. This common base enabled the Ch'an masters to instruct their Japanese disciples through an exchange of written questions and answers. The Japanese monks in China who relied on interpreters for most daily transactions preferred to conduct their private interviews with Zen masters in this manner, and the same format was also used in Japan, for example between Lan-ch'i Tao-lung and Kōhō Kennichi. Though these conversations in *hitsudan* could be awkward, Ming-chi Ch'u-chün viewed the situation poetically:

> I express my mind
>   using a brush instead of my tongue,
> and you seize my meaning
>   hearing my words with your eyes.[13]

This practice survived even when both participants were Japanese, as in a written dialogue between Daitō and Emperor Hanazono.

Besides the exchange of monks and masters, the rapid circulation of texts was another indication of the close association between the worlds of Chinese Buddhism and Japanese Zen between 1175 and 1358. Though the transmission of written works did not take precedence over the introduction of teachings and practices, one of the aims of pilgrimage was the procurement of texts. From the outset, the study and transcription of important Ch'an works was central to Zen training in Japan. The latest Chinese koan collections, biographies of eminent monks, and monastic codes were known in Japan within a few years of their distribution on the continent. Works of Japanese masters, sent to China by admiring disciples, sometimes earned appreciatory postscripts by Chinese masters. It was a high honor for a Japanese monk to have his biography written by a Chinese monk and even more prestigious if the account was included in a Chinese history of Ch'an.

The major Ch'an biographical compilations, such as the *Transmission of the Lamp* that Daitō transcribed, are found in a mid-thirteenth century catalogue of books held by Tōfukuji temple in Kyoto.[14] By the time of Daitō's death in 1337, the *Blue Cliff Record* and the *Gateless Barrier,* two classic koan collections, had also reached Japan. The exact date of the *Blue Cliff Record*'s transmission is not known, though a traditional account claims that Dōgen made a copy of it in 1227, on his last night in China before returning to Japan. Although it is unimaginable that this lengthy work could have been transcribed so quickly, the text attributed to Dōgen, known as the *One-Night Blue Cliff Record,* is housed in Daijōji temple in Kanazawa. In the early fourteenth century the *Blue Cliff Record* was republished in China by Chang Ming-yüan. Chang's edition, which was based on two previously published woodblock texts and surviving handwritten copies, reached Japan shortly thereafter, and it is the version still in use today. Daitō was among the first in Japan to focus on the *Blue Cliff Record,* commenting line by line on the entire text with capping phrases.

The introduction of the *Gateless Barrier* to Japan can be dated precisely. The Japanese monk Shinchi Kakushin (1207–1298) practiced Ch'an in China under the text's compiler, Wu-men Hui-k'ai (1183–1260). When Kakushin returned to Japan in 1254, he brought his master's koan collection with him. The émigré Chinese master Ch'ing-cho Cheng-ch'eng (Ta-chien, 1274–1339), a contemporary of Daitō, is said to have written the first commentary on this text in Japan, yet this work apparently has been lost. The *Gateless Barrier* currently in use in Japan is based on a Japanese edition of 1405.

Though the two major koan collections were transmitted to Japan by the beginning of the Muromachi era, their impact on Japanese Zen differed considerably. During the medieval period the *Blue Cliff Record,* more complex and more literary, was widely used and admired. It provided an important stimulus to the cultural movement known as "the literature of the Five Mountains" *(Gozan bungaku),* which spread beyond the confines of the Zen monasteries. The *Gateless Barrier* did not achieve comparable stature until the seventeenth century. By that time the monks' ability to read Chinese (as *kanbun*) had declined, and they found Wu-men's text to be structurally simpler and linguistically more accessible than the *Blue Cliff Record.*[15]

Genealogies of the First Transmitters

Lines of descent are of great importance in many realms of East Asian society, and they are especially emphasized in Japan. Zen is regarded by its adherents as a spiritual lineage that can be traced back through the patriarchs of China and India to Shakyamuni Buddha himself. The numerous divisions and subdivisions of the Zen school are sometimes diagramed in the manner of a family tree, and they have been compared to "cousins who accept each other's claims to membership in the extended clan, but who prefer to think of themselves as representing the most direct line of descent."[16]

During the two centuries following Kakua's return from China in 1175, various lines of Ch'an were transmitted to Japan. A 1677 exposition of this transmission, still accepted within Japanese Rinzai Zen, identified forty-six such transmissions *(den)*.[17] Among these, twenty-four were singled out as streams *(ryū)* or branches *(ha)* that took hold through a succession of disciples. The first monk in each of these streams is called a *so,* a term with a number of possible English renderings: ancestor, patriarch, founder, pioneer. The men recognized in this way were almost equally divided between Japanese pilgrims and Chinese émigrés. Twenty-one of the streams were of the Lin-chi (Rinzai) school, and three belonged to the Ts'ao-tung (Sōtō) school. The first *so* in this scheme was not Kakua but Eisai, who returned to Japan in 1191. The last master of the group was Daisetsu Sonō, the pilgrim who returned in 1358. Among the Chinese émigré masters, the first to establish a Japanese stream was Lan-ch'i Tao-lung, who arrived in 1246. And the last Chinese master to leave his mark in Japan during this period was Tung-ling Yung-yü (d. 1365), who debarked in 1351. After 1358 the intercourse between Chinese Buddhism and Japanese Zen declined, and no new teaching lines were established in Japan for another three hundred years.

Another important term used to express genealogical continuity in Zen is *shū* (Ch. *tsung*). It can be translated in English as "lineage," "school," or "sect," depending on the historical context. In China the various divisions of Ch'an were primarily a means of identifying master-disciple lineages. At times these divisions may also have signified doctrinal or institutional differences, but our knowledge of these traits is less certain. Nor is the boundary between Ch'an and other Buddhist schools always clear-cut. When speaking of early Ch'an, "lineage(s)" is perhaps the best translation; after 960 (the beginning of the Sung period), the designation "Ch'an school" becomes more meaningful. In Japan the boundaries between Buddhist schools—and the divisions within them—were more distinct than in China, so the term "sect" can be used for Japanese Zen and also for the primary divisions within it.

Recently, Bernard Faure has challenged scholars to reexamine many of the assumptions associated with the concept of lineage or sect as used in Zen and Zen studies. Giving little credence to the ideal of a spiritual bond between masters and their disciples, Faure argues that lineages are formed more from without than from within:

In other words, orthodoxy takes its shape not from its kernel—a lineage—but from its margins, the other trends against which it reacts by rejecting or encompassing them. . . . By this dissolving the contours of the "sect," a concept definitely too "substantialist," we may be able to provide a more nuanced analysis and to emphasize the various kinds of regrouping—sociological, political, strategical, doctrinal, or geographical.[18]

Recognizing the limitations of certain widely used terms, we may nonetheless identify the key figures of the transmission process and note their traditional placement in the various subdivisions of Ch'an and Zen. From the outset the streams of Japanese Zen formed a configuration that differed from the Chinese antecedents, and these differences increased with time. Dominant branches of Ch'an perished in Japan, while lines of lesser prominence eventually triumphed there. One result of this process was that masters of relative obscurity in China came to be regarded as great Chinese patriarchs by the Japanese.

Naturally, many Japanese and Chinese monks brought to Japan the stream of Ch'an that was dominant at the time. In the Southern Sung period the religious mainstream was occupied by the P'o-an line of the Yang-ch'i branch, a division of the Lin-chi school.[19] The leading figure among the Japanese pilgrims who transmitted this P'o-an line of Ch'an was Enni Ben'en (1201–1280). Enni's teacher was Wu-chun Shih-fan (1177–1249), abbot of the preeminent Ch'an temple in China, Ching-shan. Praised by a medieval Japanese text as "the number one Ch'an master in the world,"[20] Wu-chun actively encouraged the propagation of Zen in Japan. His disciple Enni aspired to be faithful to his master's teachings, but conditions in Japan did not yet permit the establishment of an independent Zen sect. Instead Enni promoted a type of Zen that incorporated elements from other schools of Chinese and Japanese Buddhism, a response characteristic of the early conciliatory phase. The most influential Chinese monk to bring the P'o-an line to Japan was Wu-hsüeh Tsu-yüan (1226–1286), another disciple of Wu-chun Shih-fan. When Wu-hsüeh arrived in 1279 he was already fifty-three years old, a senior monk who had held important positions in major Chinese monasteries. Hōjō Tokimune accordingly made him the founder-abbot of Engakuji monastery in Kamakura.

Many of the pioneers of Japanese Zen were heirs to streams of secondary influence on the continent. The earliest master in this category was Eisai, who was exposed to Ch'an in 1187 on his second pilgrimage to China. At that time an undivided Yang-ch'i branch of Ch'an was ascendant, eclipsing Huang-lung Ch'an, yet Eisai brought back second-rank Huang-lung. Untroubled by the complexities of Chinese lineage rivalries and perhaps unable to identify the special features of the

Huang-lung line, Eisai equated it with all Ch'an. He also treated Ch'an as the whole of Sung Buddhism, using designations like "Buddha Ch'an (Zen)," "Pure Ch'an," or "Tathāgata Ch'an."[21] Whereas Eisai's identification of Ch'an and Sung Buddhism has typically been seen as an oversimplification or an expedient polemical device, recent research suggests that Eisai's assessment was not without basis. That is, Ch'an permeated Sung Buddhism to such an extent that the purported distinctions between the various Buddhist schools were comparatively insignificant.[22] Upon returning to Japan in 1191, Eisai continued to regard himself as a Tendai monk, and he willingly incorporated his version of Ch'an into a Tendai framework. The established schools felt threatened nonetheless, and their resistance prompted Eisai to reply that he was reviving the "T'ang dynasty Ch'an" introduced centuries earlier by the founder of Japanese Tendai, Saichō.

Daitō's teacher Nanpo was another important early figure who introduced a less influential Ch'an line. Nanpo trained in China under Hsü-t'ang Chih-yü, a master of the Sung-yüan branch of Yang-ch'i Ch'an. Hsü-t'ang served as abbot of more than ten different temples, among them the prestigious Ching-shan, yet he never achieved the stature of Wu-chun. When Nanpo was about to return to Japan, Hsü-t'ang encouraged him with a confident prediction: "East of the sea, my heirs will increase daily."[23] Those who view themselves as part of a spiritual lineage transmitted from Hsü-t'ang to Nanpo to Daitō (a group that includes most present-day Rinzai Zen followers) believe that Hsü-t'ang's vision was in fact confirmed by subsequent developments.

Besides Nanpo, many Chinese émigré monks also represented the Sung-yüan line in Japan. The most significant figure in this category was Lan-ch'i Tao-lung, noted above, who arrived in Japan two decades before Nanpo's return. Through the patronage of Hōjō Tokiyori, Lan-ch'i became founder-abbot of Kenchōji in Kamakura, and his appointment was a harbinger of Zen's shift from syncretic coexistence to independence.

During these years of cultural and religious transmission, relatively obscure branches of Ch'an were also brought to Japan. The most notable transmitter of a lesser branch was Dōgen Kigen, an heir of T'ien-t'ung Ju-ching. Ju-ching belonged to the Ts'ao-tung (Sōtō) school, one of the classic "Seven Schools" of Ch'an. But as Dōgen himself acknowledged, by the thirteenth century Ts'ao-tung was numerically overwhelmed by the many branches of the Lin-chi school. Upon Dōgen's return to Japan in 1227, he first attempted to promulgate Zen in Fukakusa on the southern perimeter of Kyoto. Disappointed by his reception or impelled by other reasons that remain unclear, he then moved north to Echizen province and built Eiheiji monastery.[24] There he completed the *Treasury of the True Dharma Eye (Shōbōgenzō)*, the work that has since earned him a reputation as a thinker of international importance. Whereas rivalries between the various streams of Zen did not disturb Dōgen in his early teachings, after the move to Echizen he sharply attacked the Lin-chi/Rinzai school and some of its leading masters, claiming that Lin-chi "never said anything original even in his dreams."[25] The Japanese Sōtō school, which has long regarded Dōgen as its first Japanese patriarch, weathered the vicissitudes of history to become one of the two major sects of Japanese Zen.

The Development of Koans

Kōan is a Japanese pronunciation of the Chinese word *kung-an*, which literally means "public case." A koan is a spiritual puzzle that cannot be solved by the intellect alone. Though conundrums and paradoxes are found in the secular and sacred literature of many cultures, only in Zen have such formulations developed into an intensive method of religious training. What gives most koans their bite, their intellect-baiting hook, is some detail that defies conventional logic, such as the tail that cannot follow the ox through the window. Initially, a koan may be used as the focus of concentration in seated zazen. But once the practitioner is gripped by the koan, he or she becomes involved with it beyond the scheduled periods of meditation. Some practitioners report that they can continue to work on koans even during sleep. When absorption in the koan is so intense that it leads to self-forgetfulness, awakening is said to be possible.

The actual development of koan practice is difficult to trace. The word *kung-an* first appears in the discourse record of Ch'an master Huang-po Hsi-yün (d. 850?); in another early text one of Huang-po's heirs tells an approaching monk, "As a ready-made koan, I spare you from thirty blows."[26] The *Blue Cliff Record* merely states: "The koan arose in the T'ang and flourished in the Sung."[27]

Anecdotes and dialogues from the lives of notable Ch'an figures, whether recorded in early biographical collections or passed around orally by itinerant monks, provided abundant source material for the earliest Chinese koans. In these accounts, masters framed questions in paradoxical language to test their disciples, often drawing upon incidents and objects close at hand. For example, many dialogues in the *Record of Lin-chi* have a koan-like quality:

> The Master [Lin-chi] said to the steward of the temple, "Where have you come from?" "I've been to the provincial capital to sell the millet," answered the steward. "Did you sell all of it?" asked the Master. "Yes, I sold all of it," replied the steward. The Master drew a line in front of him with his staff and said, "But can you sell this?"[28]

Lin-chi did not identify any of his training methods as a *kung-an* (the word does not even appear in his *Record*), though later in Japan "Rinzai [Lin-chi] Zen" became almost synonymous with "koan Zen." By the early tenth century, practitioners were being instructed to meditate upon their predecessors' enigmatic words or deeds. Nan-yüan Hui-yung (d. 930) adapted some of Lin-chi's expressions to test his students, and Yün-men Wen-yen (d. 949) may have been the first master to assign koans in the manner that came to characterize the Lin-chi school.

By the time that koan collections appeared in the eleventh and twelfth centuries, koans were well-defined as a form of Ch'an practice and a genre of Ch'an literature. The earliest and largest collection was the *Blue Cliff Record,* compiled in two stages. Initially, Hsüeh-tou Ch'ung-hsien (980–1052) assembled one hundred koans from the records of former masters, composed an appreciatory verse for each koan, and commented on fifteen of the koans with capping phrases. About sixty years after his death, Yüan-wu K'o-ch'in (1063–1135) added an introduction to most of the koans, a prose commentary to all of them, capping phrases on individual lines of koan text, more capping phrases on each line of Hsüeh-tou's verses, and a final commentary on Hsüeh-tou's verses. The resulting book, published in 1128, was named after Yüan-wu's "Blue Cliff" residence on Mt. Chia in Hunan. It has served for centuries as a rich compendium of Ch'an teachings, lore, poetry, and wit. The *Blue Cliff Record* also reflects the confluence of Ch'an and the literati class during the Sung period. As Robert Buswell has noted, such koan collections "helped to bring Ch'an into the mainstream of Chinese cultural life and also led to a fertile interchange between Ch'an and secular belles lettres."[29]

Yüan-wu's disciple Ta-hui Tsung-kao (1089–1163) marks a peak in the development of Chinese koan practice. Ta-hui advocated introspection of the koan's kernel, a meditation technique called *k'an-hua,* "observing the [critical] phrase." Rather than pondering the koan as a whole, practitioners try to focus their attention on its most crucial word or phrase (Ch. *hua-t'ou;* Jp. *watō*). Continuously holding this phrase in the mind, one attempts to penetrate its meaning. Ta-hui claimed that this method was an effective "short-cut" to practice and a path to sudden enlightenment:

> If you want to understand the principle of the short-cut, you must in one fell swoop break through this one thought—then and only then will you comprehend birth and death. Then and only then will it be called accessing awakening. . . . You need only lay down, all at once, the mind full of deluded thoughts and inverted thinking, the mind of logical discrimination, the mind that loves life and hates death, the

mind of knowledge and views, interpretation and comprehension, and the mind that rejoices in stillness and turns from disturbance.[30]

The type of koan practice advocated by Ta-hui was transmitted to Japan before Daitō's era (and it still characterizes present-day Rinzai Zen). Thus when Daitō investigated the koan "Ts'ui-yen's Eyebrows," he focused on the single word that had been designated as the koan's *watō:* "barrier."

In 1229 Wu-men Hui-k'ai published his *Gateless Barrier,* adding brief prose comments and verses to forty-eight selected koans. As noted above, Wu-men's text was easier to approach than the *Blue Cliff Record:* it was about one-tenth the length of its predecessor; it had one compiler instead of two; it lacked capping phrases; and its style was more straightforward and less literary. The first koan in the *Gateless Barrier* came to be one of the most widely used koans in Zen:

> A monk asked Chao-chou, "Does a dog have Buddha-nature or not?" Chao-chou said, *"Mu."*[31]

Throughout the Sung and Yüan periods, masters assigned koans regularly and commented on them in lectures, in prose, and in verse. Many details of the practice, however, remain hazy. Did students have the freedom to choose koans themselves, or did masters assign them, perhaps in a standard sequence? When students needed guidance, did they see their masters individually or in groups? Was koan practice a formal or an informal part of the monastic routine? How were the literary dimensions of koan practice handled? These and other questions are not resolved by the fragmentary materials that survive from these eras.

Koans can be answered verbally or nonverbally. Naturally, verbal responses dominate the written records, though a variety of nonverbal responses were also noted—monks and masters would slap each other, prostrate, roll up a mat, lie down, wave their sleeves, and so on. Some nonverbal responses were specific to a particular situation, as in case 40 of the *Gateless Barrier:*

> Pai-chang took a pitcher, placed it on the ground, and asked, "This must not be called a pitcher. What do you call it?" . . . Kuei-shan walked up, kicked over the pitcher, and left.[32]

In the *Record of Lin-chi* there is one encounter that is completely silent:

> Ta-chüeh came to see Lin-chi. The Master [Lin-chi] raised his whisk. Ta-chüeh spread his mat. The Master threw down the whisk. Ta-chüeh folded up the mat and went into the monks' hall.[33]

Such responses still have a place in contemporary Zen: certain koans are answered by demonstrations in which the practitioner acts out his or her understanding in a spontaneous and uninhibited manner. In order to express the spirit of a koan involving an animal, for example, a student might get down on all fours and "become" that animal. Whatever the content of a verbal or nonverbal answer, a master is primarily concerned with the practitioner's understanding; if a master sees that a "correct" response does not spring from the requisite mind-state, he is not supposed to accept it. The degree to which acted-out demonstrations were used in Ch'an or in early Japanese Zen is not known. It is not safe to assume that the answers that entered the written records were the only answers given, yet it would also be a mistake to read contemporary answers or methods of koan training back into the early texts. In the *Record of Lin-chi*, Lin-chi asked Hsing-shan, "What is the white ox on the bare ground?" Hsing-shan answered, "Moo, moo!"[34] In cases such as this, we do not know what kinds of nonverbal responses might have accompanied the recorded verbal answers.

Koan Practice in Early Japanese Zen

The introduction of Ch'an to Japan stimulated fresh developments in the koan tradition. While the effectiveness of koans was recognized by all the early masters, they also saw that their Japanese students had difficulty relating to the classic Ch'an koans, which often seemed too foreign, too complex, and too literary. So they added new koans to the traditional corpus. Some were created spontaneously in response to particular situations; others were based on passages from Buddhist texts already known in Japan. For example, the pithy *Heart Sutra* included several phrases that made effective koans, and students were further challenged to condense this sutra into just "one word." A verse from the *Diamond Sutra,* spoken by the Buddha, became another koan:

> If you try to see me through form
> or hear me through sound,
> nothing you see or hear
> is where I am.[35]

In order to pass this koan, a student had to be able to demonstrate how —if not through form—one *does* see Buddha.

The earliest phase of Japanese Zen was centered in Kamakura, the site of the shogun's headquarters, and many of the koans from this era were adapted for warrior disciples. A master might ask, "If you were surrounded by a hundred enemies, how would you manage to win without fighting or surrendering?"[36] Other koans were based on incidents (or alleged incidents) from the lives of warriors. The following tale suggests the intensity with which some warriors practiced Zen:

Tadamasa, a senior retainer of Regent Hōjō Takatoki, had the Buddhist name Anzan. He was an ardent Zen follower and for twenty-three years came and went to the meditation hall for laymen at Kenchōji. When the fighting broke out in 1331, he was wounded in an engagement, but in spite of the pain he galloped to Kenchōji to see Sozan, the twenty-seventh teacher there.

A tea ceremony was in progress at Kenchōji. When Anzan arrived in full armor, Sozan quickly put a teacup in front of the warrior and asked, "How is this?" Anzan at once crushed it under his foot and said, "Heaven and earth broken up altogether." The teacher asked, "When heaven and earth are broken up, how is it with you?" The warrior stood with his hands crossed over his breast. Sozan hit him, and Anzan involuntarily cried out from the pain of his wounds. Sozan said, "Heaven and earth are not quite broken up yet."

The drum sounded from the camp across the mountain, and Anzan galloped quickly back. The next evening he came again, covered with blood, to see the teacher. Sozan came out and asked again, "When heaven and earth are broken up, how is it with you?" Anzan, supporting himself on his blood-stained sword, shouted a great "Katsu!" and died standing in front of the teacher.[37]

A student working on this koan was sometimes tested with a follow-up question: "When the elements of the body are dispersed, where are you?"[38]

Some of the koans from the Kamakura period retain the flavor of the popular literature *(setsuwa bungaku)* of early medieval Japan, a narrative genre in which Buddhism and folk religion, entertainment and moral instruction, were richly intertwined. In these Kamakura koans pilgrims have visionary dreams, supernatural beings appear and disappear, and animals assemble to hear sermons on the Dharma, their "eyes glistening with tears." For example, a Zen priest claims that the divine snake that guards his temple is also coiled day and night around his own body, visible to those with the "true eye." In another koan, a Zen monk is asked to conduct a rain-making ritual during a great drought, and he responds by urinating on the altar. The outraged officials promptly arrest him, but on the way to police headquarters the travelers are drenched by a downpour, and the monk is set free amidst warm apologies.[39]

The leading masters of Japanese Zen were involved with koan practice in various ways. Though Eisai's name is not ordinarily associated with koans, there is evidence that he was among those who created them from sutra passages. Jufukuji, Eisai's temple in Kamakura, is referred to in one early text as the "temple of the eighteen diamond koans."[40] Dōgen was exposed to the koan-centered practice of several Lin-chi lines during his five-year stay in China, and he later produced his own

compilation of three hundred classic koans. When this text was rediscovered in 1766, it was rejected as spurious by Sōtō sect adherents who
insisted that Dōgen had never used koans (the work was authenticated
in 1935). Dōgen's familiarity with koans can also be seen in his *Treasury
of the True Dharma Eye*. In the later chapters of this book, however, he
distanced himself from Ch'an advocates of koan practice, mocking Ta-
hui's understanding as "nothing but a few memorized passages from
the . . . sutras."[41] (Such comments also reflected the lineage rivalries
and political setbacks that bedeviled Dōgen after his return from
China.) Among the émigré Chinese masters, Lan-ch'i took the lead in
adapting his teaching to his listeners, using uncomplicated koans like
"The One-Word Sutra" and issuing koan-like injunctions such as "See
where life comes from!"[42] Wu-hsüeh Tsu-yüan, who reached Kamakura the year after Lan-ch'i's death, had achieved enlightenment
through a koan, and he urged his Japanese students to tackle classic
koans as well as new ones:

> At the beginning you have to take up a koan. The koan is some deep
> saying of a patriarch; its effect in this world of distinctions is to make
> a man's gaze straight, and to give him strength as he stands on the
> brink of the river bank. For the past two or three years I have been
> giving in my interviews three koans: "The Original Face before Your
> Parents' Birth," "The Mind, the Buddha," and "No Mind, No Bud-
> dha." For one facing the turbulence of life-and-death, these koans
> clear away the sandy soil of worldly concerns and open up the golden
> treasure which was there from the beginning, the ageless root of all
> things.[43]

Like Lan-ch'i before him, Wu-hsüeh received students formally in
sanzen, the private master-disciple encounter that became an indispensable part of koan training in Japan. His most prominent disciple was
the Hōjō regent Tokimune, who successfully defended Japan against
the Mongols. Because Wu-hsüeh did not speak Japanese, he had to deal
with Tokimune through an interpreter. Besides the language barrier,
Tokimune's exalted status imposed certain constraints on the master-
disciple relationship—when Wu-hsüeh wished to strike his distinguished student, he administered his blows to the hapless interpreter.[44]

5

DAITŌ ASCENDANT
AT DAITOKUJI

One night the Master [Daitō] dreamed of six
monks who looked like advanced disciples of
the Buddha. The most senior monk said:
"The time has come for you to become head
of a temple. Why do you not go forth?"

EXPLOITS OF NATIONAL MASTER DAITŌ

ACCORDING TO his biographers, Daitō's years of seclusion at Ungo-an
were ended by a revelatory dream in which six monks challenged him to
"go forth." One of the six visitors punctuated his advice by piercing
Daitō's brain with a bamboo needle. Takuan identifies the monks as
"the Six Patriarchs [of Ch'an] who transmitted the robe," and Shunsaku concludes the incident with a convincing detail: "The Master
awoke with a headache."[1] This auspicious dream is the third in Daitō's
biography—his miraculous birth had been heralded by his mother's
dream, and his enlightenment was augured in Nanpo's dream about
Yün-men. Though these visions may be biographers' embellishments,
the forty days that Daitō had just spent copying the *Transmission of the
Lamp* would be sufficient stimulus for a peculiar dream about Ch'an
monks (not to mention a headache).

The decade that Daitō spent at Ungo-an, 1309–1319, had been a
time of continued growth for Zen in Japan. In Kamakura the metropolitan Zen monasteries extended their influence under the patronage of
the Hōjō rulers. The year that Daitō settled in Ungo-an the prestigious
Ch'an master Tung-ming Hui-jih (1272–1340) arrived from China in
response to Hōjō Sadatoki's invitation. After successive appointments
as abbot of several Kamakura monasteries, Tung-ming was persuaded
by the ambitious young Go-Daigo to take over Kenninji monastery in
Kyoto. The political influence of the Hōjō clan was by then eroding,
and their decline was accelerated by Sadatoki's death in 1311, yet their
patronage of Zen was sustained by the regent Takatoki, who came to
power in 1316. During Takatoki's tenure three more émigré masters
were installed in Kamakura temples.

64

Japanese pilgrims continued to seek Buddhism on the Chinese mainland, undeterred by the traumatic effects of the recent Mongol invasions, the hazards of the sea voyage, or the hardships of life in a foreign nation. Though the Mongols who had overrun China remained hostile to Japan, they proved themselves to be enthusiastic patrons of Buddhism. In the first two decades of the fourteenth century, Japanese pilgrimage to China reached its height; in some of the Ch'an monasteries Japanese and Korean monks even outnumbered their Chinese counterparts. For instance, while Daitō was in retreat in Ungo-an, Chūgan Engetsu was waiting in the Kyushu port of Hakata for a ship that would take him abroad. He failed to secure passage on his first attempt in 1318, because the ship's quota of monks had been filled, but he succeeded a few years later.

Daitō's biographers make no mention of any attempt by Daitō to travel to China, nor do they speculate on his possible reasons for shunning such a trip. Daitō was not alone among the promising young monks who eschewed the trip to China in favor of further training in Japan, often in relative obscurity. While Daitō was living simply in Kyoto, Musō similarly spent six years in isolation outside Kamakura. In one of his poems Musō chided those who violated his solitude:

> It would be merciful of people
> not to come calling and disturb
> the loneliness of these mountains
> to which I have returned
> from the sorrows of the world.[2]

Another contemporary Zen monk who stayed in Japan was Kokan Shiren (1278–1345). Kokan believed that the best-qualified Japanese monks were no longer going to China, and he wanted to remedy the situation by going himself, but he abandoned his plans because of frail health.[3] When Kokan's teacher I-shan asked to read a history of Buddhism in Japan, Kokan was prompted to write his *Genkō [Era] Record of Buddhism (Genkō Shakusho)*. It was published in 1322, the first work of its kind.

Toward the end of Daitō's Ungo-an period there were portentous stirrings in the world of Zen and in national politics. A number of prominent Zen masters died, most notably Kōhō Kennichi in 1316 and I-shan I-ning in 1317. Their passing left vacancies at prestigious temples such as Nanzenji, opening the way for a transfer of leadership to a new generation. In 1318 Go-Daigo assumed the throne and began to influence the course of events. Musō was finally lured out of retirement in 1320 by Hōjō Takatoki. The next year Daitō received a grant of land from Go-Daigo's son Prince Morinaga, and in 1323 he had his first meeting with the recently retired emperor, Hanazono. Daitō emerged from his period of postenlightenment cultivation just when Zen was poised to assume a prominent role in medieval Japan. He became one of the new leaders who shaped Zen's rapid expansion.

Debut at Murasakino

Murasakino is a district in the northern part of Kyoto, west of the Kamo River and east of the rounded hills of Kinugasa. Known for the beauty of its fields and flowers (Murasakino means "purple fields"), the area once housed the imperial villa of Emperor Junna (reigned 823–833), and it was a favored spot for aristocratic poetry parties. In Daitō's era the district was a sparsely populated patchwork of rice paddies, forests, and wild marshes. The local peasants honored native gods at an ancient Shinto shrine called Uchiyama, a few simple structures scattered amidst stately trees. None of the buildings in the area was high enough to obstruct the dramatic east-facing view of Mt. Hiei and the Kamo River. Here Daitō undertook the construction of a new Zen monastery, which he named Daitokuji—Temple of Great Virtue. He probably made the move from Ungo-an to Murasakino in 1319, at age thirty-seven.[4] Part of Daitokuji's site was originally occupied by an older Tendai temple, Byakugō-in. Daitō's uncle Akamatsu Norimura, the provincial governor of Harima, apparently facilitated the transfer of land rights. Though records identify Norimura only as a "patron" of Byakugō-in, the temple property may have been part of the Akamatsu clan's extensive holdings.

Daitō soon began to attract influential patrons. Zen master Nanpo's sanction established his religious credentials, and in Norimura he had a valuable link to the regional power structure. At a time when political authority was beginning to shift from Kamakura to Kyoto, the prospect of a new Zen monastery untainted by the influence of the Hōjō regime appealed to a variety of potential supporters. Besides the practical advantages of association with an up-and-coming Zen master, some patrons must also have been prompted by sincere spiritual motivations and Daitō's personal qualities. Norimura's son Norisuke (1312–1371) became an early backer, as did Go-Daigo's son Morinaga, who gave provincial lands to Daitokuji in the Genkō era (1321–1323).[5] In the spring of 1324 Emperor Go-Daigo enlarged Daitokuji's compound by granting land on its south side. This tract included Emperor Junna's burial mound and another Tendai temple, Unrin-in, which had been founded in 869. Daitō wrote a letter of appreciation to Go-Daigo, promising that future generations would continue to perform memorial services at the imperial tomb.[6] In 1325, still a year before Daitokuji's formal inauguration, Daitō received a flurry of decrees from emperors

Go-Daigo and Hanazono. In the second month the retired emperor Hanazono appointed Daitokuji as an imperial prayer center, and Emperor Go-Daigo (not to be outdone) issued a similar decree five months later.[7] Other named and unnamed benefactors began to make donations in the form of money, materials, land in Kyoto, or income-producing estates in the provinces.

The "beggar at the bridge" legends portray a reluctant Daitō who was plucked from obscurity by an emperor seeking a sage. Though there may be a kernel of truth in this idealized image, it is likely that Daitō welcomed and even solicited patronage during the Ungo-an and early Murasakino periods. His connections within the Zen world and his family ties with the Akamatsu clan positioned him well for such activity.

Daitō's two imperial patrons, emperors Hanazono and Go-Daigo, were members of different branches of the royal family: Hanazono, who reigned from 1308 to 1318, belonged to the "northern" line; his successor Go-Daigo, who reigned from 1318 to 1339, was from the "southern" line. It appears that Daitō met Hanazono shortly before he met Go-Daigo. Hanazono kept a copious diary, a source of valuable information about the era's intellectual and religious milieu.[8] In this work Daitō is first mentioned on the twenty-third day of the fifth month, 1323, when Hanazono was a young man of twenty-six (and already "retired"). The entry is brief: "I met the Venerable Myōchō [Daitō]. Our conversation was similar to our previous talk."[9] (The "previous talk" was not recorded.)

By the time Hanazono encountered Daitō, he was well versed in the teachings of a number of Buddhist schools, and he also had developed a keen interest in Zen.[10] His spiritual yearnings and insights are revealed in his diary. In a passage written after his forced abdication in 1318, he lamented: "Often, because I am restless, I consider withdrawing from the world, yet my resolve is not up to it. This shows I lack a mind that seeks the Way. How pitiful! I wonder what the buddhas and heaven, with their clear vision, would have me do."[11] As he explored the doctrines and practices of the Shingon, Tendai, and Pure Land schools, Hanazono read over forty Buddhist texts, which he cited by name. Early in 1320 he met a Rinzai monk named Gatsurin Dōkō (1293–1351), also known as Myōgyō. Their conversation lasted till dawn, and Hanazono praised Gatsurin as a "dragon."[12] The two men continued to meet periodically for about three years. As Hanazono's involvement deepened, so did his admiration for Zen: "The exalted, wondrous nature of the Buddha-Dharma and the utmost principle of the Mind-ground lie solely in this one school of Zen. The teachings of the other schools of the Mahayana and the Hinayana cannot possibly equal it."[13] The retired emperor was introduced to koan practice, and he accepted Gatsurin as his teacher in a formal ceremony, but the relationship was severed abruptly when Gatsurin embarked on a pilgrimage to China.

Around this time Hanazono first met Daitō. Gatsurin and Daitō shared a past affiliation with Kōhō Kennichi, and Gatsurin may have brought Daitō's name to the retired emperor's attention.[14] Shunsaku's depiction of the initial encounter between Daitō and Hanazono later became part of Japanese Zen lore:

> The Emperor began, "The Buddha's Law facing the King's Law on the same level—how unthinkable!" The Master replied, "The King's Law facing the Buddha's Law on the same level—how unthinkable!" The Emperor's expression revealed his esteem for the Master.[15]

Hanazono's opening statement refers to the privilege Daitō has been granted: in the conventional hierarchy the emperor's position was supreme and absolute; few of his subjects were allowed even to look upon his face. In reply Daitō boldly holds up the Buddha's Dharma as a truth that underlies and surpasses all such worldly distinctions, a law that is itself "unthinkable" because it defies conceptualization. Although Hanazono was no newcomer to Zen, the bluntness of Daitō's response may have shocked him: the master had already begun to teach the retired emperor in a Zen manner. A month after Hanazono first mentioned Daitō in his diary, he penned some thoughts on this same subject: "First and foremost, the secular law and the Buddha's truth cannot be two separate things. The *Lotus Sutra* states, 'Whether governing the world or discussing meditation, one should follow the True Dharma in all cases.' More than anyone, an emperor should understand what this means."[16]

Even if Shunsaku's version of the first Daitō-Hanazono encounter is enriched by apocryphal elements, it highlights a pertinent theme and captures the spirit of the remarkable relationship that developed between the two men. As will be seen below, the retired emperor continued to train under Daitō for at least fourteen years, and he came to be acknowledged as one of the master's outstanding disciples.

About a year after Daitō met Hanazono, he first encountered his other imperial patron, Emperor Go-Daigo.[17] Daitō was forty-two, and Go-Daigo was thirty-six. The Emperor hastened to express his enthusiastic support, showering the master with imperial favors, grants, and titles. Go-Daigo also invited Daitō to participate in a religious debate, an event that dramatically accelerated the relatively unknown master's rise to prominence.

The Shōchū Debate

The Shōchū Debate, named after the era in which it occurred, reflected the rivalry between the emerging Zen institution and the established Buddhist sects. By the Shōchū period (1324–1326), Zen had planted roots in southern Japan (Kyushu) and eastern Japan (Kamakura), yet it continued to encounter active resistance in western Japan (the area around Kyoto). There the Tendai and Shingon sects and the older Nara schools had their headquarters. When the leaders of these religious groups petitioned the Emperor to halt the spread of Zen, he responded by setting up a public debate, a procedure sanctioned in Asia by countless precedents. As Yüan-wu wrote in the *Blue Cliff Record:*

> In doctrinal disputes in India the winner holds a red flag in his hand, while the loser turns his clothes inside out and departs through a side door. Those who wanted to hold doctrinal disputes in India were required to obtain royal permission. Bells and drums would be sounded in the great temples and afterwards the debates could begin.[18]

An early religious debate in Japan, authorized by Emperor Saga (reigned 809–823), is said to have lasted seventeen days and nights.

The Shōchū Debate began during the (intercalary) first month of 1325, in the Seiryōden Hall at the imperial palace.[19] Representing Zen were two disciples of Nanpo—Daitō and Tsūō Kyōen (1257–1325). Because Tsūō was Daitō's senior by twenty-five years and the abbot of the prestigious Nanzenji temple, he bore the primary responsibility for defending Zen. The established sects were represented by a number of eminent clerics; foremost among them was Gen'e, the Tendai abbot "renowned for learning beyond all men of the age." Other debaters included Kosei, the abbot of Tōji, a Shingon temple in southern Kyoto; monks from Miidera, a Tendai headquarters temple on the shores of Lake Biwa; and priests from the Nara schools.

Only fragmentary accounts of the debate have survived, and their degree of accuracy cannot be determined, yet the depiction of Daitō's role is revealing. At one point Gen'e reportedly stepped forward and asked, "What is Zen, which claims to be a separate transmission outside the teachings?"[20] His question alluded to the well-known Zen slogan that challenged the sutra-based or "doctrinal" schools of Buddhism. Daitō's reply, terse and uncompromising, was a one-line capping phrase from the *Blue Cliff Record:* "An octagonal millstone flies through the air."[21] Rather than give Gen'e a discursive explanation of

Zen or its relation to the teachings, he sought to express Zen as directly as possible, and to do that he relied on a capping phrase.

We are not surprised to learn that "Gen'e did not understand"— Daitō's image is a difficult one, and Gen'e was probably unfamiliar with the conventions of Zen encounter dialogues. Yet capping phrases are not nonsensical. At the least, the image of a flying millstone suggests something beyond ordinary experience or conventional description, traits that would fit a transmission "outside the teachings." A hard object in flight might also be destructive, even terrifying, just as Zen is considered to have an alarming power to overturn customary patterns of thought. In Zen language the activity of inanimate objects such as flying millstones often refers to the "no-minded" quality of enlightened behavior. Masters assert that if Zen awareness is brought to everyday acts, one can move freely through daily life in a manner as wondrous as "flying through the air."

The baffled Gen'e withdrew and was followed by a Tendai monk bearing a box. Daitō asked him what he was carrying, and the monk replied, "This box is the universe." Tendai doctrine held that the microcosm encompasses the macrocosm, as expressed in the teaching that "one thought is three thousand worlds."[22] Again Daitō abruptly altered the terms of debate—he took up his short staff and struck the box, breaking it. "When the universe is smashed to bits, what then?" he asked. Daitō's challenge would not have been entirely unexpected by a fellow Zen monk. A number of koans pose similar conundrums: "If all things return to the One, to what does the One return?"[23] Or: "In the roar of the kalpa fire, the whole universe is destroyed. Tell me, is This destroyed?"[24] In Zen there are ways to respond to such questions, but the hapless Tendai monk, "dazed and bewildered," was unable to answer Daitō.

Daitō's biographers report a second exchange involving Daitō, Gen'e, and several others; if this encounter was not part of the Shōchū Debate, it may have occurred about the same time.[25] The dialogue, dealing with a Confucian text, is evidence of the renewed interest in Confucianism among Japanese Buddhists:

> [Gen'e's] group heard the Master's [Daitō's] name and went to question him. "What are the methods of the Zen school?" they demanded. The Master answered, "Teaching the truth through falsehoods." The scholars of Confucianism asked, "Have the sages ever spoken falsely?" The Master said, "They have." The men insisted, "Being sages, how could they have spoken falsely?"
>
> The Master asked, "Don't you know this passage in *Mencius*? 'Hsiang [thinking he had succeeded in killing Shun] said, "I have killed Shun." But when Hsiang entered Shun's house, there was

Shun sitting on his bed playing a lute. Shun [who knew of Hsiang's murderous intentions] was pleased when he saw Hsiang come in.' Isn't it untrue [that Shun was pleased to see Hsiang]?"

The scholars of Confucianism fell into a heated discussion among themselves. Then they asked the Master, "How can we resolve the meaning of this passage once and for all?" The Master said, "Actually, Shun killed Hsiang." The scholars all bowed to the ground in the manner of disciples.[26]

In this exchange Daitō not only exhibits an impressive command of a Confucian classic, he also demonstrates the interpretive flair he applied to the texts of his own Zen tradition. Daitō's descendants cite his responses in the Shōchū Debate, especially his smashing of the box and his "octagonal millstone" answer, as epitomizing his character and his Zen style. Yet when these two portrayals of Daitō as debater are seen side-by-side, they present a fuller and more complex portrait of the man. In the first instance Daitō is enigmatic and fierce, whereas in the second he is erudite and articulate. If he had indeed been able to be discursive or nondiscursive as the occasion demanded, he would have fulfilled a peer's definition of a true Zen master, who "simply seizes upon a teaching in response to the moment, giving his tongue free rein."[27]

Political considerations inevitably colored the outcome of sponsored religious debates, and sometimes these events merely legitimated a shift of influence already under way. In Japan of 1325 the former dominance of the older sects had become tenuous; within fifteen years the balance would tip in Zen's favor, through the support of the new Ashikaga shogunate. Emperor Go-Daigo, full of his own ambitions, sought to make the Buddhist establishment, old and new, subordinate to imperial rule. For reasons of his own or in response to the debaters' arguments, Go-Daigo awarded victory to the Zen monks. To Tsūō and Daitō he granted special palanquins, which they or their descendants were invited to use whenever they visited the palace (Daitō's palanquin is still housed at Tokuzenji, a Daitokuji subtemple). Tsūō, aged sixty-seven, literally exhausted himself on behalf of Zen—in a dramatic denouement he died on his way back to Nanzenji right after the debate.

Daitō's former antagonist Gen'e was reportedly so impressed by Zen and its two representatives that he experienced a complete conversion. Shunsaku states: "Senshinshi [Gen'e] entered *sanzen* training [under Daitō]. His accomplishments were not shallow, and the depth of his faith was unsurpassed. To further the construction of the new abbot's residence, he donated his own dwelling to Daitokuji."[28]

Although Gen'e's alleged realignment symbolically reinforces Zen's triumph, it is not as implausible as it may first appear. However intense the sectarian rivalries of the day, individual monks were not irrevocably bound by their affiliations. In fact, the rapid rise in the Zen monastic population during the first half of the fourteenth century can be partly attributed to an influx of monks (and scholar-monks) who had been ordained in the older schools. Another Tendai abbot became a follower of Daitō's heir Tettō after Daitō's death. These senior monks may have been attracted to Zen by a number of factors: its preeminence in China, its association with the latest developments in continental thought, the rigor of its monastic discipline, or the caliber of its leaders. Individual conversions did not, however, diminish the established sects' official opposition to Zen. The vehemence of Tendai resistance was still evident two decades after the Shōchū Debate, when Musō opened Tenryūji temple in 1345. In that case a Tendai threat of violence had to be met by a show of Ashikaga military might, with Tendai again on the losing side.

The Inauguration of Daitokuji

For Daitō's personal career the Shōchū Debate of 1325 was an auspicious debut. To have been chosen at all was an indication of ascendant prestige, and Daitō's comportment further impressed his patrons and his peers. By the seventh month of 1325 Daitokuji had been honored by two emperors as an imperial prayer center, and donations continued to arrive from various quarters. One patron, a wealthy female disciple named Sōin, facilitated the purchase of building materials for the new temple: "They selected huge timbers and raised a wind with the whirring of their axes."[29]

Construction of a Dharma hall began in 1325 and was completed by the end of 1326. In medieval Zen the Dharma hall (*hattō*) was a square building two stories in height; besides the supporting pillars and a single dais, the interior was left bare to accommodate the congregation of monks. The hall was used in Japan in accord with Chinese precedents, as described in a Ch'an text of the Sung dynasty:

> All the monks gather morning and evening in the [Dharma] hall. The abbot enters the hall and ascends the dais. The monastery officers and the assembled monks stand in files as they listen [to the abbot's discourse]. The abbot and the monks exchange questions and answers, thereby clarifying the essential teachings.[30]

Instead of offering learned commentaries on the sutras, a Zen master was expected to express his own enlightenment, his own realization of the Dharma, in a direct and forceful manner. The absence of devotional images such as buddha figures reinforced the master's authority as a living representative of the entire patriarchal line.

In the winter of 1326, on the traditional date of Shakyamuni Buddha's enlightenment (the eighth day of the twelfth month), Daitō conducted the ceremony inaugurating the Dharma hall of Daitokuji. This event concurrently fulfilled several aims: it officially opened both the Dharma hall and Daitokuji; it installed Daitō as founding abbot and affirmed his qualifications for the post; and it served as a public demonstration of Daitō's sources of patronage. The inauguration ceremony performed by Daitō was called a *kaidō* (literally, "opening the hall"). In the traditional Chinese manner, the event began with a solemn procession from the main gate of the temple to the new Dharma hall. The abbot, dressed in his most ornate robes, wore bright red Chinese-style slippers with toes that curled upward. He was trailed by young novices, monks in training, and abbots of other temples, some bearing ceremonial objects. Ordinarily, the abbot would pause at each gate or building to offer a Zen poem in Chinese, but these other structures had not yet been built at Daitokuji.

Once inside the Dharma hall, Daitō mounted a dais by its center stairway and sat facing the assembly. One by one, attendant monks ascended the dais by a pair of flanking stairs, until the ceremonial offerings were complete. The master then addressed the audience. Traditionally, the installation of a new abbot included a lively exchange, in the manner of a final examination, during which any member of the congregation was entitled to engage the abbot in "Dharma combat." In Daitō's case the monks posed their questions in a highly deferential manner, and their master always had the last word. (In contemporary Japanese Zen this dialogue is rehearsed by the abbot and his designated interlocutor.)

Daitō's inaugural Dharma lecture adheres to convention without sacrificing vitality. Rich in the variety of its language, it includes flowery formulas in praise of emperors, personal expressions of gratitude, original poems, comments on koans, erudite allusions, and opaque paradoxes. Early in the ceremony Daitō offered incense to Go-Daigo, the reigning emperor, and to Hanazono, the former emperor, using standard Chinese Buddhist formulas: "I pray that the Emperor will live for tens of thousands of years."[31] Lighting incense for the senior government officials, he enjoined them to emulate Mencius and the model bureaucrats of ancient China. Whereas a number of Ch'an masters had resisted such formalities,[32] Daitō was undoubtedly aware that the two emperors present were also his most powerful patrons.

Because a Zen monk often trained under several masters, it was necessary for a new abbot to name the teacher who had sanctioned his enlightenment. If he had received the sanction of more than one master, he announced which line he had chosen to succeed. In Daitō's opening talk he identifies his teacher as Nanpo Jōmyō and expresses a feeling of "deep obligation for his gift of the milk of the Dharma." He alludes poetically to his own enlightenment at Kenchōji and his subsequent period of self-cultivation. Holding aloft his monk's shawl *(kesa)*, an emblem of Dharma transmission, he asked aloud: "As I reverently don this *kesa*, who can discern its true color?" Later in his address Daitō offers further statements of gratitude, lavishing praise on his benefactor-disciple Sōin. He then rejoices:

> Thanks to the high [aspiration] of the Emperor and his retainers, I have been permitted to requite my indebtedness to all the sages—past, present, and future—in the sea of great enlightenment, to all the superior friends whom I have encountered over many lifetimes in the past, to my companions in the Way who share the daily activities of monastic life, to my teachers, to my parents, to all those who have assisted me, and to all living beings.[33]

The inauguration of Daitokuji marks a significant juncture in the history of Japanese Zen. Previously, all of the major Zen temples had been founded by Chinese émigrés or by Japanese pilgrims who had acquired their credentials abroad. In the Japanese reception of Ch'an, Daitō was the first native monk trained in Japan to establish a major monastery.

Daitō held the post of abbot at Daitokuji from the time of his move to Murasakino in 1319 until his death in the winter of 1337. During that period he made one ten-day trip to neighboring Tajima province and one three-month trip to distant Kyushu. Otherwise, he remained in Kyoto to guide his monks and supervise the growth of his fledgling temple. Daitō's relative lack of mobility was unusual in the early Muromachi period, when a distinguished master would often serve as the abbot of many different temples. We have seen that Daitō's teacher Nanpo, after over thirty years as the resident master of Sōfukuji in Kyushu, was appointed abbot of Manjuji in Kyoto at age seventy-one, then abbot of Kenchōji in Kamakura two years later. Daitō's peer Musō was perhaps the most peripatetic of all—he made ten moves in the last twenty-six years of his life, becoming abbot of eight different temples.[34] Musō's ability to shift with the political tide was remarkable: he became an intimate advisor of the Ashikaga brothers as soon as they defeated his former patron, Go-Daigo; previously he had slipped away from his first supporters, the Hōjō regents, as their fortunes began to wane. Daitō never attempted to duplicate such feats of survival in the public arena. Four years before his death he assented to an imperial decree (intended as an honor) limiting the abbacy of Daitokuji to descendants of his line, and he may have assumed that he too was restricted by this edict. It is also possible that his later career would have followed a pattern similar to Nanpo's if he had lived beyond age fifty-five.

In 1330 Daitō was invited by Yamana Tokiuji (d. 1372) to inaugurate Yūtokuji, a newly built temple in Tajima province (present Hyōgo prefecture), not far from the area of Daitō's birth. Tokiuji was the governor of the province and a descendant of a distinguished warrior family. As part of the Yūtokuji *kaidō* ceremony, Daitō challenged the assembled monks:

> If you think you understand before having heard [the Dharma], you violate the command of the patriarchs. But to have an understanding of the Dharma based on [someone else's] words is also incorrect. Now, is there anyone here who can resolve this matter without committing either of these errors?"[35]

The following year Daitō was invited to Sōfukuji temple in Kyushu, where Nanpo had presided for three decades. The request came from Ōtomo Yorihisa, a marshal of the military headquarters in Dazaifu (present Fukuoka prefecture). Shunsaku reports that Daitō had to ask Go-Daigo twice for permission to make the journey. During his three-month stay Daitō performed a *kaidō* ceremony, completed a ninety-day training period, and founded a subtemple called Shinshū-an. At the end of his visit he composed a farewell poem:

> No footprints of mine are seen
> wherever I wander:
> on a tip of a hair I left the capital,
> on three drum taps I am leaving Kyushu.[36]

The Elaboration of Patronage

In its first decade Daitokuji was directly affected by the sweeping changes that accompanied Japan's transition from the Kamakura to the Muromachi period. In 1330 Kamakura was still the seat of the Hōjō shogunate, and the most prestigious Zen temples were located there. The Hōjō's official Gozan ranking system was first applied to the Kamakura Zen temple Jōchiji in 1299; then Kenchōji, Engakuji, and Jufukuji—all Kamakura temples—were given Gozan rankings in 1310. When Go-Daigo wrested power from the Hōjō regime in 1333, the political center of gravity shifted west to Kyoto. To reinforce this transition, Go-Daigo ordered major changes in the Zen institution, reshuffling the Gozan rankings in favor of Kyoto temples. Daitokuji, which he attempted to place at the very top of the Gozan system, figured prominently in his strategy. However, in less than three years power again changed hands, as Go-Daigo was ousted by his former general Ashikaga Takauji. Takauji confirmed Kyoto as the country's new capital, but he had his own plans for the Zen institution. In the first Ashikaga ranking of the Gozan, dated 1341, Daitokuji was excluded entirely from the top five positions.

Imperial patronage of Daitokuji during Daitō's lifetime can be divided into three phases. During the first phase, from 1323 to 1330, Daitō received a moderate level of support from reigning emperor Go-Daigo and former emperor Hanazono, in roughly equal proportions. Hanazono had met Daitō first; Go-Daigo judged the Shōchū Debate shortly thereafter. In 1325, as we have seen, both emperors made Daitokuji an imperial prayer center. (The Kamakura shogunate, attempting to counter Go-Daigo's influence, in 1329 designated Daitokuji as one of its own prayer temples.) In 1330 Go-Daigo awarded Daitokuji an estate that included Daitō's birthplace in Harima province; the grant specified the temple's allotment of rice income.

Throughout this initial phase of patronage Hanazono was practicing Zen intensely, and at some point he had an enlightenment experience that was validated by Daitō. An undated scroll in Hanazono's own hand poetically expresses his Zen understanding:

> A man who has endured twenty years of pain and suffering
> does not change his old wind and smoke when spring arrives.
> He just wears his robe and eats his rice.
> When one lives such a life,
> could the great earth give rise to even a speck of dust?[37]

In this verse Hanazono refers simultaneously to himself and to Daitō, who was believed to have endured austerities for twenty years.

When Go-Daigo's rebellious schemes were first exposed in 1331, he was forced to flee Kyoto, and his patronage of Daitokuji was interrupted. In 1333 he returned triumphantly to the capital and presided over the short-lived Kenmu Restoration. Go-Daigo's eager support of Daitokuji between 1333 and 1336 constitutes the second phase of patronage. During this period former emperor Hanazono continued his private contacts with Daitō but avoided public notice. Go-Daigo issued over forty decrees concerning Daitokuji, conduct that exemplified his investment in the Zen institution and his attempt to consolidate power after his return to Kyoto.[38] His continuous manipulation of Daitokuji's land rights outstripped his involvement with the holdings of any other temple. The five principal documents were issued in the space of a year; four of them have been preserved, and Daitō's written response to one of them is also extant.

The first of Go-Daigo's major decrees, dated the eighth month of 1333, limits Daitokuji's future abbots to members of Daitō's spiritual lineage. This injunction was contrary to the Gozan principle of open monasteries, whereby abbots were chosen from any Zen lineage on the basis of merit (at least in theory). Go-Daigo's text proclaimed:

Daitokuji is the nation's peerless Zen temple, where a thousand monks live in peace. I command them to pray for the everlasting welfare [of our nation]. In the succession from master to disciple, members of other branches of Zen are not permitted to become head abbot. I write this directive with special respect for the proper transmission of the Dharma, not with any feelings of prejudice. These words shall be left to distant posterity, until the time of Maitreya's appearance in the world.

Twenty-fourth day, eighth month, third year of Genkō [1333]. To Zen Master Shūhō Kokushi.[39]

In the second decree, issued less than two months later, Go-Daigo ordered that Daitokuji be included in the Gozan system.[40] The document's ambiguous wording also seemed to place Daitokuji at the top of the Gozan rankings. Shunsaku states that Daitō respectfully declined the honor (displaying the humility expected of a Zen monk). Yet in a letter to the priest of Yūtokuji, Daitō expressed his pleasure at the news and named the five disciples he would appoint to oversee the anticipated expansion of the temple.[41]

A few months later, in the first month of 1334, Go-Daigo specified in a third major decree that Daitokuji was to be ranked alongside Nanzenji at the apex of the Gozan system. He stated in part: "Daitokuji is a grand and auspicious site for the enhancement of the Emperor's destiny. . . . Its edifices please us greatly. Its ceremonies surpass those of the great temples of the past. It must be placed alongside Nanzenji in the top rank of temples."[42] In the Emperor's new ranking the top four temples were located in Kyoto: Daitokuji, Nanzenji, Tōfukuji, and Kenninji. Below them were Kenchōji and Engakuji, two Kamakura temples.

A fourth Go-Daigo proclamation, in the fifth month of 1334, confirmed Daitokuji's boundaries in Kyoto. At the time the temple extended as far as "the eastern edge of Funaoka Hill on the east, Agui Avenue on the south, the bamboo forest on the west, and the Uchiyama shrine on the north."[43] Another significant decree, in the eighth month of 1334, is known from Kokai's edition of the *Chronicle*. It completed Go-Daigo's recognition of Daitokuji by confirming the temple's provincial landholdings. After naming various estates in different provinces, the Emperor wrote:

From now on, the *kokushi* and the *shugo* [two types of provincial governors] are prohibited from requisitioning corvée labor, rice, or the like in these areas. I hope that my intention to keep the monks well nourished is fulfilled for a long time. When the King's Law and the Buddha's Law aid each other, the imperial wind and the patriarchal wind will unite forever.[44]

Daitō's response is included in his *Record:*

> All the lands held by this temple are now clearly defined. The words
> of this official certificate, once received, cannot be annulled for a hun-
> dred eons or a thousand lifetimes.[45]

It is unlikely that Daitō ever developed as close a relationship with
Go-Daigo as he had with Hanazono. We have already noted the pre-
dominantly political nature of Go-Daigo's behavior, his desire to control the established Buddhist sects, and the attention he lavished on
other Zen masters besides Daitō. For example, when Go-Daigo
returned to power in 1333, he recalled Musō to Kyoto before issuing
any of his decrees to Daitokuji. During this same period Go-Daigo also
invited eminent Ch'an monks to become abbots of Nanzenji and Kenninji, and he gave titles to other Zen masters such as Kakushin. Even
after his overthrow, Go-Daigo maintained relations with a number of
figures; for example, he formally accepted a Buddhist name from
Musō.

One of Daitō's biographers asserts, "Whenever Emperor Go-Daigo
could spare time from affairs of state, he sent for the Master [Daitō] and
questioned him about the essentials of Zen."[46] However, only two
meetings are specifically noted. According to Shunsaku, the Emperor
first invited Daitō to the palace for a ceremony; a portrait of Ch'an master Pai-chang was displayed in honor of the occasion. Go-Daigo was so
pleased by his conversation with Daitō that the next day he sent the
master "precious gold, finely woven silks, and other gifts."[47] In 1335
Go-Daigo paid a visit to Daitokuji. As patrons do, he expressed interest
in the temple's expansion, suggesting to his host that a pond be built
southeast of the abbot's quarters. Daitō "immediately directed the
monks to begin digging a pond, joining them in the work."[48]

During this second phase of imperial patronage Go-Daigo's son
Morinaga, one of Daitō's first backers, continued to demonstrate his
support of Daitokuji. In 1333 he donated a vegetarian feast to the resident monks. Daitō extravagantly thanked Morinaga, a general, by
comparing him to a martial incarnation of the bodhisattva of compassion: "The bodhisattva Kannon has thirty-two manifestations. Among
them, the general of the gods is the most true. He dissolves all obstacles,
bestows joy, seizes a hundred blessings, and rescues the destitute."[49]
The next year Morinaga added more land to the temple's holdings. In
1333 another early patron, Akamatsu Norimura, donated a private
estate in Harima and notified the Emperor accordingly.

A third phase of patronage, during which Hanazono was ascendant,
lasted barely eighteen months in 1336–1337. For several years the former emperor had skirted the political arena. In 1335 his head was

shaved in a formal Zen ceremony, an act that expressed his personal commitment to Daitō and his further withdrawal from the world. (Hanazono's snipped-off hair is preserved at Daitokuji in a small reliquary pagoda.) When Go-Daigo was stripped of his power at the end of 1336, a northern-line emperor was installed in his place by Ashikaga Takauji. For Daitokuji, Go-Daigo's previous patronage threatened to become a serious liability, whereas Hanazono's membership in the northern branch was suddenly an asset. Responding to Daitokuji's predicament, Hanazono took steps to reaffirm his support for the temple and its founder.

In the ninth month of 1336 Hanazono sent "many kinds of handmade flowers" to Daitō. It is possible that Daitō's health was already failing, though the biographies do not mention illness until the following year. Daitō's words of appreciation are found in his *Record:*

> Indra rained flowers down upon [Subhūti] and moved the earth. The retired emperor has bestowed these flowers upon us. Are these events the same, or are they different?[50]

In 1337, when Daitokuji's lands were vulnerable to confiscation by Ashikaga Takauji or his partisans, Hanazono presented the temple with a tract in Mino province (present Gifu prefecture). Only four months before Daitō's death, Hanazono issued a decree reconfirming Daitokuji's privilege of single-line succession (figure 3). His words echoed Go-Daigo's first decree to Daitokuji four years earlier:

> Daitokuji Zen temple is a special recipient of the true vein of [the Sixth Patriarch, who taught in] Ts'ao-hsi. Only Daitokuji continues to fan the wind from [Bodhidharma's temple] Shao-lin. Daitokuji truly sets the standard among all the Zen monasteries. During this kalpa, until the coming of Maitreya, the Dharma seat of this temple must be occupied only by successors of the Daitokuji lineage, never by monks from other lines. How could this decree arise from prejudicial personal sentiments? The intention is to distinguish clearly between the different branches of Zen. In the future, this commandment must never be violated.
>
> Twenty-sixth day, eighth month, fourth year of Kenmu [1337]. To Zen Master Kōzen Daitō Kokushi.[51]

Working closely with Daitō and his disciple Kanzan Egen, Hanazono sponsored the founding of another monastery, Myōshinji, to which he donated part of his country residence. After Daitō's death in 1337, Hanazono chose to continue his own Zen training under Kanzan, though he also supported Daitō's successor at Daitokuji, Tettō Gikō.

During Daitō's lifetime emperors Go-Daigo and Hanazono signifi-

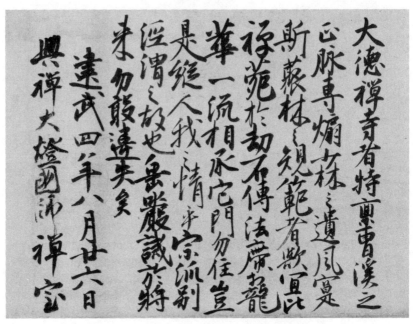

FIGURE 3. PROCLAMATION FROM EMPEROR HANAZONO TO DAITŌ, 1337.
COURTESY OF DAITOKUJI.

cantly enhanced his prestige by giving him "Kokushi" (National Master) titles. Daitō's original monastic name was Shūhō Myōchō. Hanazono awarded him the title of "Kōzen Daitō Kokushi," and Go-Daigo reportedly called him "Kōshō Shōtō Kokushi."[52] In the documents that have survived, the first use of "Kokushi" was Go-Daigo's 1333 decree ordering single-line succession, where "Shūhō Kokushi" was used as a form of address. This unusual combination of a personal name with "Kokushi" could simply have been an indication of Go-Daigo's respect for Daitō. The first complete Kokushi title appears in Hanazono's 1337 reconfirmation of Daitokuji's single-line succession, which ends with a salutation to "Zen Master Kōzen Daitō Kokushi." Granting a title at this point in Daitō's career was an appropriate final tribute to a master nearing death, and it was another way to counteract Daitokuji's loss of influence after Go-Daigo's fall (the new title may even have been the primary rationale for the proclamation).

The title credited to Go-Daigo, "Kōshō Shōtō Kokushi," does not appear on any extant document. It seems that "Shōtō" was granted during Daitō's lifetime and that "Kōshō" was awarded posthumously, when the defeated Go-Daigo was confined to the Yoshino mountains near Nara. The decree awarding "Kōshō," dated the fourth month of

1339, is addressed to Tettō.[53] This scroll is sometimes credited to Emperor Go-Murakami (reigned 1339–1368), but even so the title itself could have been determined by Go-Daigo.

A subtle rivalry developed between Go-Daigo and Hanazono, yet it was tame in comparison with the bitter divisions of the age.[54] Four years into Go-Daigo's reign Hanazono twice praised his successor in his diary.[55] His tone changed, however, in the tenth month of 1325, during the early period in which the two emperors were vying with each other in their patronage of Daitō. After describing a meeting between Go-Daigo and Musō, Hanazono criticized them both: "Everyone says that His Majesty [Go-Daigo] earnestly desires the Buddha-Dharma to flourish. So I do not understand why he tries to make a secret of his reliance on [Musō]. To treat this man as a venerable abbot is to destroy the patriarchal succession of the Zen school. One cannot help but grieve."[56] The two emperors frequently duplicated decrees to Daitō. When Hanazono designated Daitokuji as an imperial prayer center, Go-Daigo followed suit. Go-Daigo limited Daitokuji's abbacy to one lineage, and Hanazono repeated the command four years later. Hanazono granted a Kokushi title; Go-Daigo ignored it and granted his own.

It is difficult to gauge Daitō's response to the gradual elaboration of patronage. The traditional view within Zen is that he was so devoted to the training of his monks that he was oblivious to such worldly matters as politics or patronage. Early biographers claim that he protested two of Go-Daigo's major proclamations: the imperial prayer center decree of 1325 and the first Gozan decree of 1333. Japanese scholar Hirano Sōjō believes that the imperial favors were a "terrible nuisance" to Daitō and the apparent competition between the two emperors an added "headache."[57] Yet a reading of the documentary evidence, including Daitō's numerous expressions of gratitude in response to the gifts and decrees, gives the impression that he sincerely welcomed whatever support he could muster. If Daitō had really wanted to reject imperial patronage, he could have moved away from Kyoto, as a number of his predecessors and contemporaries did. Instead, he sustained the support of two "rival" emperors for a decade and a half, handling matters so adroitly that both patrons remained eager to honor him even after his death.

When Daitō moved to Murasakino in 1319, at the age of thirty-seven, he lacked institutional standing, influential patrons, and public recognition. In 1334, when the master was fifty-two, his new temple was ranked at the top of the Gozan system. During this fifteen-year period Daitō had emerged from relative obscurity to a position of authority in the expanding world of Japanese Zen. His role as founder and abbot of Daitokuji became central to his Zen legacy—for the historical event itself and for the religious interpretation given to that achievement. The Daitō depicted in the biographical materials is a figure whose search for self-realization was untainted by worldly ambition, whose development included a proper hiatus between enlightenment and a public career, and whose intentions in founding a temple were genuinely spiritual. He thus came to represent an ideal resolution of the ever-present tension between the individual Zen practitioner and the Zen institution: a free spirit who can operate skillfully within the system, bending it to unselfish purposes without allowing it to sap his energy or cloud his insight.

6

ENLIGHTENMENT AND AUTHENTICITY

WHEN GEN'E ASKED, "What is Zen?" in the Shōchū Debate, he raised a question that the pioneers of Japanese Zen needed to answer for themselves as well as others. Several factors fueled the inquiry into the essence and principal features of Zen. Zen was originally a foreign religion in Japan, recognizable as Buddhist but alien in many respects. The large Chinese-style Zen monasteries in Kamakura and Kyoto represented novel forms of architecture, ritual, dress, etiquette, and language. Monks sought not only to comprehend such unfamiliar traits but to embrace them intimately and personally. Political considerations also affected conceptions of orthodoxy and heterodoxy, as individual masters and emergent lineages struggled to gain influence. Moreover, the Ch'an/Zen tradition was itself immersed in an ongoing process of self-definition and self-examination. In one form or another, practitioners confronted challenging questions: What is a correct understanding of Zen and how is it demonstrated? What is the mainstream of this tradition and what falls outside it?

Questions of authenticity and legitimacy were also of vital concern in medieval Japanese society generally. The warriors who had displaced the nobility as the country's ruling elite were still regarded as usurpers in some quarters, and they attempted to enhance their legitimacy through any available means, from acquired titles to the trappings of culture. The legitimacy of the imperial succession became another source of tension after the imperial family split into two branches. Though representatives of the "two courts" alternated amicably for a period, political pressures generated uncertainty about the true succession and the criteria used to establish it. One courtier, Kitabatake Chi-kafusa, was impelled to reexamine the entire history of Japan's imperial descent in his treatise of 1339.

In the realm of religion, analogous issues stirred a number of Buddhist sects besides Zen. For instance, a struggle for leadership in the True Pure Land (Jōdo Shinshū) sect was couched in terms of the authenticity of spiritual succession. Kakunyo (1270–1351), unable to assert authority simply by virtue of his blood relation to the founder Shinran, further claimed to be the privileged recipient of a spiritual transmission from Shinran, allegedly passed from master to disciple over three generations. The general uncertainty about legitimacy in other sectors of Japanese society undoubtedly intensified the discourse about authenticity within Zen.

Controversy about the elements of authentic Zen was most factious early in the period of transmission; Dōgen's well-articulated and often strident stands are especially revealing. The later pioneers, Daitō prominent among them, begin to express a greater degree of consensus regarding the cardinal characteristics of Zen in Japan. In order to assess Daitō's individual approach, it is helpful first to survey the contributions of his predecessors and peers.

Conceptions of Authenticity

All religious traditions are continually required to define and redefine themselves as their circumstances change. In the face of heterogeneity and potential ambiguity, adherents want to be convinced (and to convince others) that the teachings and practices they have received are authentic in every sense of the concept—that is, original, genuine, real, true, credible, legitimate, and authoritative. The following Zen anecdote can be read as a story about authenticity:

> A wandering monk was climbing a mountain alongside a stream, on his way to the Zen monastery at the top, when he noticed a vegetable leaf floating downstream from the direction of the monastery. He thought, "It is just a single leaf, but any place that would waste it cannot be very good," and he turned to go back down the mountain. Just then he saw a lone monk come running down the path, chasing after the floating leaf. Immediately the wandering monk decided to enroll in the monastery at the top of the mountain.[1]

On the basis of a single leaf the traveling monk concluded that first-rate Zen training—and by extension genuine Zen itself—was not to be found at the mountain monastery; then a glance at a single monk convinced him that true Zen was being practiced there after all. In this case, the principle that nothing should be wasted (linked to Zen teachings such as mindfulness and the intrinsic value of all things) functioned as a decisive criterion of authenticity for the story's protagonist.

Every school of Buddhism claims to uphold the Dharma, which refers (among its many meanings) to the ultimate truth and the teachings propounded by Shakyamuni Buddha after his enlightenment. The earliest Buddhist texts contrasted the "true Dharma" *(saddhamma)* with mistaken views. A Buddhist cosmological scheme that had great impact on East Asia identified eras of true Dharma *(shōbō* in Japanese), counterfeit Dharma *(zōbō)*, and degenerate Dharma *(mappō)*. An influential eighth-century history of Ch'an lineages, the *Record of the Dharma Treasure Down Through the Generations (Li tai fa pao chi)*, was subtitled "Record in which the true and false are determined, the heterodox is suppressed, and the orthodox is revealed."[2]

In Ch'an/Zen the concept of authenticity has been expressed in many ways (a Sino-Japanese character or compound often can function as a noun, adjective, or verb, just as English has authenticity, authentication, authentic, and authenticate). The characters *shō* and *shin* mean "true," "real," and "authentic." They appear in such fixed compounds as "true Dharma" *(shōbō)*, "true school" *(shōjū)*, "true vehicle" *(shinjō)*, "true gate" *(shōmon)*, and "true enlightenment" *(shinshō)*. Ch'an master Lin-chi combines both characters to indicate "true insight" (Jp. *shinshō no kenge*).[3] *Shingi* (literally, "truth/falsity") often corresponds to the notion of authenticity, as in the following passage by Dōgen: "You should know that for a Buddhist it is not a matter of debating the superiority or inferiority of doctrines, or of choosing the depth or superficiality of teachings that matters; all we have to know is whether the practice is *authentic or not (shingi)*."[4] The words *honbun* and *honrai* can mean "primordial," "fundamental," or "authentic." Yüan-wu defines an "authentic master of the school" (Jp. *honbun no shūshi*) as one who "sets up the banner of the Dharma and establishes the essential teaching."[5] Dōgen speaks of *honbun no hito*, the "authentic" or "primordial" person.[6]

Another character *shō* is an important Zen term with a range of English renderings that include "authenticate," "enlighten," and "prove." It appears, for example, in a famous formula by Dōgen:

> To study the Buddha Way is to study the self;
> to study the self is to forget the self;
> to forget the self is to be *authenticated (shō)* by all things.[7]

The third line can also be translated: "to forget the self is to be *enlightened* by all things,"[8] testimony to the intimate link between enlightenment and authenticity in Zen.

When a religion is seeking to establish itself in a new culture, the

issue of authenticity intensifies. In the case of Ch'an's introduction to
Japan, the pioneers faced considerable difficulties. Whatever "Ch'an"
was, its dimensions seemed to be simultaneously spiritual, doctrinal,
institutional, artistic, literary, and social. In addition, the contours of
Chinese Ch'an continued to shift during a period of transmission that
spanned nearly two centuries. Lineage rivalries created internal fissures, subschools prospered or faded, styles of teaching changed, and
literary tastes evolved. The Chinese monks who claimed to represent
Ch'an, whether they remained in China or emigrated to Japan, inevitably varied in their approaches. In certain significant respects, Ch'an
presented a different tableau to each of the Japanese monks who encountered it.

Dōgen's earliest extant work, an essay called "On Practicing the
Way" *(Bendōwa)*, illustrates the early pioneers' preoccupation with the
authenticity of their Buddhism or their Zen. In the first sentence of this
work Dōgen extols the direct transmission of the Dharma from one
enlightened buddha to another, and then he declares: "That it is transmitted without deviation from buddha to buddha is by virtue of the
samādhi personally enjoyed [by the Buddha] *(jijuyūzanmai)*, which is its
touchstone *(hyōjun).*"[9] For Dōgen, genuine Zen is the rightly transmitted Buddha-Dharma, and the criterion for Dharma transmission is the
supreme enlightenment of the buddhas. In the remainder of the text,
Dōgen elaborates on this theme. As Carl Bielefeldt has shown,

> Dōgen uses the notion of the historical tradition of the Buddhas and
> Patriarchs to distinguish his Zen meditation from other forms of Bud-
> dhist practice. In fact the entire work is dominated by an acute sense
> of this tradition and of the historical significance of its transmission to
> Japan. In his introduction to the text Dōgen recites the legend of the
> transmission of the "Buddha mind seal" *(busshin'in)*, from Śākya-
> muni to the five houses of Ch'an. This tradition represents the
> "orthodox transmission" *(shōden)*, the "authentic *buddha-dharma*"
> *(shinjitsu no buppō)*, the "unadulterated *buddha-dharma*" *(jun'ichi no
> buppō)*, brought to the East by the First Patriarch, Bodhidharma, and
> spread there by the Sixth Patriarch, Hui-neng.[10]

About ten years after Dōgen wrote *Bendōwa*, he wrote an essay called
"The Way of the Buddha" *(Butsudō)* in which he addressed the authenticity of the transmission in a more sectarian fashion. He traced the
spiritual genealogy of Ch'an from the Indian patriarchs specifically to
his own Chinese teacher and asserted that the lineage he represented
was the only one that was genuine: "There is no other transmission;
there is no other school."[11]

When was authentic Ch'an first introduced to Japan? When did the

Japanese really understand Ch'an? When did Zen in Japan become truly Japanese? These questions conceal further normative issues involving the nature of "Chinese Ch'an" and "Japanese Zen." Another source of complexity is the wide range of phenomena to which the notion of authenticity can be applied. In the question "Is X's Zen authentic?" X can be replaced by a person, a temple, a text, a lineage, a doctrinal tenet, a type of practice, a style of poetry, and so on. Though many things can be described as "authentically Zen," there may not be one single criterion that will fit all cases.

Scholarly treatment of the issue of authenticity in Zen's transmission to Japan has been uneven and idiosyncratic. Widely varying criteria are cited (or assumed), and different masters are accordingly singled out for distinction. For example, the early pilgrim Kakua is described by Daigan and Alicia Matsunaga as "the first to receive proper Zen transmission."[12] Hee-jin Kim gives prominence to Dōgen: "The Kōshō-hōrinji [Kōshōji] temple, founded by Dōgen in 1233, thus had historic significance in that it was the first attempt ever made by the Japanese to establish . . . 'pure Zen.' "[13] Heinrich Dumoulin stresses the arrival of the Chinese émigré masters, because "the Zen they all brought with them was authentic."[14] Yanagida Seizan points to Daitō as "the first Japanese truly to touch the heart of the *Blue Cliff Record.* "[15] Other scholars credit other masters (e.g., Eisai, Enni, Nanpo, and Musō) with various milestones in early Japanese Zen.

In recent years the assumptions that underlie such assessments have been subjected to fresh scrutiny. Rather than searching for a "pure" Ch'an or Zen, some scholars see a dynamic and ever-present tension between orthodoxy and heterodoxy, and they are reluctant to privilege one over the other. Bernard Faure writes:

> Thus, there is no pristine purity at the origin of the Zen tradition, and the "pure Zen" advocated by Dōgen and some of his predecessors was perhaps a self-serving ideology. Zen, as a living religious tradition, has always had a syncretistic or combinatory nature. . . . There is no Ch'an or Zen tradition apart from repeated departures from the tradition.[16]

Early Japanese Zen certainly validates the observation that a religion is composed of many different voices; on some level there was a constant struggle to identify acceptable and unacceptable forms of discourse. At the same time, as we assess the doctrines and the behavior of influential religious figures, it is best not to make too sharp a distinction between the "pure" and the "self-serving." Historical realities and hermeneutical acumen may not permit us to posit a Zen that would be universally regarded as authentic. Yet it does not follow from such interpretive

complexities that the teachings of the pioneers should be viewed only as
sectarian or ideological power struggles.

Enlightenment

In the *Blue Cliff Record,* Yüan-wu poses a fundamental question:

> Jewels are tested with fire, gold is tested with a stone; a sword is tested
> with a hair, water is tested with a pole. In the school of the patchrobed
> monks, in one word, one phrase, one act, one state, one exit, one
> entry, one encounter, one response, you must see whether someone is
> deep or shallow, you must see whether he is facing forwards or back-
> wards. But tell me, what will you use to test him with?[17]

For Ch'an and Zen masters, enlightenment is the primary criterion
of authenticity, and all other criteria are linked to it in some way.
Through training and awakening, the masters assert, one can realize
one's essential nature, the ground of one's existence. The primacy of
enlightenment in Zen and other schools of Buddhism is widely recognized. D. T. Suzuki makes the point emphatically:

> Enlightenment occupies the central point of teaching in all schools
> of Buddhism, Hinayana and Mahayana, "self-power" and "other-
> power," the Holy Path and the Pure Land, because the Buddha's
> teachings all start from his enlightenment experience, about 2,500
> years ago in the northern part of India. Every Buddhist is, therefore,
> expected to receive enlightenment either in this world or in one of his
> future lives. Without enlightenment, either already realized or to be
> realized somehow and sometime and somewhere, there will be no
> Buddhism. Zen is no exception. In fact, it is Zen that makes the most
> of enlightenment, or *satori.*[18]

Although Suzuki's appraisal reflects his admiration for Zen, it
acknowledges that even within Buddhism there are many different ways
of conceiving and expressing "enlightenment." The Theravada tradition, for instance, equates it with the realization that all conditioned
things are impermanent, lack self-existence, and entail suffering. For
many East Asian followers of Pure Land Buddhism, enlightenment is
anticipated to occur after death, through the saving power of Amida
Buddha or the earnest devotions of one's living descendants. In apparent contrast, a Tibetan Buddhist might seek enlightenment through
identification with a cosmic buddha and an ecstatic transformation of
consciousness.

In the Ch'an/Zen tradition some of the oldest ways of expressing
enlightenment were metaphoric: a mirror free of dust, the dispersal of
clouds, the bright flame of a lamp, and so on. Early Ch'an texts also
offered more discursive descriptions of enlightenment, as in the following portrayal of those who have achieved buddhahood:

[They] are enlightened to the Dharma-nature and distinctly illuminate the mind that is the source [of all things]. They do not generate false thoughts, never fail in correct mindfulness, and extinguish the illusion of personal possession. Because of this, they are not subject to birth and death. Since they are not subject to birth and death, they have achieved the ultimate state of serene extinction [nirvana]. Since they have achieved serene extinction, the myriad pleasures naturally accrue to them.[19]

A time-honored Ch'an/Zen term for enlightenment is "seeing the nature" (*chien-hsing* in Chinese; *kenshō* in Japanese), which may also be rendered in English as "seeing True-nature," "seeing one's own true nature," or a comparable expression. The most important early use of this term is found in the *Platform Sutra* (compiled in the ninth century), where it plays a prominent role in the teachings attributed to the Ch'an patriarch Hui-neng.[20] To "see" one's own original nature is to discover and experience universal Buddha-nature, which is inherent in all beings whether they are enlightened or not. Another influential locus classicus of *kenshō* is the four-line stanza, traditionally attributed to Bodhidharma, that Zen has long used to define itself:

> A separate transmission outside the teachings;
> not depending on words and letters.
> Point straight at man's [own] mind;
> see [one's own true] nature and become Buddha.[21]

The most crucial line is the last, in which seeing one's true nature and the attainment of buddhahood are equated unambiguously.[22] Ironically, this cardinal Zen declaration about the inadequacy of language is presented as a memorable verse, with exactly four characters in each line.

A classic controversy that reverberated within Ch'an for centuries considered whether enlightenment was "sudden" or "gradual." The Southern School of Ch'an, which claimed to follow the Sixth Patriarch Hui-neng, was identified with sudden enlightenment, whereas the Northern School, personified by the historically influential master Shen-hsiu (606?–706), was linked to gradual enlightenment. In fact, the approaches of the two schools were closer to each other and more complex than the typology that was codified by tradition. The masters of the triumphant Southern School held that sudden awakening could transform one instantly into a buddha, though in practice they usually conceded that an abrupt insight should be followed by sustained cultivation. Formulations implying that cultivation *before* enlightenment was a means to an end were rejected for their apparent dualism.

It goes without saying that enlightenment was as central to Japanese Zen as to Chinese Ch'an. The vocabulary of Japanese Zen is replete with terms and expressions that signify enlightenment, most of them rooted in Chinese and Indian Buddhism. Besides satori and *kenshō*, one finds awakening *(kaku)*, true awakening *(shōgaku)*, perfect awakening *(engaku)*, insight *(sei)*, attaining the Way *(jōdō)*, becoming Buddha *(jōbutsu)*, opening the eye *(kaigen)*, liberation *(gedatsu)*, authentication *(shō)*, the great death *(daishi)*, self-enlightenment without a teacher *(mushi dokugo)*, great satori with full penetration *(taigo tettei)*, and peerless perfect enlightenment *(anokutara sanmyaku sanbodai)*. All these nouns have verb forms as well. Other Zen expressions too numerous to list also point to enlightenment: "To settle the one great matter," "To cut through the storehouse consciousness with one blow," "To leap directly into the land of Tathāgata Buddha," and so on.

Certain conceptions of enlightenment were universally shared among the Japanese Zen pioneers. When Bassui asserted that "the essential thing for enlightenment is to empty the mind of the notion of self,"[23] he upheld a teaching as old as Buddhism. Lan-ch'i, writing for his Japanese audience, expressed another common point: enlightenment was not based on ordinary knowledge or sensation, but, once attained, it informed the activity of the mind and the senses. He stated, "Turning the light around to shine back, knowing and seeing fundamentally inherent Self-nature, is called the eye of wisdom; after seeing one's [Self-]nature, one may then put seeing, hearing, discernment, and knowledge to use."[24] Enlightenment defied conceptualization, said the masters, and yet it could be known as intimately as one knows whether a drink of water is hot or cold. It was neither a special state nor an "experience" like other experiences. In this spirit, Dōgen spoke of enlightenment as boundless: "As for what this unexcelled enlightenment is like, even all the worlds in ten directions are no more than a fraction of unexcelled enlightenment."[25]

Several meanings of "enlightenment" were accepted in Japanese Zen, as had been the case in Chinese Ch'an.[26] (Though the focus here is historical, the same can be said of contemporary Japanese Zen.) The notion was flexible enough to embrace weighty doctrinal tenets, specific insight experiences, and advanced states of awareness. In one of its primary meanings, enlightenment was equated with inherent Buddha-nature. Musō, for example, declared that "purity, truth, awakening, nirvana, and the various perfections *(pāramitās)* all flow from total enlightenment," which he identified with the "field of Original Nature."[27] Other teachers used terms like True Mind, Original Face, Tao (Way), or Self-nature as synonyms for enlightenment.

In a second cardinal meaning, enlightenment embraced the full range of awakening experiences, from a tip-of-the-tongue taste to a profound realization. This usage highlighted enlightenment's psychological dimension as a turning point in the spiritual development of an individual. Vivid descriptions of this decisive moment, like the one in the following passage by Bassui, spurred practitioners on to greater effort:

> If you push forward with your last ounce of strength at the very point where the path of your thinking has been blocked, and then, completely stymied, leap with hands high in the air into the tremendous abyss of fire confronting you—into the ever-burning flame of your own primordial nature—all ego-consciousness, all delusive feelings and thoughts and perceptions will perish with your ego-root, and the true source of your Self-nature will appear. You will feel resurrected, all sickness having completely vanished, and will experience genuine peace and joy. You will be entirely free.[28]

In a third important understanding, enlightenment was at times equated with full awakening or full buddhahood. This conception deemphasized a particular peak experience in favor of the moment-by-moment awareness associated with the highest degree of spiritual attainment. Though such a state was said to be beyond description, its psychological attributes were believed to include a nondual awareness free from separation between self and other, a liberating lack of attachment, and a spontaneous compassion for all beings. At this level, little distinction was made between the historical Buddha, cosmic buddhas, and practitioners so advanced as to have achieved buddhahood. The émigré master Lan-ch'i asserted:

> To see [True-]nature and become Buddha is to know one's Self-nature and sever the root of sentient existence. . . . Then there is no birth-and-death or delusive passions. This is provisionally termed "becoming Buddha." Buddha is enlightenment, the realization that one has never been deluded.[29]

In actual usage the boundaries between these principal meanings of "enlightenment" were not scrupulously observed, and a given term sometimes embraced more than one dimension of the concept. The ambiguity that resulted could be justified, however, by the conviction that the various meanings of enlightenment were fundamentally congruent and even ultimately identical. By the time Ch'an reached Japan, the classic controversy regarding the "sudden" or "gradual" nature of enlightenment had yielded to a widely shared formulation that accepted the suddenness of enlightenment and the need for both prior and subsequent cultivation. Variations within this near-consensus were more a matter of emphasis than of substance. Suddenness was affirmed in similar terms by émigré Lin-chi masters such as Lan-ch'i and by Japanese Rinzai masters such as Bassui. Lan-ch'i wrote: "When delusive views have all been exhausted, you suddenly awaken from the great dream and see Buddha-nature. This is called 'great satori with full penetration.' "[30] Bassui reiterated: "When the intense questioning envelops every inch of you and penetrates to the very bottom of all bottoms, the question will suddenly burst and the substance of the Buddha-mind be revealed. . . . The joy of this moment cannot be put into words."[31]

Sudden enlightenment was accepted by the early Japanese Sōtō masters as well. Dōgen praised Hui-neng because "once he was suddenly enlightened, he left his mother and sought a teacher."[32] Dōgen's descendant Keizan taught that one enters enlightenment when "the innate inconceivably clear mind is suddenly revealed and the original light finally shines everywhere."[33] Keizan's heir Gazan is said to have awakened suddenly when he heard his teacher quote a Ch'an saying.

Postenlightenment cultivation was similarly recognized as indispensable by all branches of Zen. Because an initial awakening rarely (if ever) corresponded to full enlightenment, even those who had glimpsed their true nature were still thought to be vulnerable to pride, complacency, or self-delusion. Hence the need for further practice and the guidance of a qualified teacher. Bassui compared someone who settled prematurely for a shallow awakening to a man who finds copper and gives up his search for gold.[34] Dōgen lauded Hui-neng for seeking a teacher *after* his sudden enlightenment, and Musō extolled the postenlightenment practice of Chao-chou, who was renowned for his dedication to zazen:

> This old monk was enlightened almost from birth, yet his practice of Ch'an was [unrelenting]. You can imagine what those who are not yet fully self-enlightened must do! There is an old saying: "An unenlightened person must strive as if he were mourning his parents; an enlightened person must also strive as if he were mourning his parents."[35]

The most discordant note in this early discourse was perhaps sounded by Dōgen. Although he accepted many of the tenets embraced by his peers, he objected to the term *kenshō*. To Dōgen this expression suggested at least two false dualisms—practice versus enlightenment, and "seeing" versus "True-nature."[36] Accordingly, he criticized the famous line "see [True-]nature and become Buddha" from the stanza attributed to Bodhidharma. Although he acknowledged Hui-neng's sudden enlightenment, he also attacked the *Platform Sutra* for its endorsement of *kenshō*: "In the *Platform Sutra* of the Sixth Patriarch are the words 'to see [True-]nature.' This work is a forgery . . . not to be trusted or used by any descendants of the buddhas and patriarchs."[37] As is often the case with Dōgen, his stance can be seen as a creative refinement of Zen teachings, or a partisan attempt to discredit a rival lineage, or both.

An Elusive Touchstone?

When masters such as Dōgen identify the enlightenment of the buddhas as the criterion *(hyōjun)* for authentic Dharma transmission, they do not subject their technical terms or their doctrinal assertions to Western-style philosophical analysis. The concept of a criterion has its own subtleties; when applied to such difficult topics as Dharma transmission, enlightenment, or Zen, the complexities multiply. In this case the Zen approach and a scholarly perspective seem bound to diverge.

Within Zen, enlightenment functions as the criterion of authentic Zen because (it is believed) "enlightenment" and "Zen" do not refer to two different phenomena. D. T. Suzuki, speaking from this standpoint, asserts that "Zen and satori are synonymous."[38] It may be helpful here to distinguish between conventional and ultimate standpoints, as Buddhist and Zen teachers sometimes do. According to this approach, from the ultimate standpoint enlightenment is the one and only criterion of authentic Zen, *even if* that truth breaks down on the conventional level. In other words, Dōgen can assert unequivocally that the buddhas' enlightenment is the sole touchstone of Dharma transmission (an ultimate-level claim) and at the same time argue that without a proper certificate of transmission one cannot be considered a Dharma heir (a conventional-level distinction).

For an observer sympathetic to the Zen tradition but standing outside it, the relation between Zen and enlightenment is not as straightforward as the synonymity affirmed by Suzuki. The Zen discourse about authenticity certainly begins with enlightenment, but it does not end there. In a number of cases, enlightenment alone does *not* appear to determine or guarantee authentic Zen. One finds, for example, that certifiably enlightened Zen monks are censured as inadequate or even as heterodox on other grounds. Additional factors prevent enlightenment from functioning as a self-sufficient criterion of authenticity: it is variously experienced, it is difficult to demonstrate, and it can deepen or fade over time. Masters concede that one may even have an enlightenment experience and not recognize it as such. "Do not think you will necessarily be aware of your own enlightenment," Dōgen reportedly taught.[39] Nor is enlightenment, by itself, able to establish Zen's distinctiveness as a sect—there are awakened masters in other Buddhist and non-Buddhist traditions.

What are the criteria for enlightenment itself? Again the traditional and scholarly approaches diverge. Within Zen, genuine enlightenment is supposed to be self-authenticating *(jishō)*, as Dōgen writes in one of his later essays.[40] At the same time, Zen claims that enlightenment is objectively verifiable by those who are qualified to judge. An approximate analogy for the experience and its recognition might be a happily married mother who can tell at a glance that her daughter has fallen in love. The mother may not be able to explain "falling in love" or cause her daughter to feel it, but, since she has had the experience herself, she can recognize it in anyone she knows well. In this case, the criterion is actually the experience itself, though the specific signs will vary considerably.[41] Similarly, a master (using his own experience as the criterion) is supposed to be able to recognize a disciple's enlightenment, even if the clue is as subtle as a smile.

But, a scholar might ask, what if the mother or the daughter *thought* she had fallen in love but later concluded that she had not? Are there not degrees of depth, hidden cultural assumptions, learned patterns of behavior, and other factors that must also be considered? Zen lore is full of incidents in which monks who were absolutely certain of the authenticity of their enlightenment were sharply rebuffed by a teacher. Masters also challenge each other regularly. Eisai accused Nōnin of false self-enlightenment, and Dōgen leveled similar charges against Ta-hui. Dōgen even rejected Ta-hui's crowning enlightenment, which had been sanctioned by a distinguished master. What are we to conclude about a "criterion" that is itself the focus of such heated contention?

Scholars and practitioners may concur on one point at least: in the end, all notions of "enlightenment" become problematic. Because the word reifies that which is supposed to be beyond reification, the more it is used, the more it congeals into what it is not. For Zen monks and masters the solution is to experience enlightenment and live it, whereby these and other conceptual dilemmas come to be seen in a different light. As Lan-ch'i taught: "Delusion and enlightenment just depend on the deceiving mind—in the real mind there is no illusion or enlightenment. Sentient beings and buddhas are basically deluded or enlightened on the basis of one mind; when you comprehend its true nature, then ultimately there is no distinction between ordinary man and sage."[42]

7

CLARIFYING THE ESSENTIALS OF ZEN

As a transitional figure who bridges the evolving Zen of the Kamakura period and the established Zen of the Muromachi period, Daitō sheds light on his predecessors and his successors. In order to assess Daitō's Zen, it is instructive to consider the dialogical matrix in which he operated. Scholars are increasingly aware of the degree to which the early Zen masters were responding to each other and to the tradition, manifesting what is now called intersubjectivity and intertextuality.[1] Zen was also a "mind-to-mind transmission" in a conventional sense; inescapably, Daitō was shaped by his religious and cultural inheritance.

The discourse of early Japanese Zen was heterogeneous, characterized by discord as well as consensus. Even as they clarified their conceptions of authentic Zen, the Japanese masters continued to disagree about a number of fundamental points. For example, zazen was widely regarded as indispensable, yet masters also held divergent views about the most correct or effective type of zazen. The intensity and occasional acrimony of the early debates can be seen in the following statement by Eisai. Responding to a questioner who alludes to the Daruma school, Eisai gives his own outline of the essentials of Zen, sharply rejecting other approaches:

> This Zen school despises masters of dim enlightenment, and it abhors those who hold a false view of emptiness. They are as detestable as corpses at the bottom of the sea. To follow the perfect teaching, to cultivate complete and sudden enlightenment, outwardly to avoid transgressions according to the disciplinary code, inwardly to exercise compassion for the benefit of others—that is what we mean by the

95

Zen school, that is called the Buddha-Dharma. Those whose realization is blind and whose view of emptiness is false do not understand
this. They are thieves in the Buddha-Dharma.[2]

Eisai is forced to make a distinction between true and false enlightenment, and he is compelled to cite a number of other attributes of genuine Zen. Speaking strictly from an ultimate standpoint, masters would
deny that factors such as adherence to the disciplinary code could serve
as touchstones of real Zen—they were signs of Zen, but not Zen itself.
Speaking on the conventional level, however, masters would argue that
a certain style of zazen or a properly constructed monastery were indeed
critical features of genuine Zen. Properly understood, the two levels
were not supposed to contradict each other. This chapter surveys five of
the features most often cited as essentials of Zen: zazen, emblems of
Dharma transmission, the monastic rule, monastery construction, and
withdrawal from the world. A sixth indicator—the response to the textual tradition—will be addressed in Chapter 10, in connection with
Daitō's commentaries.

Zazen

Although most Buddhist schools employ meditation in one form or
another, *zazen* (seated meditation) is the sine qua non of Zen.[3] The
name of the Zen school is taken from the Sanskrit word for meditation,
dhyāna, which was transliterated (and shortened) in Chinese as *ch'an,* a
character that is pronounced *zen* in Japanese. In physical terms, zazen
means sitting in a proper cross-legged posture, back erect and eyes low-
ered but not closed. The mind is turned inward and placed at one point
until it is no longer distracted by random thoughts. Depending on the
type of zazen, the focus of attention is usually one of the following: the
breath, a part of the body (such as the lower belly), a koan, or awareness itself.

Though zazen was variously conceived, its centrality was stressed at
every stage of Ch'an's development. According to tradition, Bodhidharma did zazen in a cave for nine years after his arrival in China.
The Fifth Patriarch Hung-jen (600–674) advocated a type of zazen that
had much in common with other forms of Buddhist meditation: "Make
your body and mind pure and peaceful, without any discriminative
thinking at all. Sit properly with the body erect. Regulate the breath
and concentrate the mind so it is not within you, not outside of you, and
not in any intermediate location."[4] In the T'ang dynasty Chao-chou
gained renown for his lifelong dedication to sitting. He reportedly
claimed, "For thirty years in the southern regions I did zazen continuously except for the two meal periods."[5] During the Sung period the

standard monastic routine in the major Ch'an monasteries included four different sessions of zazen per day.

Within this apparent consensus, various terms were used for concentration, meditation, or seated meditation, and their interpretation was linked to the discourse about authenticity in Ch'an.[6] Most conceptions of zazen embraced the actual practice of seated meditation, but some formulations challenged the necessity of the traditional posture. Hui-neng, for example, criticized immobile sitting and redefined zazen without reference to any physical activity. Later, Hung-chih Cheng-chüeh (1091–1157) taught a "silent-illumination" zazen in which the body and the mind are completely at rest, while his contemporary Ta-hui advocated a more energetic "investigation" of koans. Though some form of zazen was universally affirmed, many aspects of the practice were not transmitted in texts; for centuries instruction in the specifics of meditation remained largely an oral tradition. The influential *Record of Lin-chi* mentions zazen only twice in passing.[7] The earliest known Ch'an meditation manual, the brief *Principles of Meditation (Tso-ch'an i)*, did not appear until 1103, as part of the *Pure Rules for Ch'an Monasteries (Ch'an-yüan ch'ing-kuei)*.[8]

The *Pure Rules* and its tract on meditation were introduced to Japan in the late twelfth and early thirteenth centuries by pilgrims such as Eisai and Dōgen. Many of the Zen pioneers also composed new or supplementary meditation manuals, recasting the Chinese models in their own voices. Eisai outlined the fundamentals of zazen in a section of his principal work, *Promulgation of Zen as a Defense of the Nation (Kōzen gokokuron)*. Dōgen composed his *Universal Promotion of the Principles of Meditation (Fukan zazengi)* sometime after his return to Japan in 1227. Lan-ch'i wrote his *Treatise on Meditation (Zazenron)* shortly after his arrival in 1246, and Kakushin drew up his *Principles of Meditation (Zazengi)* a decade later.

In these and other works, zazen was acclaimed as the core of practice and the wellspring of doctrine. Alluding to classic Ch'an formulations, the leading masters often echoed one another: Eisai and Dōgen both called zazen "the Dharma gate of great ease and joy," Lan-ch'i praised zazen as "the Dharma gate of great liberation," and Enni reiterated that "the school of zazen is the way of great liberation."[9] Lan-ch'i was praised for having "exhorted those who joined the assembly as Zen monks to devote themselves exclusively to zazen."[10] The four daily sessions of zazen were strictly enforced even in temples where the practices of more than one sect were permitted. Musō was not alone when he insisted: "With the exception only of bath days and those days on which there are meetings with the abbot, four daily sessions of zazen must be held, even at the hottest and coldest periods of the year."[11]

Zazen and enlightenment were considered to be intimately related, as inseparable as two sides of the same coin. From a conventional standpoint, zazen could legitimately be regarded as the most effective path to enlightenment. But from an ultimate standpoint, zazen and enlightenment were not to be treated dualistically; practitioners were supposed to grasp that the activity of zazen took place within enlightenment and that enlightenment was fully embodied in zazen. In this spirit, Lan-ch'i taught: "When you sit once in meditation, you are a buddha for that sitting; when you sit for a day in meditation, you are a buddha for a day; when you sit in meditation all your life, you are a buddha all your life."[12] Dōgen's formulations of the matter were more emphatic. For example, in a well-known passage from *Bendōwa* he asserted: "Because one's present practice arises from enlightenment, one's initial treading of the Way is itself the whole of original enlightenment."[13] In an apparent attempt to express his stance in the most radical possible terms, Dōgen explicitly equated the seated posture with ultimate enlightenment: "Sitting is itself the treasury of the eye of the true Dharma and the mystic mind of nirvana."[14]

Together with the shared understandings of zazen, there was also considerable variation in regard to its specific content. Besides the basic breath practices, some teachers stressed the classic Chinese koans, some devised new koans for their warrior students, and some favored forms of self-inquiry such as "What is this Mind?" or "Who is it that hears?" Dōgen advocated a type of objectless awareness that he called "just sitting" *(shikantaza)*. One persistent issue concerned the relation of zazen to practices advocated by other Buddhist sects, especially the recitation of sutras and the invocation of Amida Buddha's name *(nenbutsu)*. In Sung China, zazen was one of many practices taught at the large public monasteries designated as "Ch'an," and in Japan these other practices were also accepted by many masters. For Lan-ch'i, *nenbutsu* and sutra chanting were a source of benefits in future lives, notably "great wisdom" and rebirth "in a Buddha-land."[15] Jakushitsu Genkō (1290–1367) went so far as to assert that *nenbutsu* practice and Zen practice "have different names but are essentially the same."[16] But Dōgen expressed a different view:

> Intending to attain the Buddha Way by foolishly working your lips in incessant thousand or ten thousand–fold recitations is just like pointing the thills of your cart north when you want to go south. . . . Lifting your voice in endless recitation is like the frogs in the spring fields, croaking from morning to nightfall . . . without benefit.[17]

At our historical distance it is often difficult to assess the relative force of agreement or disagreement in the discourse of early Japanese Zen.

Whether Dōgen's approach to zazen differed significantly from that of his peers or predecessors is one of the issues that continues to engage scholars. Recent research has shown that Dōgen borrowed extensively from the *Pure Rules for Ch'an Monasteries* in his *Principles of Meditation.* Hee-jin Kim concedes that "the external form of Dōgen's zazen was not much different" from the zazen taught in the *Pure Rules,* and Carl Bielefeldt notes that Dōgen introduced his meditation manual with statements that "could have been said by virtually any Ch'an master from the mid-T'ang on."[18] Kim nonetheless attributes to Dōgen "a radically different conception of zazen in its content and significance."[19]

Emblems of Dharma Transmission

Zen teaches that genuine enlightenment, in any age, is essentially the same enlightenment that Shakyamuni Buddha experienced. As Wumen asserted, someone who has awakened can "see with the same eyes and hear with the same ears" as the "whole line of patriarchs."[20] This spiritual continuity is often conceived as a transmission (Ch. *ch'uan;* Jp. *den*) of Mind or Dharma or the "lamp" of enlightenment. More than an initiation, Zen transmission is described as a direct and nonverbal communication of truth between master and disciple, a mutual recognition and a mutual confirmation. The tradition stipulates that nothing is handed down—even a great master cannot bestow enlightenment on someone else.

The principle of mind-to-mind transmission also played a central role in Ch'an's early attempts to define itself. In eighth-century China, adherents of Ch'an teachings sought to differentiate themselves from other Buddhist followers, most of whom had already set up lineages identifying their spiritual predecessors. Ch'an developed a comparable lineage to demonstrate that it had faithfully transmitted the Dharma in an unbroken line from Shakyamuni. The earliest known Ch'an reference to the concept of mind-to-mind transmission is found in an epitaph for the monk Fa-ju (638–689): "The transmission [of the teaching] in India was fundamentally without words, [so that] entrance into this teaching is solely [dependent on] the transmission of the mind."[21]

The many accounts of Dharma transmission from master to disciple were an essential element of Ch'an and Zen. According to tradition, Shakyamuni initiated the process when he silently held up a lotus flower during a sermon. Only Kāśyapa, a senior disciple, smiled in comprehension. Shakyamuni then proclaimed (in the version that became standard) that he was entrusting "the true Dharma eye, the marvelous mind of nirvana" to Kāśyapa.[22] Another significant point in the traditional lineage was the transmission from Bodhidharma to his Chinese heir, Hui-k'o (487–593). When Bodhidharma asked his three senior disciples to express their understanding, the answers of the first two disciples were adequate, and the master told them that they had attained him in his "flesh" and his "bones," respectively. The last disciple to respond was Hui-k'o, who said, "Fundamentally, there are no delusive passions; from the very beginning [the mind] is enlightened." Bodhidharma replied, "You have attained me in my marrow."²³ In a later version of this story, there were four disciples, each with new answers. Bodhidharma told the first three disciples that they had attained him in his skin, flesh, and bones. When Hui-k'o's turn came, he bowed deeply to his master and silently returned to his place. Again Hui-k'o attained Bodhidharma in his marrow and became the Dharma successor.²⁴

Within Zen the marks of enlightenment can be as subtle as a twinkle in the eye or a mien of deep composure, yet the Zen institution also needed some standard means of identifying those whose enlightenment had been sanctioned authoritatively. Accordingly, spiritual succession in Ch'an and Zen was often substantiated by a variety of symbols. The Fifth Patriarch instructed his heir, Hui-neng, "The robe is the proof and is to be handed down from generation to generation."²⁵ Huang-po Hsi-yün (d. 850?) similarly offered his former teacher's armrest to his principal heir, Lin-chi.²⁶ By the Sung period, almost any object associated with the master could serve as an insignia of transmission: a robe, an alms bowl, a staff, a prostration cloth, a whisk, a book, an impromptu verse, or a portrait. Formal documents of succession and seals of enlightenment had a practical as well as a spiritual value: recognized by civil authorities as legal documents, they provided aspiring masters with the equivalent of a license required to ply a trade. A new abbot, upon his inauguration, customarily named the teacher who had sanctioned him, and those credentials figured prominently in any assessments of him or his temple. Griffith Foulk has argued that the most reliable indicator of a "Ch'an master" in Sung Buddhism, at least from an institutional standpoint, was not his adherence to particular doctrines or practices, but his possession of a Ch'an inheritance certificate.²⁷

A seal of enlightenment *(inkajō, denbōin)* was a master's written confirmation of a disciple's attainment, which was supposed to equal or even exceed the master's own insight. These texts varied in format, sometimes combining praise, "censure," obscure allusions, and specific advice. As we have seen, Nanpo responded in writing to Daitō's enlightenment poems: "You have already cast away brightness and united with darkness. I am not equal to you. Because of you, my school will become firmly established. Before making this sanction public, you must continue your spiritual cultivation for twenty years."²⁸ Documents of succession *(shisho)* were charts depicting the traditional Ch'an/

Zen lineage. They began with Shakyamuni or the "seven Buddhas of the past," went on to list twenty-eight Indian patriarchs, six Chinese patriarchs, the Chinese masters of a particular branch, the monk's own master, and lastly the monk himself. For example, a document presented to Enni Ben'en featured him as the fifty-fourth heir to the transmission, following his teacher Wu-chun.[29] One Zen pioneer who valued such documents was Dōgen. During his stay in China he managed to inspect five "secret" lineage charts, and upon his return he insisted: "In the Buddha Way, whenever the Dharma is inherited there must be a document of succession. Unless the Dharma is handed down, the heresy of spontaneous [enlightenment] arises. . . . For one to become a buddha, there must be the document of succession that is transmitted from buddha to buddha."[30]

A portrait *(chinsō)* of one's master was also used as proof of Dharma transmission. The master's pose seldom varied: he sat in an oversized lacquer chair, his legs crossed in the full-lotus position under his ceremonial robe, his expression dignified and stern. If the portrait bore the master's personal inscription, it was even more valuable. Before Nanpo returned to Japan, he received a *chinsō* of his master Hsü-t'ang; it included an inscription that began, "The succession is now unmistakably assured."[31] Hsü-t'ang seems to have been unusually generous with his portraits; so many were brought back to Japan that Ikkyū later discovered one in a secondhand store.[32]

Another important emblem of succession was the monastic robe or shawl *(hōe, kesa),* usually a large rectangle of pieced panels, about five feet by nine feet, worn across one shoulder. The oldest known Ch'an *kesa* in Japan was brought from China by Saichō in 805. Dōgen's teacher Ju-ching had refused to wear the symbolic robe in China, but he reassured the departing Dōgen: "There is nothing to prevent you from wearing the Dharma robe in your home country, Japan."[33] Robes of elegant Chinese silk worn by such figures as Wu-chun Shih-fan, Wu-hsüeh Tsu-yüan, and Zekkai Chūshin (1336–1405) have been reverently preserved in Japanese Zen temples.[34]

Dainichi Nōnin illustrates the plight of those with inadequate certification. As noted earlier, he began teaching Zen on his own authority, using the Ch'an texts that had been transmitted within the Tendai sect. When his opponents challenged his credentials, he sent two disciples to China with a letter or a poem that expressed his Zen understanding. Fo-chao Te-kuang (1121–1203), an heir of the famous Ta-hui Tsung-kao, responded favorably to Nōnin's entreaty and validated his enlightenment. The two disciples reportedly returned with a Dharma robe, an inscribed picture of Bodhidharma, and an inscribed portrait of Te-kuang. This incident may prompt questions about "mind-to-mind transmission," but it shows the significance accorded to insignia of Dharma succession. Perhaps in response to insecurity about its status, Nōnin's Daruma school embraced the popular Asian practice of handing down jewel-like grains believed to be the remains of great masters or bodhisattvas. Possession of such relics *(shari)* was a persuasive means of establishing authenticity.[35]

In their attempt to clarify the essential elements of Zen, the early Japanese pioneers accorded considerable significance to emblems of Dharma transmission. For several hundred years there were no well-known masters who deliberately spurned traditional forms of certification. By the mid-fifteenth century, however, abuses had become apparent, and some masters no longer regarded these emblems as meaningful indicators of genuine Zen. Ikkyū Sōjun reportedly ripped his seal of enlightenment to pieces, and when his students tried to repair the document he then burned it.[36] In further protest of the system, Ikkyū refused to certify any of his own disciples.

The Monastic Rule

The operation of a Zen monastery was governed by time-honored traditions, precepts, and codes. The "pure regulations" (Ch. *ch'ing-kuei;* Jp. *shingi*) of the monastic rule shaped all aspects of monastic life: the daily schedule; the procedures for meditation, work, sleep, and other activities; the duties of monastic officers; the policies regarding absence and guests; the management of landholdings; and the administration of branch temples. The various elements of the monastic rule were not regarded as arbitrary or imposed from outside, but as natural expressions of an enlightened mind, handed down from Shakyamuni Buddha and the Zen patriarchs. Though historians now suspect that "Ch'an" monasticism was actually standard Sung Buddhist monasticism, the Japanese pioneers treated this institutional framework as an essential feature of authentic Ch'an/Zen. "Monks of a single generation should bear in mind the thousand-year legacy," declared Musō in reference to the regulations.[37] For Dōgen, "Ch'an" monasticism preserved the entire Buddhist monastic tradition:

> You should know that the monastery layout and ritual procedures found in today's so-called Ch'an cloisters are all [in accord with] the instructions of the patriarchs themselves. They are the direct transmission of the true [Dharma] heirs. Therefore, the ancient [monastery] arrangement of the Seven Buddhas is found only in Ch'an cloisters. . . . The ritual procedures followed in these cloisters today are in truth the authentic transmission of the buddhas and patriarchs.[38]

The concrete aspects of the monastic rule allowed it to be replicated with relative certainty; many details of daily life in the larger Japanese monasteries conformed to Chinese precedents by the end of the Kama-kura period.

The first communities associated with Ch'an teachings were estab-lished during the seventh century in the mountains of south-central China, though scholars no longer assume that the early adherents of Ch'an constituted a distinct sect. Pai-chang Huai-hai (720–814) is tra-ditionally revered as the founder of the monastic rule, yet none of the surviving monastic codes can be reliably attributed to him. The earliest description of Ch'an monastic life appears in a text of 1004 called *Regu-lations of the Ch'an Approach (Ch'an-men kuei-shih),* and the oldest full-scale monastic code is *Pure Rules for Ch'an Monasteries,* dated 1103. The latter text was brought to Japan in the twelfth century; by 1330 four other Chinese codes had also been transmitted. Using these works as models, many of the pioneers of Japanese Zen compiled their own monastic codes.[39]

Dōgen, one of the most outspoken advocates of the monastic rule, left extensive essays governing the daily behavior of monks. Because his *Treasury of the True Dharma Eye* has come to be regarded as a classic of Zen thought, one tends to forget that about a third of this text is devoted to guidelines regarding meditation, study, dress, meals, bathing, and sleep. In another work Dōgen cites the Buddha as an authority on den-tal hygiene:

> Next we take up a toothbrush and say with our hands clasped:
>
>> As I lift this toothbrush,
>> may all beings be uplifted;
>> may the correct Dharma reach their ears
>> and purify their minds. . . .
>
> The Buddha says, "The thicker end of a toothbrush should not be frayed more than one-third of its length." In polishing our teeth or scraping dirt off our tongues, we must follow the Buddha's teach-ings.[40]

Such passages were intended not only to teach monks how to behave; masters also sought to imbue every act with spiritual significance. A Sōtō Zen maxim interpreted this orientation in extreme terms: "Eti-quette is the Buddha's teaching; ritual propriety is the essential princi-ple of our school."[41]

At least two controversial points were also related to the monastic rule. One was the validity of Zen training for lay people in an era when the monastic character of Zen predominated. Some masters explicitly stressed the advantages and virtues of monkhood. In his "Final Admonitions," Nanpo declared:

> Those who enter the gate of Buddhism should first of all cherish a firm faith in the dignity and respectability of monkhood. . . . Its respectability is that of the fatherhood of all sentient beings; no parental respectability belonging only to the head of a little family group equals it. . . . The shaven head and the dyed garment are the noble marks of a bodhisattva.[42]

At the same time, Ch'an had a long tradition of eminent laymen, and in Japan the émigré Chinese masters freely accepted warriors as disciples, certifying the enlightenment of sevcral prominent figures. Most of the other Zen pioneers continued to encourage lay practice, for women as well as men. Jakushitsu Genkō justified this approach in the following terms:

> If you misunderstand your mind, you are an ordinary man; if you realize your mind, you are a sage. There is no difference at all whether man, woman, old, young, wise, foolish, human, animal, whatever. Thus, in the Lotus of Truth assembly, was it not the eight-year-old Nāga girl who went directly south to the undefiled world Amala, sat on a jewel lotus flower, and realized universal complete enlightenment?[43]

The tension between the two sides of this issue could also be seen in the thought of one person. Dōgen initially taught that enlightenment was equally accessible to all: "In the comprehension of the Buddha-Dharma there must be no distinction between man and woman, high and low. . . . It is simply a question of whether the will is there or not."[44] Reversing his position after his move to Echizen in 1243, he proclaimed that only monks were qualified to practice Zen and that no layman in the history of Buddhism had ever achieved genuine enlightenment.[45] "Even if a monk violates the precepts, he is superior to a layman who does not violate the precepts," Dōgen argued.[46] Although Dōgen may have been adapting his rhetoric for different audiences, such vacillation suggests that his perceptions of Zen were far from static.

A second subject of dissension was the role of the Buddhist precepts, which were an important part of the monastic rule. The precepts proscribed killing, theft, unchastity, lying, intoxication, and other transgressions. "After receiving the precepts, one should always uphold them," the *Pure Rules* stated. "It is better to keep the rules and die than to have no rules and live."[47] In Zen the precepts were regarded as direct expressions of enlightenment, not as a set of commandments imposed by divine authority or social exigency. Eisai, still identifying himself with the Tendai tradition, sought to restore the precepts to prominence in all forms of Japanese Buddhism, and he was alarmed to find his compatriot Dainichi Nōnin teaching a style of Zen that openly challenged the precepts. Nōnin's adherents reportedly claimed, "There are no precepts to follow, no practices to engage in."[48]

The position associated with Nōnin was branded as heterodox, and this particular controversy soon subsided. In fact, references to the precepts or to broad ethical issues are scarce in the writings of the early Japanese masters. On a doctrinal level, Zen claimed to *precede* morality, and the prescriptive interpretation of the precepts was considered secondary. On a practical level, a certain standard of behavior was simply assumed. In the closely supervised communal environment of a monastery, a monk who committed an offense would soon be exposed and disciplined. Another factor in the fading of the precept issue may have been the instrinsic Japanese reluctance to make sharp ethical judgments about "good" and "evil." Excessive preoccupation with moral codes tends to open a gap between the sacred and the secular, and to discredit those people whose lives may involve transgressions that monks are able to avoid. Whatever the reasons, morality rarely functioned as a principal or independent standard of authenticity in early Japanese Zen.

Zen monastic life revealed sharp contrasts between extremes of restriction and freedom. The Zen way was supposed to nurture a mind unfettered by convention or conventional thinking, and the tradition esteemed those who expressed their spiritual liberation through eccentricity. At the same time, the routine of a typical monk was tightly circumscribed by daily, monthly, and annual schedules; a rigid hierarchy based on seniority; and the austere simplicity of the monastic lifestyle. The constrained and unconstrained dimensions of Zen life can be clearly seen in the private meeting between master and disciple, especially as it developed in the Rinzai sect. Though most aspects of this encounter were governed by etiquette and ritualized procedures, during one crucial interval both participants were free to act in any way that enabled them to demonstrate their Zen, even if that called for rudeness, violence, silliness, or irrationality. On a larger scale as well, the pressures created by the monastic rule were deliberately heightened to induce spiritual breakthroughs. Ideally, this form of training enabled a Zen monk to transcend any disjunction between "outer restriction" and "inner freedom." A person could express spiritual liberation in the observance of the daily routine, performing ordinary tasks wholeheartedly. A well-known Zen saying makes this point concretely: "Carrying water and hauling wood—how mysterious, how wonderful!"[49]

Monastery Construction

The need to clarify the essentials of Zen was also evident in the construction of the first Japanese Zen monasteries. Bypassing indigenous architectural forms and shunning temple designs used in the older Japanese Buddhist sects, the Zen pioneers were determined to replicate the type of monastic architecture then current in China, a style they identified with Ch'an. A monastery was supposed to be the optimal environment for teaching and training, perfected over countless generations by awakened masters. Dōgen was not alone in depicting the monastic layout as "the direct transmission of the true [Dharma] heirs."[50] In a similar spirit Nanpo affirmed, "The temple buildings with all their ornamental fixtures are the honorific emblems of Buddhist virtue. They have nothing to do with mere decorative effects."[51]

Many of the Japanese pilgrims studied the specifications of Sung monastic architecture as eagerly as they applied themselves to Zen training. After their return, they sometimes dispatched disciples to China to acquire further designs, and they arranged for skilled Chinese carpenters and sculptors to be escorted to Japan. These efforts, sustained throughout the early phases of transmission, resulted in the faithful reproduction of many aspects of Chinese temples: massive masonry foundations, tiled floors, stone pedestals for the wooden columns, solid walls, swinging doors, graceful bell-shaped windows, and sweeping tiled roofs supported by curved wooden brackets.

The standard layout of a Sung Ch'an monastery was also duplicated whenever possible. Though Dōgen and others sought to emphasize the differences between Ch'an and non-Ch'an monasteries, in Sung China the leading Ch'an, Discipline (Lü), and Doctrine (Chiao) monasteries had essentially the same physical layouts.[52] The Japanese preserved a central, south-facing axis composed of an entrance gate, a Buddha hall, and a Dharma hall. The monks' hall and latrine were on the west side of this axis, the kitchen-office and bathhouse were on the east, and the abbot's residence was usually located near the apex of the configuration. A typical compound also included a reading room, a bell tower, an attendants' hall, a pagoda, and storehouses. In some cases, subtemples on the premises had extensive facilities and gardens of their own.

The assumption that the presence of a particular building enhanced authenticity led to consideration of the relative importance of different structures. At least according to the records that have survived, Eisai stressed the walls and gates, Dōgen the monks' hall, and Musō the abbot's quarters. Wu-hsüeh gave prominence to a Buddha hall at Engakuji, whereas Daitō inaugurated Daitokuji with just a Dharma hall. The strong motivation to uphold precedents in the layout and construction of monasteries stemmed from the conviction that such details were a vital feature of genuine Zen.

The first structure one encountered as one approached a Zen compound was the entrance gate *(sanmon)*. An imposing two-tiered building with heavy, upward-curving eaves, it often had outside stairways leading to a usable second story. Originally, this gate was linked to a walled enclosure. For Eisai, the gates and walls of the monastery performed a vital task: "There should be walled cloisters on all four sides with no side gates and only a single gate to permit entrance and exit. The gatekeeper must see to it that the gate is closed at dusk and opened at dawn. Nuns, women, or evil people should on no account be permitted to stay overnight."[53] Not only "women and evil people" but even outside monks were ordinarily banned from staying overnight, so that the routine of the resident monks would not be disturbed.

The Buddha hall *(butsuden)*, positioned some distance behind the entrance gate, was a large, nearly square building two stories tall. Its open interior had an impressive vertical quality that reflected the Chinese fondness for height. A Buddha hall typically housed figures of Shakyamuni and several attendant bodhisattvas, who were venerated in public and private devotional services. The lacquered wooden tablets in front of these images bore such worldly inscriptions as "Long Live the Emperor" and "Prosperity and Good Fortune to Patrons," standard Chinese Buddhist formulas that also had relevance in their new Japanese setting. At the head of the central axis was the Dharma hall *(hattō)*, similar in construction to the Buddha hall. The principal furnishing inside this hall was the dais used by the abbot when he delivered his Dharma lecture; otherwise the interior was left bare to accommodate the congregation of monks.

Ch'an traditionally gave the Dharma hall precedence over the Buddha hall, in deference to the master's status as a "living buddha." The subordinate role of the Buddha hall was supposed to distinguish Ch'an from the doctrinal schools, but Buddha halls were found in all of the large Sung monasteries, and they were accordingly accepted in Japanese Zen. In 1270, when Nanpo became abbot of Kōtokuji in Kyushu, he alluded critically to two T'ang masters who had opposed Buddha halls: "Tung-shan and Yün-men saw only the point of the awl; they did not see the squared tip of the chisel. My approach is different. At the entrance gate, I place my hands palm-to-palm; in the Buddha hall, I light incense."[54]

Near the top of the central axis was the abbot's residence *(hōjō)*, one of the few buildings in the monastic compound that reflected Japanese architectural styles. There the master lived apart from the trainees, waited upon by one or more attendant monks. Because the master often conducted his private interviews with disciples in the *hōjō,* it too was highly valued. Musō gave the abbot's quarters priority even over a Dharma hall in a middle-sized monastery: "It is not essential to establish a Dharma hall. . . . If the abbot truly has the capacity of the great masters of the past, then he may sit squarely in his own quarters and instruct those who visit him there."[55]

A final structure, the monks' hall *(sōdō),* eventually became the spiritual and institutional heart of the Zen monastic system in Japan. Inside this hall were long wooden platforms where the monks communally meditated, slept, chanted sutras, ate certain meals, and participated in various rituals. For these activities each monk was allotted a space less than three feet by six feet on a section of the platform. Direct exposure to life in Ch'an monks' halls made a deep impression on the Japanese pilgrims who went to China. As Dōgen recalled: "I personally saw in great Sung China Ch'an monasteries in many areas, each built to include a meditation hall, wherein from five or six hundred to one or two thousand monks were housed and encouraged to devote themselves to zazen day and night."[56] The monks' halls that Dōgen built at Kōshōji and Eiheiji in the mid-thirteenth century appear to have been the first Sung-style *sōdō* in Japan.[57] "The cardinal monastic buildings are the Buddha hall, Dharma hall, and monks' hall," Dōgen wrote, and among them "the monks' hall is most vital."[58]

Withdrawal from the World

The marks of genuine Zen could be as tangible as the layout of a monastery or as intangible as a spirit of detachment from the affairs of the world. Because various forms of seclusion had long been extolled in many Asian cultures, this trait was by no means associated exclusively with Zen. Nonetheless, transcendence of the mundane world was both an aim and an indication of the Zen life. To become a Zen monk one "left home" *(shukke),* an act that originally signified a withdrawal from society and its obligations. *Shukke* also meant seeing the illusoriness of the world of relativity, "leaving" it to dwell in the formless Dharma realm. A person with the "Dharma eye" *(hō no manako)* was supposedly free of attachment to wealth, power, recognition, and other worldly enticements.

The fact that the Zen institution itself was very much in society added a level of complexity to this ideal. During the period of Zen's introduction to Japan, there was a need to stabilize and strengthen the institution rather than to restrain or reform it. Nearly all of the early masters embraced the argument that Zen would contribute significantly to the welfare of the nation. For individual practitioners, many aspects of life within a monastery could be just as worldly as what went on outside the monastery's gates. Here other interpretations of *shukke* became operative: it was taught that one could even be actively engaged in secular or religious affairs and remain free from attachment or defilement. Like the proverbial lotus flower that was rooted in mud yet blossomed beautifully above it, a true Zen devotee—monastic or lay—aspired to transmute the given conditions of life into a path of liberation. The unworldliness prized by Zen was not simply world-denying.

The favored signs of inner detachment have included poverty, seclusion, and eccentricity. Several important Ch'an figures were associated with these traits, in accounts that may have been more legendary than factual. Bodhidharma was renowned for his alleged nine years of zazen inside a remote mountain cave. The T'ang master Fen-chou Wu-yeh (762–823) stressed that the ancient sages "erased their traces and completely forgot the world" for twenty or thirty years.[59] Chao-chou repeatedly refused offers of financial assistance from his supporters: "When the broken-down walls of his meditation hall let in the harsh winter winds of North China, and when his preaching platform collapsed from rot and decay, he merely patched them up with old planks and pieces of rope."[60] The roster of unworldly exemplars also included laymen such as P'ang Yün, who gave away his house and sank his possessions in a river. Lung-ya Chü-tun (835–923) declared, "Only after studying poverty and becoming poor can you be intimate with the Way."[61]

Withdrawal from the world is variously depicted in the *Record of Lin-chi*. In a sermon Lin-chi declares that the powers of a buddha include "entering the world of color yet not being deluded by color; entering the world of sound yet not being deluded by sound; entering the world of odor yet not being deluded by odor . . . entering the world of dharmas yet not being deluded by dharmas."[62] One of Lin-chi's companions, P'u-hua, embodies another aspect of this ideal. He is described as "acting like a lunatic." Invited to dine at a patron's house, P'u-hua kicked over the dinner table. When he was ready to die, he reportedly got into his coffin and asked a passerby to nail it up.[63] Such was the behavior of the free spirits who were thought to have transcended the world.

The early Japanese Zen masters similarly embraced the themes of withdrawal and detachment, linking them implicitly or explicitly to genuine Zen. Keizan extolled the "uncommon person who has transcended [the world]" *(chōzetsu no ijin)*.[64] "Be satisfied with simplicity," Musō exhorted his monks, adding that "past seekers of the Way sat on rocks and under trees, preferring isolated valleys and craggy ledges."[65] Dōgen, who frequently quoted his Chinese master's indictment of worldliness, wrote that "buddhas and patriarchs have never desired

halls or pavilions."[66] "From the time of the Buddha till the present,"
Dōgen also stated, "we have never seen or heard of a true practitioner
of the Way who possessed wealth."[67]

Dōgen is traditionally depicted as having fulfilled a yearning for
seclusion "among the deep mountains and still valleys" when he built a
temple in distant Echizen province.[68] Yet the historical evidence suggests that Dōgen actively pursued political patronage during the first
thirteen years after his return from China and that he retreated reluc-
tantly to Echizen only after failing to establish himself in Kyoto.[69] It is
difficult to determine which masters, if any, withdrew from the world in
a literal as well as a spiritual sense. When Bassui was an itinerant
monk, he reportedly refused to stay overnight in large temples,
declaring that "temples are not the only sites of Buddha-Dharma or the
vocation of monkhood."[70] Kakushin, summoned to Kyoto by the court,
protested that he was "not virtuous enough to be the teacher of an
emperor," and he left the capital at the first opportunity.[71] Declining a
similar invitation to serve as founder of Nanzenji, Kakushin was apparently content to remain the abbot of a small mountain temple in Kii
province.

The biography of the reclusive Kanzan Egen has for a long time been
augmented by colorful legends. Before his appointment as founder-
abbot of Myōshinji, Kanzan allegedly had to be retrieved from an
obscure country village. His residence at Myōshinji was said to be so
humble that the roof leaked whenever it rained. A story from Zen lore
involving Kanzan and Musō expresses the ideal of unworldliness by
contrasting the two masters:

> Musō was constantly making visits to the court. This was out of his
> concern for the country—his good intention to do something to
> reunite the northern and southern courts. The way to and from the
> palace ran right past Myōshinji temple, so it seems he often passed its
> back gate. On the one hand there he was, riding past in a carriage, a
> figure of luxury. On the other hand, there was Kanzan, tending rad-
> ishes or carrying a shoulder-pole weighted into a crook. Seeing that
> figure from within his carriage, Musō himself said that his Buddha-
> Dharma would be replaced by Kanzan's.[72]

A century after Daitō's era, Zen master Ikkyū railed against the cor-
ruption he saw at the top of the Zen establishment. Paradoxically, Ikkyū
sought to demonstrate his authentic unworldliness by immersing himself in worldly activities normally shunned by Zen monks. Appointed to
the abbacy of a Daitokuji subtemple, he resigned in less than a fort-
night, with the following envoi:

Only ten fussy days as an abbot,
And already my feet are tangled in red tape.
If, someday, you want to look me up,
Try the fish-shop, the tavern, or the brothel.[73]

Conclusion

Our investigation has revealed the breadth and complexity of the discourse about authenticity in early Japanese Zen. The repercussions of this issue affected nearly every facet of the religious life, from the way a monk meditated to the way a meditation hall was built. Given the array of features considered essential and the variation within them, it is not surprising that individual conceptions of authenticity flourished. Though the notion of tradition is prone to reification, at any given moment a living tradition is undergoing change. Cultural transmission brings a tradition's mutability and diversity into greater relief. Indeed, some of the Japanese masters' most forcefully argued positions can be seen as deliberate attempts to shift or expand the prevailing conceptions of "Zen."

All tenets about orthodoxy or authenticity become unstable in Zen, because on some level they are dualistic: authenticity must stand against inauthenticity, orthodoxy is defined in opposition to heterodoxy. The masters believed that such dualities had to be denied (or denied and affirmed simultaneously). Even Dōgen, who so strongly emphasized true Dharma transmission, cautioned against either/or formulations of the matter. For example, he radically reinterpreted the traditional account of Bodhidharma's transmission to his four disciples. In the accepted Chinese version of the event, the first monk attained Bodhidharma "in his skin" and the last, Hui-k'o, attained Bodhidharma "in his marrow." Hui-k'o became the Second Patriarch, the others did not. But Dōgen rejected the assumption that the best answer invalidated the other responses. Collapsing the distinction between proximity and distance, he argued that all four students ultimately received the Patriarch's "body-mind": "Even the 'in my skin' must be a transmission of the Dharma. The Patriarch's body-mind is the Patriarch—his skin-flesh-bones-marrow. It is not the case that the marrow is intimate and the skin distant."[74]

This same principle can be applied to the search for the essentials of Zen in medieval Japan. Though certain stances eventually gained acceptance and others came to be branded as "outside the Way," they functioned as interlocking pieces of the same mosaic. In that sense at least, the masters' various positions were equivalent and mutually dependent, whatever differences there may have been.[75] Given these complexities, the discourse about authenticity may at times appear to deconstruct itself. With nothing substantial to put one's finger on, one might surmise that ultimately there are no criteria of authentic Zen or that authenticity in Zen is somehow tied to the *absence* of unvarying criteria. Yet the writings and the actions of the early Japanese masters do not support this line of reasoning. However subtle the indications, however prone to deconstruction the discourse, the pioneers were confident of their ability to identify the essentials of genuine Zen.

8

DAITŌ'S ZEN: THE PRIMACY OF AWAKENING

WHEN WE ATTEMPT to describe the teachings of a Zen master, we may be unable to detect a unified system of thought, a dominant theme, or even a prevalent phrase. Most Zen masters are not philosophers (in the usual sense, at least), and their works are not conventionally philosophical. What we do find may seem insubstantial at first: a preference for a particular type of practice, an exceptional ability to train disciples, a determination to introduce Zen to a new audience, or a heightened aesthetic awareness. In Zen, the fundamental consistency of Dharma transmission is assumed, and the tradition discusses the distinctive features of a master or a lineage in terms of style *(kafū)*. The clue to a particular style may emerge only after considerable exposure, personal or textual, to a master's teachings. There are occasional exceptions—masters who do embrace a conspicuous theme or compose texts that might be called philosophical—but Daitō is not among them.

In response to the ongoing debate about the essentials of Zen, Daitō worked out his position regarding most of the salient points. He made little attempt to articulate the links between the various elements; it was taken for granted that underlying integration was provided by enlightenment. The configuration forged by Daitō is historically significant because it came to represent the classic or orthodox style of Rinzai Zen in Japan. Within Zen, it is believed that Daitō's style triumphed because of its inherent spiritual vitality, more specifically the depth and force of his enlightenment. Historians (including those who give credence to the religious impact of Daitō's teachings) are compelled to add that Daitō's Zen also fulfilled polemical functions during the master's

113

lifetime and for centuries afterward. Because the dialogical matrix of early Japanese Zen shaped the Zen of each individual master, the rubric developed in the preceding two chapters will provide an initial framework for our exploration of Daitō's teachings.

Enlightenment

The essence of Daitō's Zen is succinctly conveyed in a scroll, preserved over the centuries, that he wrote himself:

> Once you suddenly smash through, and go on to make the leap beyond, you will find that everything around you and all that you do, whether active or at rest, is the scenery of the fundamental ground, the original Mind. There will be not a hairsbreadth of difference between you and other things—there will be no other things.[1]

In speaking of Daitō's Zen, one must speak of enlightenment before all else, for this is the "fundamental ground" where Daitō stands, the "original Mind" that he attempts to express in all his writings. As we have seen, awakening has been the primary criterion of authenticity throughout the history of Ch'an and Zen, so Daitō's preoccupation with it does not, in itself, set him apart from other masters. Yet the ways in which Daitō expresses enlightenment are unusually powerful and evocative, and the Japanese Zen tradition singles him out as a paradigmatic embodiment of profound self-realization.

One way Daitō stresses the primacy of awakening is by referring frequently to the satori experiences of the Ch'an/Zen patriarchs. However the circumstances may differ, he asserts, the awakening is essentially the same:

> The Second Patriarch Hui-k'o stood in the snow, cut off his arm, and awakened. The Sixth Patriarch heard someone recite the *Diamond Sutra* phrase "arouse the mind without its abiding anywhere," and he awakened. Ling-yün saw a peach blossom and awakened. Hsiang-yen heard a tile fragment strike bamboo, and he awakened. Lin-chi was given sixty blows by Huang-po, and he awakened. Tung-shan noticed his own reflection when he was crossing a river, and he awakened. In each case, these men met the Master.[2]

The bellwether of all enlightenment experiences is, of course, Shakyamuni Buddha's. Daitō chose to inaugurate Daitokuji on the day that this event was commemorated, the eighth day of the twelfth month. During the ceremony he offered the following verse, based on the tale in which Shakyamuni awakened in the snowy Himalayas:

> One glance at the morning star, and the snow got even whiter.
> The look in his eye chills hair and bones.

> If earth itself hadn't experienced this instant,
> Old Shakyamuni never would have appeared.[3]

This poem celebrates the oneness of Shakyamuni and the universe. Because they achieve enlightenment together, even the snow becomes whiter at that triumphant moment. Daitō's intimate (and somewhat irreverent) reference to the Buddha as "Old Shakyamuni" reminds his listeners that the Buddha's experience is accessible to them as well.

Daitō speaks of enlightenment in several senses. When he recounts the incidents that precipitated the awakening of the patriarchs, he highlights the sense of "smashing through"; on other occasions he offers lyrical depictions of the enlightened mind itself:

> This mind, perfectly and fully realized, moves with a clear, tranquil spiritual awareness. It encompasses heaven, covers the earth, penetrates form, and rides upon sound. It is a boundless openness; it is a summit rising with forbidding abruptness. . . . It is a radiant light shining from the crown of your head, illuminating wherever you are; it is an awesome wind, rising up at each step you take, enveloping all things. . . . If you are able to make this mind your own, then even though you do not seek excellence yourself, excellence comes to you of its own accord. Without seeking emancipation, you are not hindered by a single thing.[4]

Portrayals of the enlightened mind inevitably shade into descriptions of universal Mind, because the two are ultimately one. For Daitō, this Mind is "originally silent and still."[5] It has neither color nor shape, yet "it fills the world" and its radiance exceeds the brightness of "a hundred thousand suns and moons."[6] It is unborn, undying, free from the wheel of transmigration, beyond any aspect of past or future. Even if the universe were destroyed, it would not be affected.[7] Though Daitō claims that Mind cannot be reached through words or silence, he cannot refrain from extolling it verbally:

> Before the beginningless beginning, prior to the appearance of the first Buddha, already its bright and radiant light shone forth. It illuminates heaven and stands as a perfect mirror on earth, embracing and manifesting all things. The sun, moon, stars, and planets, lightning flashes, thunderclaps—everything without exception receives its benevolent influence.[8]

In his repeated references to awakening, Daitō does not favor one particular expression. As we have noted, the term *kenshō*, "seeing one's [True-]nature," was widely accepted in Japanese Zen; its authoritative sources included the *Platform Sutra* and the classic stanza attributed to Bodhidharma. Daitō uses the expression freely in the two sermons he wrote in vernacular Japanese, equating it with the highest level of realization: "When you actually see your True-nature, you transcend *saṃ-sāra* and nirvana and reside in fundamental buddhahood."⁹ Or again: "If you desire to meet the real Buddha, you must see your True-nature. Unless you see your True-nature, even if you recite the Buddha's name, read sutras, and uphold the precepts, you will just be wasting your time."¹⁰ Although the term *kenshō* does not appear in Daitō's formal discourse record, he must have used it orally in the guidance of his monks. In Takuan's biography of the master, a monk asks, "What is this 'seeing one's nature and becoming Buddha'?" Daitō replies, "The snow melts and the bones of the mountain appear."¹¹

Daitō delights in using numerous Buddhist synonyms for awakening or True-nature. Though the names may differ, the referent does not: "It is just the same as when a baby is born—originally it has no name, and afterwards various names are given to it."¹² In one relatively brief sermon he uses at least twenty different terms interchangeably: the Way, Buddha-Dharma, Self-nature, Buddha, Mind, Emptiness, True Body of Emptiness, True Body of Mind, Original Face, Original Face before your parents' birth, Buddha-body, Dharma-body, Master, Original Master, Buddha-nature, True Buddha, Buddha Way, One Mind, Mind-Buddha, and "the place that cannot be known."¹³ Elsewhere, in light verse, Daitō reiterates his lack of attachment to any of these expressions:

> "Delusion," "enlightenment"—
> just fox-words fooling
> Zen monks everywhere.¹⁴

Daitō underscores the primacy of enlightenment in his "Final Admonitions." In many Rinzai monasteries this text is still chanted by the monks before they go to bed, night after night, and it has engendered a sense of intimacy with Daitō among countless generations of Zen practitioners. The "Admonitions" are actually a combination of two short passages found in Takuan's biography of Daitō;¹⁵ the second portion states:

> After I have moved on, some of my followers may preside over splendid temples bustling with many monks, where the Buddhist gates and sutra scrolls are inlaid with gold and silver. Other followers may chant sutras, recite *dharanis*, and sit in meditation for long periods without lying down. They may eat their single meals before noon and worship Buddha at the six appointed hours of the day.
>
> In any case, if the untransmittable wondrous Way of the buddhas and patriarchs is not in their hearts, their karmic connection with their predecessors will be lost, the true wind of Zen will sink into the earth, and they will join the tribe of malignant spirits. After I have left the world, they must never be considered my descendants.

However, if there is one person who leads an upright life in the open fields, dwelling in a simple thatched hut, eating vegetable roots boiled in a broken-legged pot, and devoting his time to single-minded investigation of himself, then this person will meet me face-to-face each day and requite his spiritual obligations. Is there anyone who can afford to be negligent? Press on, press on![16]

Again Daitō makes it clear that awakening takes precedence over all other aspects of the religious life and that these other aspects are meaningless unless one actualizes "the untransmittable wondrous Way of the buddhas and patriarchs." Zen followers who lack enlightenment not only will suffer personally; they will also imperil the transmission of the Dharma. Conversely, anyone who is practicing sincerely, in accord with the spirit of awakening, is the master's true descendant and companion.

When Daitō speaks from the ultimate standpoint, he insists that enlightenment is the sole criterion of authentic Zen, and he accords little significance to other elements such as zazen or monastery construction. When he speaks from the conventional standpoint, however, he embraces additional factors as essential features of Zen; without them he would be unable to administer a temple or instruct a disciple. The primacy of enlightenment notwithstanding, it is possible to identify salient dimensions of Daitō's thought in his approach to the other essentials of Zen.

Zazen

The centrality of zazen was not questioned by Daitō. The monastic routine at Daitokuji included several sessions of meditation each day, and lay followers were similarly urged to "devote themselves exclusively to zazen at the beginning" of practice.[17] Daitō's definition of Zen meditation was succinct: "Zazen means to sit in the full- or half-lotus posture, open the eyes halfway, and see the Original Face before your parents' birth."[18] He used a number of traditional metaphors to describe the process further:

"Sweep away thoughts!" means one must do zazen. Once thoughts are quieted, the Original Face appears. Thoughts can be compared to clouds—when clouds vanish, the moon appears. The moon of suchness is the Original Face. Thoughts are also like the fogging of a mirror—when you wipe away all condensation, a mirror reflects clearly. Quiet your thoughts and behold your Original Face before you were born![19]

Daitō sometimes uses the term *kufū* in place of "zazen" to denote the sustained exertion of Zen meditation. Two phrases from his "Final Admonitions" can also be regarded as roughly synonymous with zazen.

"Coming or going, day or night, you must just strive to face the incomprehensible,"[20] Daitō exhorts his monks in that text. Facing the incomprehensible *(murie no tokoro ni mukatte)* is the fundamental task of zazen, a probing attitude that practitioners are supposed to maintain throughout all activities. The "Admonitions" also commend "single-minded investigation of oneself" *(koji o kyūmei-su)*,[21] another description of the zazen mind-state. A person devoted to this intense self-inquiry will meet his master "face-to-face" each day, Daitō asserts. Though he does not elaborate on the two expressions or use them elsewhere in his writings, they entered the vocabulary of Japanese Zen and were cited by twentieth-century Japanese philosophers such as Nishida Kitarō (1870–1945) and Nishitani Keiji (1900–1990).

Daitō identifies several mistaken approaches to Zen meditation. For example, the cessation of thought is not a goal of proper zazen: "Your notion that thoughts arise leads to a notion that you must prevent them from arising. These conflicting ideas are both wrong."[22] Daitō alludes to Ta-hui when he asserts that a "no-thought *samādhi*" is an "outside path" and "false Zen."[23] Rather, one should "look well at the source beyond mental activity."[24] Another erroneous approach is to practice zazen in the hope that enlightenment will arrive sooner or later: "The Way transcends any aspect of going or coming, movement or quiescence, so one cannot realize satori by waiting for it."[25] Nor should zazen be seen as a precondition for awakening. "You may conclude that without doing zazen you will never see your True-nature, but that would be a mistake," Daitō cautions.[26]

In the same spirit, Daitō rejects conceptions of zazen that limit it to the immobile sitting posture: "Great Master Yung-chia said, 'Walking is Zen, and sitting is Zen. Whether one speaks, remains silent, moves, or rests, the body is at peace.' He meant that walking, sitting, or talking are all Zen."[27] True zazen can be carried on as one goes about one's daily business: "That which is called the Original Face is present in active and quiet places alike."[28] In a verse entitled "Zazen" Daitō suggests that zazen-in-activity surpasses quiet sitting:

> How boring to sit idly on the floor,
> not meditating, not breaking through.
> Look at the horses racing along the Kamo River!
> That's zazen![29]

Daitō tolerated Buddhist practices other than zazen in certain contexts. For example, he sanctioned a variety of devotional practices as expedient means for those of "shallow roots." People who help to build a temple or erect a Buddha figure thereby gain religious merit, strengthen their karmic links with the Way, and eventually "arrive at the real temple and see the real Buddha."[30] In the "Admonitions" he lists several practices ordinarily considered meritorious, such as chanting and regular worship of the Buddha, but then he rejects these activities as futile unless they reflect a genuine aspiration for enlightenment.

Daitō's understanding of meditation does not deviate in any significant way from mainstream Ch'an/Zen. What distinguishes his approach to practice is his intense involvement in koans. A koan is even embedded in his definition of zazen, cited above: "Zazen means to sit in the full- or half-lotus posture, open the eyes halfway, and see the Original Face before your parents' birth." Daitō was apparently attracted to koans as a young monk. He questioned his first teacher, Kōhō Kennichi, about the koan "An Ox Passes Through the Window," and he supposedly solved "nearly two hundred koans" in one year as a student of Nanpo. He was struggling with the koan "Barrier" when he came to deep enlightenment. Koans accordingly suffuse Daitō's lectures and dialogues during his fifteen years as abbot of Daitokuji. In the *Record of Daitō* the master may quote a classic koan for his listeners and then comment on it himself; more often a monk will cite a koan and publicly question the master about it line by line. In other works Daitō comments on the hundred koans of the *Blue Cliff Record,* annotates his own collection of one hundred twenty koans, and responds to assorted koans from additional sources.

Tradition also credits Daitō with the creation of an original koan:

> In the morning our eyebrows intertwine; in the evening we rub shoulders. What am I?
> The pillar moves back and forth all day long. Why am I immobile?
> Those who penetrate these two turning words will have completed one lifetime of Zen training.[31]

In Zen, a "turning word" is a word or phrase that has the capacity to transform a person's awareness or even to precipitate enlightenment itself. This conundrum, known as Daitō's "three turning words" *(santengo),* was transmitted orally for nearly a century before being recorded by Shunsaku in 1426. Nonetheless, it is one of the first Chinese-style koans created by a Japanese master. Though Daitō may have used it only in private sessions with disciples, he alluded to it in his discourse record:

> I have three crucial koans. If you get the first, I allow you to lift the sun and the moon over the tip of my staff. If you get the second, you may do a headstand on the tip of my whisk. If you get the third, I'll ask you whether the wheat in front of the mountain has ripened or not.[32]

Today Daitō's *santengo* is considered an advanced koan, assigned only to monks with ten or more years of experience. For each of the three parts, which are taken up separately, the practitioner must first give his own response and then offer a suitable capping phrase. Although Daitō added at least one original koan to those he inherited, he believed that a person who thoroughly penetrates even a single koan has fathomed them all: "We say that there are 1,700 koans and 17,000 kernels of koans, but they are all meant to reveal the Original Face."[33]

Emblems of Dharma Transmission

For Daitō the principle of Dharma transmission was corroborated by personal experience. Once he resolved Yün-men's koan "Barrier," he felt that he too was nourished by the "life-artery of the heroic patriarchs."[34] One of the earliest texts in Daitō's hand is his transcription of the *Transmission of the Lamp,* which traces Zen's spiritual lineage from Shakyamuni and his Indian successors through the Ch'an patriarchs and their Chinese heirs. Daitō returned to this theme throughout his teaching career; the year before his death he told his monks: "It has come down to the present day but still it flows broad and unbroken. Truly, our school is deep at its source, long and vast in its flow. Therefore it has been said that 'it will never diminish for a million ages; it is clear and unmistakable right before your eyes.' "[35]

Kokai's biography identifies fourteen followers of Daitō who "personally received his seal and inherited his Dharma."[36] When Daitō's own teacher Nanpo added words of praise and advice to Daitō's two enlightenment poems, he had in effect created a seal of enlightenment, and Daitō ceremoniously passed this document on to Tettō Gikō, his successor at Daitokuji. He also gave Tettō his personal robe and a document that declared:

> My senior monk [Gi]kō has followed me faithfully for a long time. The thoroughness of his enlightenment is something that everyone already knows. He is to succeed me as resident abbot of Daitokuji and to teach the assembled monks with compassion. In addition, I give him the Dharma robe that I have always used. My thoughts for him are filled with deep gratitude.[37]

Kanzan, Daitō's other principal heir, did not receive a comparable document. However, when Kanzan resolved the koan "Barrier," Daitō recognized his disciple's enlightenment by giving him a new name and a scroll to prove it. On an occasion of this significance, Daitō characteristically composed a verse:

Kanzan

Where the road is blocked and utterly impassable,
cold clouds in a timeless belt encircle green peaks.

> Though Yün-men's one word conceals its vital working,
> the true eye discerns it, beyond the farthest summits.

> I bestow the religious name "Kanzan" on the temple clerk Egen. Written in the third month of the fourth year of Karyaku [1329], by Shūhō Myōchō of the Dragon Peak Mountain [Daitokuji].[38]

Daitō bequeathed Nanpo's robe to the monks of Daitokuji and instructed them as follows:

> Take the purple Dharma robe that was transmitted to me by the National Master [Nanpo] and place it in a memorial chamber. Take it out and use it only once each year, on the day [of my death] when the members of the congregation gather at the temple. This directive must never be disobeyed.[39]

In other inscriptions Daitō validated the enlightenment of disciples who may not have been sanctioned as Dharma heirs. For example, he responded in writing to a request from an elder nun named Chishō, asserting, "She has realized the Way where birth and death are one."[40] He also used formal portraits of himself as insignia of transmission, though the original recipients are not always indicated. Six portraits of Daitō are extant, four of them bearing inscriptions by the master.

Clearly Daitō accepted emblems of Dharma transmission as an essential feature of genuine Zen. Besides valuing the robe and written sanction he received from Nanpo, he granted certificates, inscriptions, robes, and portraits to his own followers. He did not, however, exalt these emblems in his writings (as Dōgen did) or distribute them profusely (as Hsü-t'ang did). Over the centuries Daitō's descendants were inspired and reassured by these original insignia, which they treasured as proof of the authenticity of their lineage and their Zen.

Monastery Construction and the Monastic Rule

Since about the age of ten, when he was first sent to a Buddhist temple, Daitō led a monastic life. He was formally ordained as a Zen monk when he was about twenty-two, and he trained in several of the most important Zen monasteries of his era. Daitō was the first Japanese monk to establish a major Rinzai monastery without having been exposed to Chinese monasticism. He served for fifteen years as abbot— cultivating patrons, supervising temple construction, and training the resident monks. In Japanese Zen a monastery founder is given the honorific title *kaisan,* one who has "opened the mountain."

Though Daitō greatly valued a place to train Zen monks in the traditional manner, in his writings he does not discuss the construction of monasteries or the relative importance of various buildings. Daitokuji's records are similarly silent regarding the initial construction of the temple. Whereas other lineages take pride in the history of their monks' halls, the earliest reference to this building in the Daitokuji archives is vague and undated: "Initially it was built to the west of the Buddha hall."[41] Contemporary scholar Yanagida Seizan sees significance in Daitō's choice of a Dharma hall over a Buddha hall as Daitokuji's first major building. Because Dharma halls were originally given precedence in Ch'an monasteries, Yanagida speculates that Daitō was aiming to recapture the spirit of early T'ang dynasty Ch'an, "an unbridled, ambitious aspiration."[42] More mundane considerations, such as limited funds, may also have affected the choice of buildings.

Whereas many of his predecessors and peers composed extensive monastic codes, Daitō left only one terse list of regulations. It probably served as a supplement to the standard codes then available:

1. Contact with guest monks is not permitted.
2. The times for the three daily services and the bell and drum signals cannot be changed.
3. Monks in administrative positions must not be selfish when handling accounts for food and the like.
4. During periods of temple construction, any details involving lumber, nails, and so on are one's own responsibility; do not burden other people with such matters.
5. If monks in official positions violate the rules, I will turn my back on them forever. A novice who breaks the rules is not allowed to read sutras in the Buddha hall for a day. Those who violate these regulations will be expelled immediately.
6. For young and old alike, there must be no idle conversation.
7. Novices, postulants, and young trainees must stop misbehaving when they are not attending the three daily services; instead they should devote themselves to study. Those who violate these rules will be struck five times with a stick and denied meals for a day.
8. Those who do not memorize the sutras and *dharanis* used in the three daily services are to be deprived of their robe and bowl and expelled.
9. In the kitchen-headquarters *(kuri)*, senior monks Sōrin and Sōtetsu are in charge of rice, money, meals, salt, and miso. In the Buddha hall and the abbot's quarters, senior monks Sōren and Sōju are responsible for the three daily services and cleaning. Senior monk Sōnin is responsible for cleaning the latrine. Novice Sōgen should accompany and assist the senior monks working in the Buddha hall, kitchen-headquarters, latrine, and elsewhere. When novices or postulants misbehave, disciplining them is the duty of senior monk Sōrin.
10. Novices, postulants, and young trainees should not loiter in the kitchen-headquarters. Those who break this rule will be struck five times with a stick and denied meals for a day.

These regulations accord with the intentions of buddhas and patriarchs. Keep an eye on your companions, and do not hesitate to report offenders. These are the established rules.[43]

Daitō's use of personal names in this code suggests that he was not addressing a large monastic community; he may have compiled these rules at an early stage of Daitokuji's development. The recurrent references to punishment are consistent with the master's reputation as a strict disciplinarian. The modest scope of this original code compelled Daitō's successor, Tettō, to fill the breach: around 1368 Tettō composed three sets of regulations, one for Daitokuji and two for Daitokuji subtemples.

The relative validity of monastic and lay practice was variously interpreted by Daitō's predecessors and peers, as we have seen. Though it is sometimes difficult to ascertain the audience being addressed, Daitō appears to have taken a broad-minded approach to this issue. Whereas his teacher Nanpo had extolled the virtues of monkhood in his "Final Admonitions" and other texts, Daitō often reproached those who were monks in name only. In the following passage he claims Bodhidharma as his authority:

> Great Master Bodhidharma was asked, "What is the essence of leaving home to become a monk *(shukke)*?" He answered, "Don't think that leaving home is just cutting your hair, shaving your beard, and wearing a monk's robe. Someone who shaves his hair, puts on a robe, and dons a *kesa* has not really become a monk unless he has awakened. Until then, he does not differ from an ordinary householder."[44]

Daitō welcomed lay people and nuns as students, and he seems to have demanded of them what he demanded of his monks—a strong aspiration for self-realization. A woman named Sōin, Daitō's disciple and patron, was influential in the early construction of Daitokuji. Daitō wrote a sermon in vernacular Japanese for the consort of an emperor and composed a similar tract for an unnamed layman. Among his extant calligraphic works, three are addressed to nuns, two to lay men, and one to a lay woman. In these texts he warns his lay followers not to cling to status or wealth: "Shakyamuni abandoned his kingly rank; Layman P'ang sank his precious jewels in the ocean."[45] Nor should responsibility for parents or children be an obstacle to practice. Rather, a true practitioner must actualize the Way whatever his or her circumstances may be: "Wearing clothes, eating meals, walking, standing, sitting, or lying down" are not separate from the "true body of emptiness."[46] Asked if householders can achieve spiritual liberation without conquering "lust," Daitō replies, "With *kenshō*, lust becomes void and ceases of its own accord."[47]

Daitō may or may not have valued monastery construction as an essential feature of Zen: he exerted himself to build a new monastery, yet he does not address the topic in his writings. Similarly, his views on the monastic rule remain indistinct: though devoted to the training of his monks, he left the barest of monastic codes, and he encouraged lay practitioners. While Daitō's admirers glorified Daitokuji's "lofty towers and imposing gates" or exalted its "thousand monks living in peace,"[48] the master sought to point beyond the external forms of institutional Zen. During the ceremonial inauguration of Daitokuji, he brandished his monk's shawl and asked, "As I reverently don this *kesa,* who can discern its true color?"[49]

Withdrawal from the World

Daitō embraced the theme of withdrawal in prose, in verse, and in practice. Even after he had assumed the abbacy of Daitokuji he wrote of himself:

> So many years of begging,
> this robe's old and torn;
> tattered sleeve chases a cloud.
> Beyond the gate, just grass.[50]

Unworldliness meant establishing one's distance not only from society but also from the Zen institution itself. Accordingly, Daitō defines a "true temple" as the purification of one's own body-mind and a true Buddha image as the realization of inherent Buddha-nature.[51] His most famous statement in support of this ideal is again found in his "Admonitions," where he explicitly contrasts an abbot of a flourishing temple with a recluse living in poverty. His true spiritual heir is the person "dwelling in a simple thatched hut," not the abbot whose "sutra scrolls are inlaid with gold and silver."[52]

Zen lore magnifies Daitō's unworldly reputation, depicting him as a beggar who found shelter under Kyoto's Gojō Bridge during twenty years of self-imposed deprivation. Ikkyū and Hakuin were especially attracted to this image, and their portrayals of Daitō as an outsider strongly influenced later generations. Though the beggar story is undoubtedly exaggerated, it contains a kernel of truth—after his enlightenment Daitō did withdraw to an obscure temple near the Gojō Bridge, remaining there for at least a decade.

The worldly dimensions of Daitō's life are more easily documented, because most of his career took place within Zen's institutional mainstream. He came to enlightenment in a major metropolitan monastery, accepted patronage from two emperors for nearly twenty years, and became founder-abbot of Daitokuji. His faithful observance of the annual monastic calendar is confirmed by the dated entries in the *Record of Daitō*—for example, he gave formal talks on the ninth day of the ninth month for seven years. In theory at least, a monk could fulfill his social and institutional responsibilities while remaining free of ambition and attachment. Just as zazen amidst activity was esteemed, this detached involvement was in some ways a higher ideal than simple withdrawal. Indeed, Daitō is revered in the Rinzai sect as a deeply enlightened monk who mastered the Zen institution without sacrificing his spiritual strength. If that assessment is accepted, the beggar image also symbolizes an inward orientation that historical facts alone cannot reveal.

Several of Daitō's contemporaries and near contemporaries offer revealing comparisons in this context. Musō rose to the pinnacle of the Zen world, served as an advisor to shoguns, and gained recognition in literary circles. Yet within Zen his stature as a master is somewhat diminished: posterity concluded that his worldly successes were won at some cost to his inner life. A contrast of a different sort is Shinchi Kakushin, whose depth of insight was widely acknowledged but who eschewed influential posts and had little impact on Zen's institutional development. Similar issues were highlighted a century and a half later in the bitter rivalry between Ikkyū Sōjun and Yōsō Sōi. Yōsō, a prominent abbot of Daitokuji, was vilified as corrupt by Ikkyū, who attempted to avoid all positions of authority. Whereas Daitō became an exemplar of the successful integration of the individual and the institution, these later figures symbolize less rounded stances, leading to deviance or degeneration.

Daitō as Teacher

As the leader of an expanding monastic community, Daitō interacted regularly with his students. He gave Dharma talks to the assembled monks, engaged members of the audience in public dialogue, met privately with individual disciples, and corresponded with several followers concerning their Zen practice. His monastic regulations confirm his strictness as an abbot and bespeak his intimacy with the senior monks, to whom he refers by name. Throughout the years that Daitō spent establishing a temple, running it, and arranging for an orderly succession, he remained singleminded in his advocacy of awakening. Most Zen masters of Daitō's stature are associated with one or more telling anecdotes—factual or legendary—that epitomize their Zen teaching style. Tan-hsia burns a wooden Buddha to warm himself, Chü-ti cuts off his attendant's finger, Eisai gives a starving man the halo from a Buddha figure, Ikkyū parades a skull on a pole through the streets of Kyoto, and so on. In Daitō's case, the vignettes most often recalled are the bright-eyed beggar under the Gojō Bridge, the self-possessed teacher conversing with two emperors, and the indomitable master who breaks his own leg to die in the full-lotus posture. For further hints about Daitō's deportment as a Zen teacher, we may turn to several documents that have been preserved by his descendants.[53]

By his own account, Daitō confronted his disciples in the manner of a formidable adversary. In the inscription on one of his portraits, he describes himself as follows:

> His eyes glare angrily. His mouth turns down in scowling wrath. He is an enemy of buddhas and patriarchs, an arch-enemy of Zen monks. If you face him, he delivers a blow. If you turn from him, he emits an angry roar. Bah! Who can tell whether the blind old monk painted here is host or guest? But never mind that, Inzen. Just bow to the floor before your mind begins to turn.[54]

Powerful as this language may be, it is also traditional, reflecting the assumed link between severity and authenticity in Ch'an/Zen. If Daitō wished to be seen in this light, his contemporaries and successors readily complied. Soon after his death, Emperor Go-Daigo extolled the master in similar terms. In an inscription on another Daitō portrait (figure 4), the Emperor wrote:

> Swifter than a flash of lightning, he brandishes his stick as he pleases. Faster than ever before, he forges buddhas and patriarchs on his anvil. When he deals with his monks, there is no place for them to seize hold. He was a teacher to two emperors, yet never once revealed his face to them. His severe and awe-inspiring manner made it impossible for anyone to approach him. A single point of spiritual radiance—who presumes to see it?[55]

Another extant document preserves a brief written exchange between Daitō and Emperor Hanazono. On this scroll, half of an undated pair, the master challenges his patron-disciple: "We have been separated for thousands of eons, yet we have not been separated for even an instant. We are facing each other all day long, yet we have never met. This truth is found in each person. I now humbly request a word from you: What is the nature of this truth?" The Emperor wrote his reply on the same scroll: "Last night, during the third watch, the temple pillar told you all there is to know."[56] This text, a rare and verifiable artifact of Daitō's Zen teaching, fails to supply its own setting. Were the two men together when they composed the scroll, or was it conveyed between them by messenger? Might Hanazono's reference to "last night" indicate that he had already been tested (and passed) by Daitō in a previous encounter? Even out of context, Daitō's provocative question has endured, and modern Japanese philosophers still cite it in discussions of the "dialectical relation" between the present and eternity.[57]

Hanazono's diary indicates that Daitō guided the former emperor

FIGURE 4. PORTRAIT OF DAITŌ. COURTESY OF DAITOKUJI.

through advanced koan practice, using the *Gateless Barrier,* the *Blue Cliff Record,* and other texts. The two men discussed Zen teachings, meditated together, and went to visit other Zen monks. After Hanazono passed a certain koan, his teacher praised his "profound" understanding of the Way.[58] Though the diary does not include descriptions of confidential sessions, Daitō's biographer Takuan reports (or imagines) a number of encounter dialogues between the master and his royal disciple. In one, Daitō responds in a classic Zen manner, and Hanazono delivers two Zen shouts:

> Retired emperor Hanazono said to the Master [Daitō], "I won't ask about the chrysanthemums blooming under the fence, but how about the fall foliage in the forest?" The Master said, "Thousand-eyed Kannon does not see through it." The Emperor gave a shout and said, "Gone where?" The Master bowed respectfully and replied, "Please consider the heavenly mirror, hanging down from on high." The Emperor said, "You must not go through the night, but you must arrive by dawn." The Master indicated his assent. The Emperor gave a shout, swung his sleeve, and left.[59]

Whatever Takuan's sources, he was doing his best to convey a sense of Daitō's forceful teaching style to readers of the *Chronicle.*

In some of Daitō's own correspondence he assigns koans and gives instructions about koan practice; these materials shed further light on his comportment as a teacher. In the following letter, for example, his tone is characteristically energetic and persistent:

> If you wish to bring the two matters of birth and death to conclusion, and pass directly beyond the Triple-world, you must penetrate the koan "This very mind is Buddha." Tell me: What is its principle? How is it that this very mind *is* Buddha? And "this very mind"—just what is it like? Investigate it coming. Investigate it going. Investigate it thoroughly and exhaustively. . . . All you have to do is keep this koan constantly in your thoughts.[60]

Daitō refers to another koan on an extant scroll that bears the single character *mu* and the following information in smaller script:

> Zen-man Ryō responded, "One slab of iron stretching ten thousand miles." I said, "What is this one slab of iron?" He said nothing.
>
> Written by Shūhō, in response to the Zen-man's request.[61]

Mu (literally, "no") is the kernel of the well-known koan in which a monk asks master Chao-chou whether a dog has Buddha-nature. This scroll apparently records a *mondō* about *mu* between Daitō and a student known only as Ryō. The student's answer to the koan is a capping phrase, one that Daitō favored in his written commentaries. Rather than attempting to explain *mu* in discursive language (perhaps as emptiness or Buddha-nature), Ryō offers a metaphoric image of something infinite, indestructible, seamless, and essentially beyond imagination or discrimination—"one slab of iron stretching ten thousand miles." When pressed further by Daitō, the student remains silent. Though silence often indicates an inability to answer, in some contexts it can also be a correct Zen reply, depending on the respondent's demeanor and other clues. Since Daitō agreed to record the exchange, it is likely that he endorsed Ryō's nonverbal answer and the spiritual insight it represented. Cryptic as this record may be, it depicts Daitō testing a student on a classic Chinese koan and accepting a capping phrase as an apt response. In addition, the scroll itself suggests how readily Daitō (and other Zen monks) rendered a spiritual experience as an aesthetic one, through calligraphy.

Inevitably, essential elements of Daitō's teaching style remain obscure. For example, it is not known whether private encounters with him were required or optional, scheduled or spontaneous, lengthy or abrupt. Such questions multiply in regard to koan practice. Did Daitō rely on either of the two major koan collections, or did he prefer to select koans from other sources, including oral ones? Did he assign koans in some order or permit students to exercise their own discretion? Did he allow students to work on numerous koans before a *kenshō* experience, or did he initially limit them to one of the "breakthrough" koans, such as "Mu"? Many aspects of the master-disciple relationship were strictly confidential, so there are limits to what can be known. Zen followers claim that a master's teaching methods defy categorization anyway. According to Daitō's colleague Musō,

> Clear-eyed Zen masters do not equip themselves with a stock of invariable doctrines. They simply seize upon a teaching in response to the moment, giving their tongues free rein. Zen masters do not hole up in any fixed position. When people ask about Zen, the master may answer with the words of Confucius, Mencius, Lao-tzu, or Chuang-tzu. Or he may expound the teachings of the doctrinal schools. On other occasions he will answer with popular proverbs, or draw attention to something close at hand. Then again, he may use his stick, shout loudly, raise a finger, or wave a fist. These are the methods of Zen masters, the unfettered vitality of Zen. Those who have not yet reached this realm cannot fathom it through the senses and intellect alone.[62]

9

CAPPING-PHRASE COMMENTARY IN THE WORKS OF DAITŌ

WHEN DAITŌ became enamored of capping phrases, he joined a long line of distinguished Ch'an predecessors. Ch'an master Yün-men Wen-yen (d. 949), one of Daitō's models, may have been the first master to answer classic koans with capping phrases, inaugurating an activity that has remained a vital part of Ch'an and Zen training for ten centuries. Capping phrases are scattered throughout the two oldest "histories" of Ch'an: *A Collection from the Halls of the Patriarchs* (*Tsu-t'ang chi*, compiled in 952), and the *Transmission of the Lamp* (*Ching-te ch'uan-teng lu*, published in 1011). Another important text in the genre's early development is the discourse record of Fen-yang Shan-chao (947–1024), who systematically added capping phrases to one hundred classic koans and one hundred original koans. For example, he wrote, "I vow to attain supreme enlightenment," and then asked rhetorically, "How is it attained?" His answer was a capping phrase: "The Son of Heaven does not cut grass."[1]

The appearance of koan collections in the eleventh and twelfth centuries notably enhanced the scope and stature of capping phrases. Yüan-wu K'o-ch'in, compiler of the influential *Blue Cliff Record,* gave the genre its classic configuration. As noted previously, this complex work includes several levels of commentary. Hsüeh-tou, the first compiler, composed interlinear capping phrases for fifteen of the hundred koans he selected. About sixty years later, Yüan-wu added a considerable amount of new material, including interlinear capping phrases for all hundred koans and for Hsüeh-tou's verses. Never before had one master so ambitiously attempted to cap an entire text. For example, the ninth koan of the *Blue Cliff Record* is based on a single exchange:

> A monk asked Chao-chou, "What is Chao-chou?"
> Chao-chou replied, "The east gate, the west gate, the south gate, the north gate."

Yüan-wu augmented this brief text with a series of provocative capping phrases, as follows:

> A monk asked Chao-chou, "What is Chao-chou?"
> *North of the river, south of the river. No one can say. There are thorns in the soft mud. If it's not south of the river, then it's north of the river.*
> Chao-chou replied, "The east gate, the west gate, the south gate, the north gate."
> *They're open. When we're reviling each other, I let you lock lips with me. When we're spitting at each other, I let you spew me with slobber. It's a ready-made koan, but do you see? I strike!*[2]

Yüan-wu's exuberant and colloquial style (however inscrutable it may appear initially) represents a peak in the literature of Ch'an. Within a century after Yüan-wu's death the capping-phrase exercise was transmitted to Japan. Practitioners began using traditional and spontaneous capping phrases to answer koans.[3] One of the earliest works written in Japan to include capping phrases is a commentary by Lan-ch'i Tao-lung on the *Heart Sutra*. The transitional nature of this work can be seen in its unusual mixture of commentarial genres. The following excerpt consists of Lan-ch'i's gloss on one line of the sutra; his capping phrase is italicized:

> "Form does not differ from emptiness"
>
> Form is originally generated from emptiness. The deluded person sees form as being outside of true emptiness. Form arises from the mind. [The enlightened person] comprehends that the mind is originally without the characteristic of form. If you revert to the senses, you will understand; if you follow their illuminations, you will not.
> *Let them have heads of ash and faces of dirt!*[4]

The passage highlights the difference between a doctrinal style of Buddhist exegesis and a "sutra-free" style of Zen commentary, as represented by the capping phrase. It also suggests that a combination of the two is problematic (Lan-ch'i may have been constrained by the limitations of his Japanese audience).

Daitō represents the next highpoint in the genre's development. The spiritual and literary affinity Daitō felt with his predecessors Hsüeh-tou and Yüan-wu is evident throughout his discourse record, capping-phrase commentaries, and other works. Besides compiling his own koan collections and commenting on them in the manner of these two masters, Daitō borrowed more capping phrases from the *Blue Cliff Record* than from any other source.

Front-side Words and Back-side Words

In Japanese Zen, over a dozen terms are used to designate various types of capping phrases. Most of these terms originated in Ch'an texts; in the *Blue Cliff Record* alone the following five expressions appear:

1. Attached words (Ch. *cho-yü;* Jp. *jakugo*). The most common term for capping phrases in the *Blue Cliff Record,* used for the comments inserted by Hsüeh-tou. *Jakugo* is also the general word for capping phrases in contemporary Japanese Zen. *Jaku* is sometimes equivalent to *chaku,* "to arrive, reach," and, by extension, "to attain." Both *jaku* and *chaku* are also used as particles to indicate completed action (perfect tense).
2. Given words *(hsia-yü; agyo)*. Originally an abbreviation for the phrase "to give one turning word." *Agyo* was the term preferred by Daitō.
3. One turning word *(i-chuan-yü; ittengo)*. A word or succinct phrase that expresses one's own realization and/or has the power to turn another's mind toward enlightenment.
4. Different words *(pieh-yü; betsugo)*. A response to a koan that differs from an answer already given by someone else.
5. Alternate words *(tai-yü; daigo)*. An answer given on behalf of another person (i.e., when a monk in a recorded dialogue cannot answer the master's question).[5]

Several additional terms have gained currency in Japanese Zen:

6. Playful [words] *(nenro)*. A traditional phrase or verse that sheds light on a given koan. Both characters in this expression mean "to twist" or "to play with"; the unstated object is the words of the ancients.
7. Vernacular words *(sego)*. Phrases and verses that originated in Japan rather than China. These have been collected in a work entitled *Anthology of Zen Phrases in Japanese (Zenrin segoshū).*[6]
8. Plain words *(heigo)*. Ordinary Japanese expressions, taken from daily life rather than published anthologies.
9. Preliminary words *(zengo)*. A phrase that presents only one aspect of a koan.
10. Main words *(hongo)*. A phrase that caps a koan in a final or comprehensive manner.

There are also "front-side words" *(omote no go),* which are used to comment from a conventional standpoint; "back-side words" *(ura no go),* which are used to comment from an absolute standpoint; and "combined words" *(sōgo),* which are supposed to express the integration of the ultimate and the conventional.[7]

No single expression in English can be expected to convey the range and complexity of these terms. Even the single word *jakugo* has been variously translated into English as capping phrase, capping words, capping verses, attached comments, and annotation. All the expressions cited above are Zen technical terms, used only by monks and specialists, whereas "capping phrase" in English has a wider currency (and may therefore mislead to some degree). The English word "capping" nonetheless suggests some of the functions of a Zen *jakugo:* to cap means "to match, to complete, to surpass," and even (in a 1937 *Webster's*) "to surprise, to puzzle, to perplex."[8]

Though the capping phrases found throughout Daitō's works potentially afford access to his Zen style, the genre is notoriously resistant to interpretation. Daitō's discourse record—full of koans, capping phrases, and encounter dialogues—was so forbidding that only a master like Hakuin would venture to take its measure. Neither the intended audience nor the specific application of Daitō's written commentaries has been established with certainty. He may have composed these texts for himself, revealed them to a select group of disciples, used them freely in the training of his monks, or addressed them primarily to posterity.

Furthermore, the usual exegetical techniques, even in the hands of knowledgeable commentators, often seem reductive and unsatisfactory. For example, one of Daitō's better-known capping phrases, "An octagonal millstone flies through the air," has elicited widely varying explanations. Distinguished scholar Yanagida Seizan writes: "An octagonal millstone is a massive millstone turned by a team of eight oxen or horses. It can pulverize all manner of things. This phrase describes such a huge millstone spinning across the sky, a terrifying sight."[9] Zen master Shibayama Zenkei's gloss of the same phrase is more abstract: "the free functioning that arises from satori."[10] And Jon Covell paraphrases the troublesome expression as a statement about ineffability: "Everyone knows that a meteor rushes across the sky, yet they cannot explain it in words."[11]

Such explanations, however skillful, restate an utterance in conventional language or familiar categories, thereby serving to confirm our ordinary understanding of reality. In that way they tend to subvert Zen language, because the perplexity that explication hastens to eliminate is just what most Zen language is trying to foster, at least initially. The aim of Zen training is not to acquire a "correct" picture of the world; it is to shed whatever notions of the world one may hold. Interpretations that construe the meaning of a Zen passage only in terms of its assumed content or message are missing the text's transformative potential and soteriological intent, which are "not dependent on words." No wonder the resulting exegesis frequently falls flat, like explanations of jokes.

Further implications of Zen language will be examined in the following chapter, but in the interim we may identify at least one principle related to interpretation: for most Zen utterances a single meaning rarely exhausts the possibilities. The multifaceted nature of Zen language can be seen, for example, in the capping phrase *ryōsai issai,* which has been used by Ch'an masters, by Daitō, and by contemporary Rinzai monks. The phrase can mean "two faces of one die," as in the English expression "two sides of the same coin."[12] In other contexts, it can also signify "two victories, one game."[13] In the *Record of Lin-chi* a master uses this expression to comment on an incident involving three monks. Rendered as "two victories, one game" and applied to that particular situation, the phrase supports several interpretations: (a) one of the three players won twice, (b) two of the players won, or even (c) all three players won in their relations with each other.[14] In Zen language multiple meanings may coexist even if they seem mutually contradictory.

An Introduction to Daitō's Capping Phrases

The most straightforward way to introduce Daitō's capping-phrase commentaries is to draw upon certain conventional modes. Once we have considered a sample of Daitō's phrases and some representative passages, we will be better able to discuss his Zen style and related interpretive issues. Initially, it is helpful to remove Daitō's capping phrases from their original context and rearrange them in a more accessible fashion.[15] For example, some of the capping phrases that Daitō quoted or composed can function as aphorisms:

> *Under a good general, one is certain to find brave soldiers.*
> *If you hear it incorrectly, you will mistake a bell for a cooking pot.*

Other capping phrases favored by Daitō create vivid scenes or capture subtle moods.

> *Under a peony, a kitten naps.*
> *His mouth is like a bowl of blood.*
> *Walking together on the Ch'ang-an Road, hand-in-hand.*
> *The pine accompanies the sound of the wind.*

A common use of the genre is to express admiration or censure. When Daitō is pleased, his praise is unstinting.

> *Just so, just so.*
> *I am not equal to you!*

When critical, he is especially blunt.

Shame on you!
He doesn't know the smell of his own shit.
Why doesn't he get control of himself and leave?

Inevitably, many of Daitō's comments allude to aspects of Zen practice and the spiritual path, though they are flexible enough to take on additional meanings in other contexts. A devotee's initial exposure to Buddhism is considered highly significant.

An opportunity hard to come by.

However ardent the student, early stages of practice may be plagued by doubt and confusion.

Stumbling without knowing it.
Watch your step!

For monks in a monastery, the schedule is relentless and the discipline severe.

The drum beats, the bell rings.
Three thousand blows in the morning, eight hundred blows in the evening.

Obstructions are encountered at every turn, as in Daitō's own struggle with the koan "Barrier."

Iron wall, silver mountain.
No road to advance upon, no gate to retreat through.
The exhausted fish is stuck in shallow water.
The shrimp cannot leap out of the wooden dipper.

Yet those with true aspiration manage to persevere whatever the obstacles.

Though the Chien-ko Road is steep,
travelers are even more numerous at night.

Entering the master's chambers and confronting him face-to-face can be a fearful experience even for a Zen adept.

A wild tiger sitting right on the path.

What can one do?

Lie flat in the tiger's mouth.

Eventually, after years of searching and questioning, something happens, perhaps unexpectedly.

Losing one's way and running into Bodhidha ma.

At this critical point one must push on until one ignites an inner explosion or attains a state of unprecedented clarity.

When the clouds disperse, the cave becomes bright.

Now the world takes on an entirely new quality—even the most ordinary things seem wonderfully alive.

Scoop up water, the moon lies in your hands;
   toy with a flower, its fragrance soaks your robe.

As one's understanding continues to deepen, one may enter realms known only by a few.

Where the white clouds are deep, a golden dragon dances.
A close friend understands, but who else understands?

The ancient patriarchs, no longer revered from afar, can be taunted affectionately.

Hsüeh-tou has not yet gotten that far.
Master Shakyamuni's eyeballs pop out.

How can this precious reality be described?

The sky cannot cover it, the earth cannot uphold it.
One slab of iron stretching ten thousand miles.
The blue sky is not blue, the white clouds are not white.

In the end, words fail.

Knead it but it won't form a ball.
A mute eats bitter melons.

And yet it must be passed on, one way or another.

Two stone statues whisper into each other's ears.

Someone who can do this is a practitioner of eloquent Zen, whose language—however strange—mysteriously hits the mark.

To insert the needle where it hurts.
His tongue has no bones.
A real Zen master!

We may now turn to some passages that reveal Daitō's actual use of capping phrases. The first passage is just two sentences in its entirety:

Huang-po struck Lin-chi sixty times.
The sun appears and the moon disappears.[16]

The italicized second line is Daitō's capping phrase on the scanty text that precedes it; together they make up one of the briefest entries in

Daitō's *One Hundred Twenty Cases (Hyakunijussoku)*.[17] Huang-po and his principal heir, Lin-chi, were two great Ch'an masters. As a comment, Daitō's phrase does not refer in a conventional manner to the original text, so one must ruminate a bit to find some connection. In nature, when does the sun appear and the moon disappear?—at dawn, the shift from darkness to light, a transformation that is also a natural symbol of enlightenment. So Daitō's comment may suggest, poetically and non-discursively, that Huang-po's beating of his disciple Lin-chi precipitated Lin-chi's enlightenment. Of course, Zen tradition offers an informed interpreter valuable clues: Daitō himself refers elsewhere to sixty blows in connection with Lin-chi's awakening. What else might be suggested by the capping phrase in this particular context? The sun may also stand for Lin-chi, the illustrious successor, and the moon for Huang-po, the teacher who has done his job and can now fade away. One further implication is that Lin-chi surpassed Huang-po (for a disciple to outdo his master is valued in Zen).

The well-known koan "Mu" also appears in Daitō's *One Hundred Twenty Cases,* as follows:

A monk asked Chao-chou, "Does a dog have Buddha-nature or not?"
His tongue is already long.
Chao-chou said, *"Mu."*
To buy iron and receive gold.
Completely fills emptiness.
To throw a holeless iron hammer head right at him.[18]

By its placement, Daitō's first capping phrase refers to the monk's question—that is, he faults the "long"-winded monk for posing the problem in such a heady and dualistic manner. Zen asserts that Chao-chou's answer, which literally means "no," is ineffable truth itself;[19] how then can Daitō annotate it? The first of his three responses is "To buy iron and receive gold." Someone who pays for iron but gets gold has certainly made a successful transaction. Likewise, a monk who asks a poor question but gets an enlightening reply from a master has gotten more than he bargained for, something as precious as gold. Rather than try to comment on *mu* itself, Daitō focuses intially on the interaction between the koan's protagonists.

Daitō's next phrase, "Completely fills emptiness," applies equally to *mu* and to Chao-chou's answer. In Zen, emptiness is not nihilism or vacuity: because form and emptiness interpenetrate, emptiness is completely filled and form is completely emptied. Chao-chou's powerful answer similarly fills the universe because it is not separate from the universe. Daitō's last capping phrase is "To throw a holeless iron hammer head right at him." A holeless hammer head is a contradiction—without a hole, there is no place to stick the handle. The image is a fitting symbol for truth (or Buddha-nature or *mu*), which cannot be grasped using any of our customary handles. Chao-chou has thrown this ungraspable *mu* right at the monk, and Daitō does nothing to impede its continuing flight.

Oral Commentary in the Record of Daitō

Daitō's discourse record *(goroku),* first printed between 1426 and 1467, includes a variety of material: the master's formal lectures and informal talks, his dialogic encounters with his own monks, a written capping-phrase commentary, a set of verses in *kanbun,* and a brief biography. Traditionally, a discourse record was supposed to be a master's principal work, though in many instances a master's best-known or most original writings are found in other sources. Because Daitō's Zen style can be seen throughout his corpus, consideration must be given to his discourse record, his capping-phrase commentaries, and his poetry.

The *Record of Daitō* contains two types of capping-phrase commentary: one is (ostensibly) oral, and the other is written. Throughout the *Record,* Daitō's monks question him about specific koans and texts, often line by line. Almost all the master's responses are capping phrases of one kind or another. If the traditional description of the *Record*'s composition is given credence, these encounter dialogues were transcribed soon after they occurred. The master himself may have participated in the composition process at times. Several extant manuscripts in Daitō's own hand appear as Dharma talks in his discourse record, and it is possible that he wrote or edited some of the dialogue sections as well.

The following passage from the *Record of Daitō* depicts Daitō using capping phrases to respond orally to a series of questions from one of his monks. During the inauguration ceremony for Daitokuji in the twelfth month of 1326, an unnamed monk cited a well-known incident that appears as a koan in the *Blue Cliff Record.* In this story, P'ang Yün—a layman and an advanced Ch'an practitioner—is leaving a temple after having spent many years there, and he is escorted to the gate by some less experienced students. It is winter, and snow begins to fall. The dialogue in the *Record of Daitō* involves four people—Layman P'ang and a student named Ch'üan from the original incident, plus the responses of Daitō and the Daitokuji monk. (For the sake of clarity, "the Master" will be translated as "Daitō.") The inauguration ceremony is already under way when Daitō begins a new dialogue:

> Again Daitō said, "Is there anyone else with a question?"
> Another monk came forth and inquired: "I recall that when Lay-

man P'ang was taking leave of Yao-shan, he pointed to the snow falling from the sky and said, 'The beautiful snowflakes, one by one, do not fall in different places.' What did he mean?"

Daitō said, "Something so difficult to grasp surely follows certain laws."

The [Daitokuji] monk continued: "At that time there was a Ch'an student named Ch'üan who asked P'ang, 'Where do they fall?' P'ang slapped him. How about this?"

Daitō said, "An octagonal millstone flies through the air."

The monk said: "The student said, 'Layman, don't be so abrupt!' P'ang responded, 'You may call yourself a student of Ch'an, but a person of understanding would not tolerate it.' How should this be understood?"

Daitō said, "My teeth are clenched."

The monk said: "The student Ch'üan said to P'ang, 'What about you?' and P'ang slapped him again. What was P'ang's intention?"

Daitō said, "Giving generously, holding back little."

The monk said: "The Patriarch Hsü-t'ang said, 'Though there were two slaps, one expressed praise and one expressed censure, one snatched up and one released.' How can they be distinguished?"

Daitō said, "It has arrived here and is being put into practice on a grand scale."

The monk said, "You have been teaching us with great compassion. How would you succinctly express the highest teachings of our school?"

Daitō said, "A thousand snowy peaks, ten thousand caves swept by cold wind."

The monk said, "Master, you are indeed a great teacher of people and gods," and he bowed.

Daitō said, "I permit you to return to your place."[20]

All of Daitō's responses in this passage are capping phrases, verbal jabs that prod the hearer or reader to probe more deeply. (Daitō's final remark indicates that the dialogue is over.) Each answer is indirect—not only are common-sense explanations avoided, but subjects, objects, and other referents are left unnamed. And yet within Zen these answers are also considered to be incomparably direct, once one sees where they point. Let us take a closer look at each segment of the passage.

Again Daitō said, "Is there anyone else with a question?"

Another monk came forth and inquired: "I recall that when Layman P'ang was taking leave of Yao-shan, he pointed to the snow falling from the sky and said, 'The beautiful snowflakes, one by one, do not fall in different places.' What did he mean?"

Daitō said, "Something so difficult to grasp surely follows certain laws."

The unusual nature of Layman P'ang's opening remark draws attention to the snow as a manifestation of Buddha-nature itself. From an ultimate standpoint, there is not even any "place" for the snow to "fall." In the same spirit, Daitō's first capping phrase indicates that the snow connotes deeper mysteries—for instance, the path of each flake demonstrates the unfathomable intersection of causation and freedom that is also manifest in the path of a human life. Daitō's comment also applies to P'ang's seemingly inscrutable remark, which surely has something behind it.

> The [Daitokuji] monk continued: "At that time there was a Ch'an student named Ch'üan who asked P'ang, 'Where do they fall?' P'ang slapped him. How about this?"
> Daitō said, "An octagonal millstone flies through the air."

By asking, "Where do they fall?" the student Ch'üan reveals that he is still caught up in a common-sense view of the matter. P'ang's slap was not only a rebuke but also a Zen answer: that momentary experience of pain is where the snow falls, the snow falls upon *you,* the snow *is* you. We recall that Daitō used this "octagonal millstone" image in the Shōchū Debate, responding to the question "What is Zen, which claims to be a separate transmission outside the teachings?" Applied to this koan, the image works in new ways. P'ang's hand, flying through the air, has the potential to pulverize the student's most cherished assumptions. The capping phrase may also allude to the multicornered snowflakes flying through the air. However light and fragile, each flake bears the full weight of reality, of the universe itself, and if *that* strikes you, it will indeed feel as if you have been hit by a millstone. Because Daitō regards this capping phrase as an apt expression of Zen, he is also validating P'ang's Zen as authentic.

> The monk said: "The student said, 'Layman, don't be so abrupt!' P'ang responded, 'You may call yourself a student of Ch'an, but a person of understanding would not tolerate it.' How should this be understood?"
> Daitō said, "My teeth are clenched."

The student in the koan misses the point again, and this time P'ang criticizes him verbally. (The version of P'ang's retort cited by the Daitokuji monk differs slightly from the orginal koan, but it has the same force.) Daitō's clenched teeth indicate that he too will not open his mouth to call Ch'üan a real Ch'an student. Daitō's refusal to elaborate may also apply to his Daitokuji interlocutor: "Figure this part out yourself."

> The monk said: "The student Ch'üan said to P'ang, 'What about you?' and P'ang slapped him again. What was P'ang's intention?"
> Daitō said, "Giving generously, holding back little."

Ch'üan's question to P'ang—"What about you?"—has two implications: "Would *you* call me a Ch'an student?" and "Are *you* a person of understanding?" In either case, Ch'üan is still entangled in the duality of this-or-that. Thus Yüan-wu commented in the *Blue Cliff Record:* "Again he's asking for a beating. From beginning to end this monk is at a loss."[21] P'ang obliges by slapping him again. (In the original he adds, "Your eyes see like a blind man, your mouth speaks like a mute.")[22] Daitō's capping phrase, "Giving generously, holding back little," interprets the second slap as an act of kindness—a bonus beating, so to speak.

> The monk said: "The Patriarch Hsü-t'ang said, 'Though there were two slaps, one expressed praise and one expressed censure, one snatched up and one released.' How can they be distinguished?"
> Daitō said, "It has arrived here and is being put into practice on a grand scale."

The koan proper having ended, the Daitokuji monk cites a comment by Hsü-t'ang Chih-yü, the Chinese master of Daitō's teacher Nanpo. Whatever the implications of Hsü-t'ang's remark, Daitō refuses to discriminate between P'ang's two slaps. Instead, he introduces a larger theme, asserting that "it"—the Way of Hsü-t'ang and P'ang and the other masters of Ch'an—has been transmitted to him. Such a claim would not have been out of place in an inauguration ceremony like the one Daitō was conducting; the establishment of Daitokuji was in fact a benchmark in Ch'an's transmission to Japan.

> The monk said, "You have been teaching us with great compassion. How would you succinctly express the highest teachings of our school?"
> Daitō said, "A thousand snowy peaks, ten thousand caves swept by cold wind."

The Daitokuji monk requests a crowning declaration from the master, and Daitō answers poetically. The possible responses to such a question include silence, action, ordinary language, or nonordinary language; Daitō used all of these rejoinders at different points in his teaching. But his response here is a fine example of his eloquent Zen style: a capping phrase that qualifies as a line of poetry, a line of poetry that doubles as a capping phrase. Incorporating the snow motif from the koan and the height motif from the question, he depicts the ineffable absolute as an austere and forbidding place inaccessible to humans. At the same time his image serves as a description of his own clear and unapproachable mind-state. In conclusion, the monk offers formulaic praise, and Daitō dismisses him:

> The monk said, "Master, you are indeed a great teacher of people and gods," and he bowed.
>
> Daitō said, "I permit you to return to your place."

Though this passage purports to record a spontaneous exchange between Daitō and one of his monks, Daitō's responses are directed more to the text than to his interlocutor. The monk quotes portions of the original koan and then prompts the master with questions that are functionally equivalent: "What did he mean?" "How about this?" "How should this be understood?" and so on. The one time that the monk asks a more specific question—"Were there two kinds of slaps, as Hsü-t'ang claimed?"—the master sidesteps it. Depending on Daitō's assessment of his disciple's performance, his final dismissal could be approving, critical, or neutral, but here it is hard to tell.

Written Commentary in the Record of Daitō

The *Record of Daitō* includes a rare capping-phrase commentary on a seminal Ch'an text, the only work of its kind in the Japanese discourse records of the Kamakura and Muromachi periods. Daitō was drawn to Hsüeh-tou Ch'ung-hsien, the first compiler of the *Blue Cliff Record* and a master of literary Ch'an. Focusing on two volumes of the *Record of Hsüeh-tou (Hsüeh-tou lu)*, Daitō added copious comments between lines and within sentences. The resulting work, *Essential Words for Careful Study (Sanshō goyō)*, was deemed worthy of inclusion in the authorized compendium of Daitō's teachings. Daitō begins his commentary midway through the first volume of Hsüeh-tou's text, with the inauguration ceremony of "Hsüeh-tou Ch'an temple" in Ming province (present Chekiang). In the following translation, Daitō's capping phrases are italicized:

> On the day of his installation as the new abbot, Hsüeh-tou stood in front of the Dharma seat and looked out upon the assembly of monks.
>
> *Please drink this cup of wine;*
>   *beyond the Western outpost you'll find no friends.*
>
> Hsüeh-tou said, "In order to speak about the fundamental matter, it is not necessary to ascend the jeweled high seat."
>
> *Just so, just so.*
>
> Hsüeh-tou pointed
>
> *A command that cannot be disobeyed.*
>
> and said, "Everyone, look where I am pointing. Countless Buddha-lands are simultaneously manifest there. Each one of you, look carefully at them.

Blind!

"If you cannot see how far those Buddha-lands extend, you will remain stuck in the mud."

Who?

Thereupon Hsüeh-tou ascended the high seat.

Thrust out so suddenly it's hard to handle.

The prefect finished reading the official letter. The precentor struck his gavel and announced, "The dragons and elephants present at this Dharma assembly should look at the cardinal principle." Then a monk came forward.

An opportunity hard to come by.

Hsüeh-tou seized him and said [to the assembly]: "The treasury of the true Dharma eye of the Tathāgata is fully present here today. Release it and tiles and stones give off light; grasp it and true gold loses its color.

One in front, one in back.

"I hold in my hand the hilt [of a sword]—now is the moment of life or death [for this monk]."

The monk must know the right timing himself.
His life hangs from a thread.

"If there is a person of understanding here, let's dispose of this matter together."

There are just a lot of [ordinary] people.

The monk said, "I have come far from the seat of Master Ts'ui-feng and arrived here at Hsüeh-tou's place of practice. Are these one or two?"

It plugs the ears of everyone on earth.

Hsüeh-tou replied, "A horse cannot catch the wind [even if he chases it] for a thousand miles."

The wind blows and the grass bends.

The monk said, "In that case, the clouds have dispersed and the moon shines into each house."

Would Hsüeh-tou [stoop to] fight with you?

A monk asked, "Te-shan's blows and Lin-chi's shouts are already clear. Master, how do *you* guide people?" Hsüeh-tou said, "I'll spare you just this once."

The buddhas and patriarchs hold their breath.

The monk hesitated, and Hsüeh-tou gave a shout.

It's hard to save people from false Dharma.

The monk said, "That's fine, but don't you have anything else [to offer]?" Hsüeh-tou replied, "I shot my arrow at a tiger, but the tiger wasn't real. I just wasted the effort and lost the [arrow's] feathers."

The first arrow went in lightly; the second arrow went deep. [23]

As we unpack the language of this difficult passage, we will see how Daitō reacts to the interplay between Hsüeh-tou and his monks. Because Daitō had presided over the inauguration of his own temple (and two others), he responds to Hsüeh-tou's ceremony as an experienced participant-observer, at times putting himself in Hsüeh-tou's place. Before Hsüeh-tou utters a word, Daitō interjects his first capping phrase:

On the day of his installation as the new abbot, Hsüeh-tou stood in front of the Dharma seat and looked out upon the assembly of monks.
Please drink this cup of wine;
beyond the Western outpost you'll find no friends.

Ordinarily, an abbot does not address the assembly until he is seated in a large chair on the rasied dais, but Hsüeh-tou is about to depart from this convention. Daitō's comment quotes a verse by Wang Wei (699–759), in which the poet bids farewell to a friend traveling to a less-civilized region of the Chinese empire. With equal intimacy, Daitō dispatches Hsüeh-tou on his journey into uncharted spiritual realms, suggesting that few will truly understand his Dharma teaching. Daitō can also be addressing the assembled monks (directly or on Hsüeh-tou's behalf), because they too are supposed to be embarking on a solitary inner voyage.

Hsüeh-tou said, "In order to speak about the fundamental matter, it is not necessary to ascend the jeweled high seat."
Just so, just so.

Daitō concurs that true Dharma teaching has nothing to do with the ritual trappings associated with the role of abbot.

Hsüeh-tou pointed
A command that cannot be disobeyed.
and said, "Everyone, look where I am pointing. Countless Buddha-lands are simultaneously manifest there. Each one of you, look carefully at them."
Blind!

The direction of Hsüeh-tou's pointing is unspecified, yet it does not matter—his pointer is itself Buddha-nature, and he is urging those in attendance to see for themselves. Daitō compares Hsüeh-tou's injunction, the essential directive of all Zen teachers, to the "command" of a general or a king. Daitō's one-word capping phrase "Blind!" exemplifies the polysemy of the genre. Initially, it suggests that the monks are blind because they do not see Buddha-nature, but it resonates on other levels as well. Because Buddha-nature cannot be seen in the manner of a discrete sense-object, even Hsüeh-tou's fleshly eyes are blind. Ultimately, Buddha-nature itself is blind, a finger that does not point.

> "If you cannot see how far those Buddha-lands extend, you will remain stuck in the mud."
> *Who?*

Here Daitō implies that Hsüeh-tou himself is still stuck in the mud—if not the mud of ignorance, then the inevitable entanglements of daily life. Through such capping phrases a Zen exegete seeks to show that he does not defer to anyone, however venerable, or follow any text, however authoritative.

> Thereupon Hsüeh-tou ascended the high seat.
> *Thrust out so suddenly it's hard to handle.*

Hsüeh-tou's taking his seat is yet another demonstration of this visible/invisible Buddha-nature. For Daitō, the abbot's simple action is so sudden and powerful it demands a response, as if a child had unexpectedly darted in front of an oncoming vehicle.

> The prefect finished reading the official letter. The precentor struck his gavel and announced, "The dragons and elephants present at this Dharma assembly should look at the cardinal principle." Then a monk came forward.
> *An opportunity hard to come by.*

The official letter is the invitation that brought Hsüeh-tou to the temple in Ming; "dragons and elephants" is an honorific reference to the monks in attendance. Daitō's capping phrase applies to both protagonists in the text: the monk who has presented himself has a rare chance to ask a master about the Dharma, and Hsüeh-tou has an excellent opportunity to demonstrate his Zen.

> Hsüeh-tou seized him and said [to the assembly], "The treasury of the true Dharma eye of the Tathāgata is fully present here today. Release it and tiles and stones give off light; grasp it and true gold loses its color."
> *One in front, one in back.*

The original passage does not indicate how Hsüeh-tou seized the monk or when he released him. Using the seizure of the monk as a point of departure, Hsüeh-tou extends the theme of apprehension and release to the Dharma. The import of his next comment is unclear—perhaps both approaches are expedients. Daitō's phrase, "One in front, one in back," refers simultaneously to the two alternatives in Hsüeh-tou's statement and to the two players in the scene being enacted by the abbot and the monk.

> "I hold in my hand the hilt [of a sword]—now is the moment of life or death [for this monk]."
> *The monk must know the right timing himself.*
> *His life hangs from a thread.*

The predicament that Hsüeh-tou has created recalls the famous koan involving Nan-ch'üan P'u-yüan (748–835), who grabbed a cat in front of his monks and threatened to cut it in half unless someone offered a timely word of Zen. Daitō's comment reinforces Hsüeh-tou's claim that the monk's spiritual life is in the balance (to save him it might be necessary to *cut* the thread).

> "If there is a person of understanding here, let's dispose of this matter together."
> *There are just a lot of [ordinary] people.*

Hsüeh-tou invites someone to say or do something that will win the monk's release, but Daitō does not expect anyone in attendance to produce a satisfactory response.

> The monk said, "I have come far from the seat of Master Ts'ui-feng and arrived here at Hsüeh-tou's place of practice. Are these one or two?"
> *It plugs the ears of everyone on earth.*

Here the original Chinese text is ambiguous on two counts: the monk speaking may be the one who was seized or another who has just come forward, and the unstated subject also permits "we have come far" or "you have come far." By asking, "Are these one or two?" the monk alludes not only to the two locations and the two masters but also to such (apparent) dualities as past and present, far and close, you the abbot and me the monk. Daitō remarks that this question plugs everyone's ears. In some contexts his comment could indicate praise (something so powerful it deafens), but here it seems to mean "spare us such a fatuous question."

> Hsüeh-tou replied, "A horse cannot catch the wind [even if he chases it] for a thousand miles."
> *The wind blows and the grass bends.*

In Hsüeh-tou's reply, he is the wind, and the horse who cannot catch him is the inquiring monk or even Ts'ui-feng, the other master. So Hsüeh-tou has the spiritual confidence required of a Ch'an abbot. Daitō, continuing the wind imagery, quotes a famous line from the *Analects* of Confucius: Hsüeh-tou is so masterful that the assembled monks submit to his teaching like grass bending in the wind.

> The monk said, "In that case, the clouds have dispersed and the moon shines into each house."
> *Would Hsüeh-tou [stoop to] fight with you?*

The monk lauds Hsüeh-tou's Dharma wind, which disperses everyone's clouds of delusion and thereby exposes the moon of truth or insight. The monk's declaration is also a way of ending the dialogue, equivalent to "we thank you for your excellent teaching." For Daitō, this final remark fails to narrow the gap between Hsüeh-tou and his questioner. The capping phrase is unusual in specifying a protagonist by name— ordinarily, referents are only implied. By this point Daitō has become so involved with the text that he responds as if he were addressing the monk directly. Daitō's text here omits a comment by Hsüeh-tou that appears in the original: "A fellow with a dragon's head and a snake's tail."[24] That is, the monk made a promising start but ended weakly.

> A monk asked, "Te-shan's blows and Lin-chi's shouts are already clear. Master, how do *you* guide people?" Hsüeh-tou said, "I'll spare you just this once."
> *The buddhas and patriarchs hold their breath.*

Another monk comes forward, cites the teaching style of two great predecessors, and asks Hsüeh-tou how he instructs his disciples. Because a master is expected to demonstrate his Zen rather than explain it, the monk has exposed himself to a direct response such as a slap. Though Hsüeh-tou "spares" him by substituting a verbal warning, Daitō depicts the buddhas and patriarchs as braced for Hsüeh-tou's painful blow.

> The monk hesitated, and Hsüeh-tou gave a shout.
> *It's hard to save people from false Dharma.*

Even Hsüeh-tou's powerful Zen shout is not enough to edify this particular monk.

> The monk said, "That's fine, but don't you have anything else [to offer]?" Hsüeh-tou replied, "I shot my arrow at a tiger, but the tiger wasn't real. I just wasted the effort and lost the [arrow's] feathers."
> *The first arrow went in lightly; the second arrow went deep.*

The monk recovers and challenges the master again, but Hsüeh-tou laments that his shout was a wasted arrow. He compares the monk to a fake tiger and in effect suggests that he return to his place. Severe as Hsüeh-tou's assessment may sound, there is still a possibility that it contains a hint of approbation, in accord with the Zen convention of praise-by-slander: even a paper tiger can alarm an unsuspecting hunter. Daitō concludes that Hsüeh-tou's second arrow—the verbal jab —was more effective than his shout, perhaps bringing the monk closer to some kind of insight.

Conclusion

The oral and written capping-phrase commentaries in the *Record of Daitō* disclose vital aspects of Daitō's verbal style: the power and fluency of his Zen language, his exegetical zeal, his determination to avoid discursive modes of teaching, and so on. Considered in its entirety, however, the *Record* is an uneven work. Some sections scintillate, but others seem to lag or falter. Like most discourse records of its period, Daitō's text adheres closely to the exigencies of the *goroku* genre. Talks are scheduled according to the monastic calendar, ceremonies follow standard protocol, predictable topics are taken up at certain times of year, and encounter dialogues conform to traditional patterns.

For example, Daitō gave formal talks on the ninth day of the ninth month for seven years. On each of these occasions Daitō or one of his monks introduced the seasonal theme of chrysanthemums, then alluded to a particular Chinese poem about chrysanthemums (five different times) or a certain Chinese saying about chrysanthemums (twice).[25] On the annual double-nine date the discourse records of Nanpo and Musō refer with comparable frequency to the chrysanthemum motif and the two Chinese allusions. We recall that the Japanese masters of the period were compelled to give their lectures and converse with their monks in *kanbun,* the cumbersome form of Japanized Chinese that was neither Japanese nor Chinese. The drawbacks of *kanbun* and the constraints of the discourse-record format are at least partially responsible for the stilted, overly textual quality of many recorded lectures and "dialogues."

Daitō, making a virtue of necessity, found in capping phrases a way to surmount the linguistic and interpretive challenges he faced. Although a Zen master cannot bestow enlightenment, he can inspire students, point them in a certain direction, correct missteps, destabilize deluded notions, and provide well-timed triggers. Remarkably, capping phrases can be used in all of these ways. Capping phrases enable masters and practitioners to respond to texts, oral koans, or live situations in a manner consistent with fundamental Zen assumptions about language and understanding. By not restating the paradoxical or poetic language of a Ch'an/Zen passage in more conventional terms, capping phrases avoid the reductive effect of most commentary. Because they do not explain discursively, they force readers (or listeners) to keep going back to the text itself. In a live encounter, they do not rob a situation of its power to generate insight. Rather than say, "The master gave a superb answer to the monk's poor question," Daitō caps, "To buy iron and receive gold." He thereby gets more from language and more from readers. Similarly, when he was asked about Zen in the Shōchū Debate, he answered with a capping phrase that threw the question back to the questioner.

Capping phrases offset the impulse of Zen devotees to sanctify honored texts as infallible scripture, just as they inhibit whatever scholastic tendencies a Zen commentator might have. In Japan the inclination to preserve inherited traditions in set forms was especially strong, and Daitō may have seen capping phrases as a means of forestalling this tendency in Zen. If someone's statement is vulnerable, if a predecessor's interpretation leans to one side, Daitō promptly "inserts the needle where it hurts." He expresses the irreverent reverence of Zen, capping the discourse record of the distinguished master Hsüeh-tou with such phrases as "Hsüeh-tou has opened only one eye," "Hsüeh-tou has not yet gotten that far," or "Do not make a mistake because of Hsüeh-tou."[26] And he applies this principle to himself as well: each time he reconsiders a koan, he caps it freshly, without reference to his earlier responses.

Daitō's attraction to capping phrases must also be assessed in the context of Ch'an's transmission to Japan. Though the Japanese pioneers were doubly distanced from Ch'an classics—by history and by culture —their search for authentic Zen compelled them to grapple with these foreign texts. Not only did Daitō read the works of the masters in Chinese, he attempted to annotate them in Chinese as well. In this light, capping phrases had obvious virtues: they were short, relatively comprehensible, readily memorizable, sanctioned by the tradition, and exempt from certain interpretive pitfalls. Daitō's use of capping phrases was conservative in some respects. He adopted a hermeneutical device that came ready-made as part of Ch'an. He did not attempt to modify the genre in any substantial way nor reach beyond Ch'an to cap other kinds of texts, religious or secular. Nonetheless, Daitō expressed a characteristically Japanese type of creativity—selectively borrowing a "foreign" element, he adapted it to a new context and continued to refine it.

Daitō's style emerges not only in his mastery of the capping-phrase genre but also in his specific responses to individual texts. Each time that he comments on the question of a monk or the answer of a master, he is exposing his Zen. Each time that he caps a line of a Ch'an discourse record, he is putting himself on the line as well. Daitō's written capping phrases are the textual equivalent of the live demonstrations that take place in the master-disciple encounter. As he caps a text, he enters into a dialogue with that particular work and with the Ch'an/Zen tradition as a whole. At times this engagement is as intimate as it can be: he speaks directly to the protagonists of a koan or to the master of a discourse record. Because many capping phrases leave subjects, objects, and other referents unnamed, when they are out of context they must be translated into English with infinitives or gerunds: "To insert the needle where it hurts" or "Losing one's way and running into Bodhidharma." Once Daitō uses these phrases in specific contexts, however, they can often be translated in accord with his dialogic involvement: "You're inserting the needle where it hurts" or "You lost your way and ran into Bodhidharma." In challenging the text and allowing it to challenge him, Daitō recaptures its original catalytic power.

10

"HIS TONGUE HAS NO BONES"

DURING THE early decades of the twelfth century, before Ch'an was introduced to Japan, Chüeh-fan Hui-hung (1071–1128) accused his fellow Ch'an monks of degeneracy: "Their teaching of the Dharma has fallen to utter ruin; everywhere Ch'an is taken to be the mere discarding of written words and letters, and the 'subtle particularity' of Ch'an is thought to consist only in oral transmission."[1] To counteract the antiintellectual tendencies that dismayed him, Chüeh-fan advocated *wen-tzu Ch'an,* a "literary" or "lettered" Ch'an that sought to integrate spiritual practice, learning, and literary pursuits. Though some of Chüeh-fan's ideas were realized through the continued interaction between Ch'an and secular Chinese culture, an unabashedly literary style of Ch'an was sharply rejected by Chüeh-fan's influential contemporary Ta-hui Tsung-kao.[2] From then on, the term *wen-tzu Ch'an* (*moji Zen* in Japanese) carried negative connotations: a wordy or overly conceptual Zen.[3] The vocabularies of Ch'an and Zen thus lack a neutral, commonly accepted name for literary Zen. For Western observers at least, "literary Zen" refers to any attempt to express Zen in a manner that has literary value. In some cases, the term may also indicate the search for commonalities between Zen and literature, especially poetry.

Eloquent Zen, a related concept, also lacks a direct equivalent in the lexicon of Ch'an/Zen. In the West, eloquence aims to "appeal to the reason or move the feelings," and it derives much of its force from "appropriateness."[4] Eloquence in Zen is something quite different: it appeals neither to reason nor to emotion, and it seeks to transform rather than to persuade, often by disrupting rational thought and defy-

151

ing conventional language. Though eloquent Zen and literary Zen are synonymous in some contexts, the distinction between the two can be significant. For example, later Rinzai monks praised Daitō as a master of eloquent Zen but denigrated Musō as a master of literary Zen.

Daitō was heir to a Ch'an/Zen lineage renowned for its skill in articulating the Way. Two of his religious ancestors, Yün-men and Hsüeh-tou, were greatly esteemed for their verbal prowess; the affinities Daitō felt with both men have already been noted. If Yün-men was the first Chinese master to respond incisively to koans with capping phrases, Daitō was the first Japanese master to respond incisively to Ch'an classics with capping phrases. To that degree at least, Nanpo may have been justified in calling his most promising disciple a "second Yün-men." Hsüeh-tou, a direct-line descendant of Yün-men, was no less influential than his predecessor. According to Yanagida Seizan, Hsüeh-tou represents a turning point in the development of Ch'an and its literature: "Before long, Hsüeh-tou of the Yün-men school created a unique Zen literature, and with this the course of Zen history was altered. The change in the history of the Zen school after Hsüeh-tou was, in a word, a shift toward the literary rather than the philosophical."[5] Daitō's early and unerring recognition of Hsüeh-tou's importance is a mark of Daitō's own significance. Among the pioneers of Japanese Zen, only Daitō created koan commentaries in the manner of Hsüeh-tou, and Daitō alone prepared an annotated edition of Hsüeh-tou's discourse record.

A more immediate influence on Daitō was his teacher's teacher, Hsü-t'ang Chih-yü. Hsü-t'ang had been a prominent figure in a group of Chinese monks and literati who were interested in the links between Ch'an and poetry. Some members of Hsü-t'ang's circle went so far as to claim that the way of Ch'an and the way of poetry were one: writing a poem could therefore be a legitimate form of spiritual practice.[6] In his own work, Hsü-t'ang artfully used natural images to convey religious messages and moods. Many of his verses lack any explicit reference to Buddhist topics; others allude to Buddhism only through subtly coded conventions. The following stanza illustrates Hsü-t'ang's style:

Listening to Snow

Cold night, no wind, bamboo making noises,
noises far apart, now bunched together,
    filtering the pine-flanked lattice.
Listening with ears is less fine than listening with the mind.
Beside the lamp I lay aside the half scroll of sutra.[7]

In its movement from evocative imagery to the expression of a religious truth, this poem exemplifies the synthesis of literature and Zen to which Daitō aspired. One of the implications of the poem is that the voice of the Buddha can be heard so clearly in the rattling of bamboo that the written scriptures may be put aside. Yet there is also an inescapable paradox here. The poem, like the abandoned sutra, uses words to express a realization that is beyond words.

Hsü-t'ang enhanced his reputation as a master of Ch'an language by capping his own compilation of a hundred koans (using one final capping phrase per koan).[8] This text, brought to Japan by Nanpo, undoubtedly stimulated Daitō, though Daitō preferred interlinear capping phrases to final ones. Hsü-t'ang was not without critics: colleagues such as Lan-ch'i reproached him for being excessively literary. But his impact on Japanese Zen has endured for centuries. Ikkyū, a distinguished poet in his own right, singled out Hsü-t'ang as the reincarnation of the celebrated Chinese poet Hsü Hun (791–854). In contemporary Rinzai Zen, quotations from Hsü-t'ang's works permeate the standard capping-phrase anthologies, and his koan collection is still used in the advanced training of monks.

The Ch'an/Zen tradition is not the only context in which the literary dimensions of Daitō's Zen style can be apprehended. In the early fourteenth century, members of Japan's cultured elite were animated by new forms of artistic expression, especially in poetry. Some of these developments had been partially stimulated by exposure to Zen, but others were the outcome of native movements. Like the Chinese, the Japanese had for centuries been interested in the relation of poetry to religion. They too had come to regard the practice of poetry and the practice of Buddhism as mutually reinforcing, if not fundamentally congruent. Problems associated with the verbal expression of enlightenment (and other religious experiences) had been investigated in literary circles as well as Buddhist ones. During Daitō's lifetime the poets, priests, and courtiers of Kyoto were captivated by *renga,* or linked verse. In intimate gatherings and in groups of up to a hundred, they created long sequences of linked poems by responding to each other in turn. What had once been an entertaining capping-verse exercise became a sophisticated poetic genre and a vehicle for the expression of religious devotion. One of the men who played a pivotal role in the cultural milieu of the day was Daitō's patron and disciple Emperor Hanazono. As we will see below, Hanazono and Daitō contributed jointly and independently to the era's extended exploration of Zen, literature, and exegesis.

A Proper Response to the Textual Tradition

In order to appreciate the position of Daitō's written works in the development of Japanese Zen, we must return briefly to the theme of authentic Zen. The Japanese pioneers regarded enlightenment as the principal criterion of Zen, and they identified several other essential components of Zen: zazen, emblems of Dharma transmission, the monastic rule, monastery construction, and withdrawal from the world. Another indicator of genuine Zen during the transmission period was a proper response to the textual tradition. Sutras, which represented the teachings of Shakyamuni Buddha, could clarify or deepen one's understanding at any stage of the path. The Ch'an corpus, as shaped by Sung bibliographers, was believed to reveal the enlightened awareness of the masters through their words and behavior. Koans, the most peculiar of texts, were intended to function as expressions of enlightenment, triggers to enlightenment, and vehicles for the exploration of specific aspects of enlightenment.

Much can be learned from the Japanese pioneers' struggle to clarify their stance toward the Buddhist scriptures. Willingly or unwillingly, they became embroiled in a long-standing dispute that had been inherited from their Chinese predecessors. As we have seen, Ch'an/Zen defined itself as "a separate transmission outside the teachings" (Ch. *chiao-wai pieh-ch'uan;* Jp. *kyōge betsuden*), according to the classic verse attributed to Bodhidharma. In this phrase, *chiao (kyō)* implied several related referents: the Buddhist teachings, the sutras, and the doctrinal schools. All Buddhist schools besides Ch'an and Zen, such as Hua-yen in China or Tendai in Japan, were classed as doctrinal.

A rival approach within Ch'an/Zen advocated "the unity of the teachings and Ch'an/Zen" (Ch. *chiao-ch'an i-chih;* Jp. *kyōzen itchi*), in which Zen and the teachings were seen as different but equally valid expressions of the same truth. Because literal translations are cumbersome here, let us call these two streams sutra-free Zen and sutra-linked Zen, respectively. The masters who upheld sutra-linked Zen often used sutra quotations and doctrinal explanations, and they accepted the practices of other Buddhist schools in their temples. An early and influential advocate of this approach was Tsung-mi (780–841), honored by doctrinal and Ch'an lineages alike. Sutra-linked Zen reached its peak in the early Sung period; its most complete exposition is found in the *Mirror Record of the [Ch'an] School (Tsung-ching lu),* a treatise of one hundred chapters completed in 961.

Eisai was one of the first Japanese masters to be troubled by Zen's relation to the sutras. The Ch'an he had embraced in China gave precedence to sutra-free Zen but also recognized sutra-linked Zen. On his return to Japan, Eisai was alarmed to see that sutra-free Zen was (allegedly) being interpreted by Nōnin in an antinomian way, risking the provocation of the powerful Tendai sect. In Eisai's main work, *Promulgation of Zen as a Defense of the Nation,* an unnamed questioner asks him:

It is said that this [Zen] school is "not dependent on words." This is close to the false view of emptiness, similar to one type of obscure realization. If so, the Tendai school opposes it. . . . It is said in the *Hsüan-i [Profound Meaning (of the Lotus Sutra)]*: "If a man who contemplates his mind thinks that his adherence to his mind is correct, that he himself is thereby equal to Buddha, and that he does not need to consult the sutras and treatises, he will fall into arrogance. This is like burning oneself with one's own torch." . . . How could the Zen school's "not depending on words" avoid this difficulty?[9]

Eisai answers by saying that those who truly understand Zen have no need to reject the sutras, and he proceeds to quote a wide range of Buddhist scriptures. Of the few Ch'an texts that Eisai cites in this tract, his favorite is the classic of sutra-linked Zen, the *Mirror Record of the Ch'an School*. Yet he also endorses the "separate transmission" slogan of sutra-free Zen.[10] Perhaps frustrated by his inability to adopt a stance that was theoretically consistent and politically viable, Eisai concluded that both elements of the traditional dichotomy should be transcended: " 'Teachings' and 'Zen' are just names; 'practice' and 'study' are also just provisional names. . . . The Zen school is . . . inconceivable, ultimately ungraspable."[11]

Whereas Eisai's strategy was to embrace as many positions as possible, Dōgen chose a different tack. In his diary he reports the following conversation with his master Ju-ching:

> I asked: "Now priests everywhere speak about the 'special transmission outside the scriptures.' This, they declare, is the real meaning in the First Patriarch Bodhidharma's coming from the West. What do they mean?"
> Ju-ching taught: "How could the great Way of the buddhas and patriarchs have anything to do with 'inside' or 'outside'? . . . The world could not have two Buddha-Dharmas."[12]

Dōgen interpreted this answer as a rejection of sutra-free Zen. In later writings he condemned sutra-free Zen as a "fallacy," insisting that "an enlightened person always masters the sutras to full advantage."[13] Thus when Dōgen built a temple, he included a building for sutra study. However, Dōgen censured forms of practice that combined elements from other Buddhist schools, thereby shunning the eclecticism associated with sutra-linked Zen.[14]

Musō was the most prominent master to be criticized in his own day for leaning too far toward sutra-linked Zen. Someone asked him point-blank: "If you are a descendant of Lin-chi, why do you always lecture on the sutras instead of teaching the fundamental matter to the monks?"[15] Emperor Hanazono condemned Musō's Zen style as "still bound by the rope of doctrine."[16] Like Eisai, Musō defended himself by attempting to transcend the terms of the debate: "The Buddha did not call himself only a man of doctrine *(kyō)* nor did he call himself only a man of Zen. Nor did he separate his teachings into a doctrine portion and a Zen portion, because Buddha's inner realization cannot be equated with either of them."[17]

Other concerns are also discernible beneath the surface of this discourse, which was more than a debate about the relation between enlightenment and written expressions of enlightenment. One can hear the masters' uncertainty about what voice to adopt in their teaching and writing. The sutras were authoritative, relatively accessible, and revered in common by many Buddhist schools, so there must have been some reluctance to abandon this corpus for the stranger works of Ch'an, as the *kyōge betsuden* principle seemed to require. Consciously or not, the Japanese pioneers were also working out the relationship between Japanese Zen and Chinese Ch'an. Which styles and streams of Ch'an were most correct, and to what degree were the Japanese compelled to adhere to them? The controversy about Zen's stance toward texts touched upon other crucial issues as well: What was distinctive about Zen in comparison with the other ("doctrinal") schools of Buddhism? What was Zen's proper relation to those other schools? Even if such questions had been settled satisfactorily in China, they had not yet been resolved in Japan.

It was against this backdrop that Daitō developed a Zen style that was faithful to certain streams of Ch'an, free from overreliance on texts, and also adaptively Japanese. On the one hand, he is identified as a master of sutra-free Zen, because he stressed that genuine awakening far surpasses any textually derived forms of understanding. On the other hand, he developed a Zen style that was both eloquent and literary. Though he did not expound the sutras, he extensively interpreted the classics of Ch'an. Whereas Eisai and Musō attempted to surmount the distinction between "Zen" and "teachings" in a manner that seems largely rhetorical, Daitō found a way to transcend the problem in practice, through a new commentarial approach and through poetry. In this task he was aided by some native Japanese literary developments, to which we now turn.

Japanese Influences on Daitō's Zen Style

In Japan, as in other Asian cultures, poetry has played a central role in cultural life, and it has long been valued as a form of religious expression. In the century preceding Daitō's birth, certain ideas about the relation between poetry and Buddhism were articulated with new confidence. Members of the priesthood and the literati class cultivated a

genre known as *Shakkyō-ka,* "poems on the Buddha's teachings."[18] In
some circles, poetry was placed on a level with Buddhist doctrine, and
the Japanese language was equated with the canonical languages of the
sutras. For example, Mujū Ichien argued that a *waka* (a five-line Japanese verse) could be equivalent to a *dharani* (a Buddhist spell using foreign sounds):

> When we consider *waka* as a means to religious realization, we see
> that it has the virtue of serenity and peace, of putting a stop to the dis-
> tractions and undisciplined movement of the mind. With a few words
> it encompasses its sentiment. This is the nature of mystic verse, or
> *dharani.* . . . Japanese poems do not differ from the words of the Bud-
> dha. . . . Had the Buddha appeared in Japan, he would simply have
> used Japanese for mystic verses. . . . Though Japanese poetry also
> uses the ordinary words of the world, when we use *waka* to convey our
> spiritual intentions, there will surely be a favorable response. And
> should it embody the spirit of the Buddha's Law, there can be no
> doubt that it will be a *dharani.* [19]

Once such correlations were invoked, others followed. The writing of
poetry was likened to the practice of meditation and to the recitation of
Buddhist sutras. Poems were regarded as suitable offerings to temples
and shrines, and there was serious discussion about whether or not the
composition of verse could advance one along the path to enlightenment.[20]

Japan also had its own capping tradition, centered on verses rather
than the pithy phrases characteristic of Zen. In the oldest history of
Japan someone successfully answers a test question with a capping
verse. A poem in Japan's first poetry collection has a "head" composed
by one person and a "tail" composed by another.[21] A poetic game popular among the aristocracy of the Heian period (794–1185) bears some
resemblance to the capping exercise that would later be brought to
Japan as part of Zen. As Donald Keene explains,

> Often a riddle was presented in the *maeku* (first verse) and the poem
> was completed by another person with a *tsukeku* (added verse) of wit
> and ingenuity. The more complicated or absurd the situation de-
> scribed in the *maeku* ("a deer is standing in the middle of the sea"),
> the greater the achievement of the person who could make sense of
> the whole by adding a cleverly explicative two lines ("the reflection of
> the mountain is cast on the waves").[22]

Linked verse attained unprecedented popularity, in the form of *renga,*
during the years that Daitō was teaching at Daitokuji. Following conventions derived from *waka,* the participants in a *renga* session took turns
writing lines, cooperating (and sometimes competing) to produce a

work that muted individual voices for the sake of the whole. *Renga* involved a complex form of capping: the end of any poem in the link also served as the beginning of the next in a sequence that could be expanded indefinitely. There is no record of Daitō having participated in *renga* sessions, though he was undoubtedly familiar with the genre. His early teacher Kōhō, his fellow master Musō, and his disciple Hanazono all enjoyed linked verse; according to one source, Kōhō and Musō "composed *renga* night and day."[23]

A degree of literary ability was expected of ordinary monks. Yanagida has claimed that "without a high level of competence in poetry, it was impossible even to begin Zen practice."[24] Though this may be overstating the case, masters and senior monks commonly tutored younger students in poetry composition. Kokan Shiren, a leading Zen figure and one of Daitō's contemporaries, described the process:

> I have some pupils who fool about, joke, chaff, and won't recite their lessons. When I prod and scold them to write poetry, they say, "But we don't know the rules of tone and meter." When I tell them to forget the rules and just write out lines with the correct number of syllables, they grumble and complain. But I do not become upset, and in spite of themselves they present me with some lines. Their poems may be halting, uneven, doltish, and clumsy, and sometimes make no sense at all; but still, they are often filled with a self-possessed purity and integrity that make me marvel.[25]

Japanese Zen monks began to face questions that had also vexed their Chinese predecessors. Was literary prowess an indication of advanced spiritual development? Would progress in one's practice improve the quality of one's poetry? Those who set great store by the literary dimensions of Zen construed the relation between the two realms as follows: a lack of verbal skill in expressing the Dharma is a salient indication that the highest level of realization has not yet been attained.[26] A number of Daitō's capping phrases make this point more tersely (in context): "His tongue is already long" or "His tongue has bones." A century and a half after Daitō's death, Zen attainment and poetic skill were equated in emphatic terms. "The one flavor of poetry and Zen" became a popular slogan. Around 1500, Chūhō En'i claimed, "Anyone who has mastered Zen will be able to write good poetry,"[27] and another monk argued, "Outside of poetry there is no Zen, outside of Zen there is no poetry."[28]

As might be expected, some Zen monks were harshly criticized for literary tendencies that seemed excessive. Passionate accusations were rebutted with equal intensity. When I-shan I-ning recited a Chinese poem on a ceremonial occasion, a monk objected, "You aren't talking about Zen Buddhism! You're only talking about literary matters!"

"Blind fool," retorted I-shan. "It is you who do not see the Way! I recite my poetry for those who can understand it."[29] Musō was well known in his time as a gifted poet, yet he blamed others and was himself blamed for being unacceptably devoted to letters. When he ranked his own disciples, Musō placed poetry-loving monks in the lowest category, branding them as "shaven-headed laymen" and "robed ricebags."[30] Unlike I-shan and Musō (and Hsü-t'ang), Daitō was never accused of being too literary. Whereas Musō was one of the originators and leading figures of the "literature of the Five Mountains" *(Gozan bungaku)*, Daitō is conspicuously absent from the poetic anthologies of the period.

Emperor Hanazono gives voice in his diary to certain notions that Daitō must also have pondered; it is reasonable to assume that the two men discussed some of these matters with each other. Hanazono describes in considerable detail his efforts to express his understanding of Buddhism in his poetry. In one revealing passage of 1332, several years after his awakening had been sanctioned by Daitō, the former emperor acknowledges his debt to Daitō and identifies one of his poetry mentors, Kyōgoku Tamekane (1253–1332). Kyōgoku had taught Hanazono that "there cannot be any sense of distinction between the Dharma and poetry." When Kyōgoku praised Hanazono's poetry as reflecting the "true essence" of the Dharma, Hanazono was greatly pleased.[31] Far from being a dilettante, the former emperor made significant contributions to medieval culture. He served as an initial conduit for Zen's considerable influence on Japanese poetry, and he was one of the first to express his Zen understanding in the form of a *waka*.[32] Andrew Goble believes that Hanazono also used Buddhist ideas to reconceptualize the role of the imperial family in Japanese society.[33] We know that Daitō taught the former emperor how to work on koans and use Zen capping phrases; it is not difficult to imagine that Hanazono influenced Daitō in a reciprocal manner.

Daitō's Poetry

Daitō was not only a dynamic teacher and an astute exegete; he was also a talented poet. His poetry and his capping-phrase works are closely related, and both genres exemplify his literary/eloquent Zen style. Like most Japanese monks of his period, Daitō wrote various kinds of poetry in two different languages. When he sought to express himself in a traditional and dignified manner, he wrote in Sino-Japanese *(kanbun)*, using only Chinese characters. Forty-eight commentarial stanzas composed in this manner (known as *juko*) are included in the *Record of Daitō*. Daitō similarly used *kanbun* for most of the poems addressed to his disciples, whether delivered orally or brushed onto a calligraphic scroll. He also wrote lighter verse in Japanese; about seventy poems in this vein are traditionally attributed to him, though their sources cannot always be verified.

Within the Zen tradition, Daitō's poetry has been highly acclaimed. Hakuin expressed his appreciation using colorful metaphors:

> These commentarial verses *(juko)* are the golden mallet that smashes apart the curtains of unrealization and self-proclaimed realization. They are the old mirror which distinguishes the true and the false in those who haven't penetrated and those who have. They are precious vessels that enable those who search in inner mystery to penetrate profoundly the abysmal depths.[34]

One of Daitō's poems prompted Hakuin to add: "This whole verse is like a great ball of flaming metal, a red-hot iron stake. It's impossible to get at it, no matter what you do. Who among you knows that the National Master [Daitō] lost his body and his life when he achieved these lines?"[35]

Most of Daitō's poems refer explicitly to some aspect of Zen or Buddhist tradition: koans, doctrinal concepts, religious lore, and so on. Often Daitō cites his source material as a headnote or a title. The following poem is about the beginning of Shakyamuni's religious quest and, by extension, the first step on anyone's spiritual path. In this version of the legend, Shakyamuni is summoned by the god Śuddha-āvāsa:

> Śuddha-āvāsa, hands palm-to-palm, appears at the window.
>
>> Full moon in the palace pond a gem
>> though it's not yet autumn;
>> this quiet night he knows the ripples have changed.
>> From here he'll walk the path as if deluded,
>> huge Dantaloka Mountain hard as iron.[36]

The opening two lines of Daitō's poem suggest Shakyamuni's inherent completeness (even before the start of practice), and the third line connotes the first wave of spiritual aspiration, the arising of the mind that seeks the Way. Not only will Shakyamuni's intense exertions make him appear crazed, but as a teacher he will eventually spend forty years "selling water by the river." For Daitō, Shakyamuni's aspiration and determination seem as lofty and unshakable as Dantaloka Mountain, where the former prince is said to have endured death-defying austerities. Reading this poem centuries later, Hakuin was reminded of Hsüeh-tou, who composed the commentarial verses in the *Blue Cliff Record:* "What a pity that Ming-Hsüeh [Hsüeh-tou] could not have seen this verse. Even one glance would have given him goose bumps."[37]

Other poems by Daitō begin with a Buddhist reference but move away from a densely allusive mode. The following verse uses a quotation from Ch'an master Nan-ch'üan as its headnote/title:

Nan-ch'üan said, "I don't know anything about buddhas in the three worlds."

> If he had known buddhas exist
>   in the three worlds,
> suddenly no spring flowers,
> no full moon in the fall.[38]

Daitō uses some natural imagery here, but the thrust of the poem is doctrinal. His point (rephrased in philosophical language) is that if one has a dualistic notion of buddhas existing apart from the natural universe, then one will not be able to see or appreciate things as they are. For those who have perceived the Buddha-nature of spring flowers, the next step is to forget about Buddha-nature and just see the flowers as flowers.

Some of Daitō's poems avoid explicit references to Zen or Buddhism yet continue to resonate with Zen-like implications. In one of his lighter verses he tells of an unexpected rainshower:

> No umbrella, getting soaked,
> I'll just use the rain as my raincoat.[39]

Out of context, the following verse by Daitō seems to have shed all traces of Zen:

> The spring hills are blue,
> the spring waters green,
> the spring clouds are scattered,
> the spring birds chirp ceaselessly.[40]

However, in this case appearances are deceptive. The poem not only alludes to an earlier verse by Hsüeh-tou;[41] it also was used by Daitō to test his monks. The poem's original context is disclosed in the *Record of Daitō*. Addressing the assembled monks, Daitō says:

> The spring hills are blue,
> the spring waters green,
> the spring clouds are scattered,
> the spring birds chirp ceaselessly.
>
> I ask all of you: In our school, is this affirmed? Is this denied? Return to your chambers and grope for an answer.[42]

In some of Daitō's poems, especially those in Japanese, his voice is more personal:

> It's over, the "buddhas and patriarchs" disease
> that once gripped my chest.
> Now I'm just an ordinary man
> with a clean slate.[43]

Assuming the poem is sincerely autobiographical, one wonders at what point in Daitō's life it was composed. Many Zen monks have reported that a bout with disease sparked a Zen insight, though these lines could also be the thoughts of a seasoned monk nearing the end of his life.

For Daitō, poetry and capping phrases were often interchangeable: both genres aimed for concision, suggestiveness, and depth. Daitō composed his own poetic capping phrases, used the poetry of others as capping phrases, and used capping phrases in his poetry. In one context he might respond to a koan by writing a verse; in other contexts he would comment on the same koan with capping phrases.[44] And sometimes he did both, annotating a Ch'an text first with a capping phrase and then with a stanza.[45] The convergence of the two genres can be seen in the following poem:

> Nan-ch'üan Cuts the Cat
>
> Holding up the cat for everyone to see,
> cutting it one, two, three—
> a hammer head without a hole.[46]

The first line cites the well-known Zen koan in which master Nan-ch'üan (allegedly) kills a cat because his monks cannot provide an appropriate Zen response to their master's threat. The second line, "cutting it one, two, three," sounds much like a capping phrase: numbers in series are used frequently by Daitō in his capping-phrase commentaries. The third line is indeed a capping phrase, one of Daitō's favorites. We noted, in the preceding chapter, that a holeless hammer head can serve as a metaphor for the ungraspable truth. Here it is also effective in other ways, suggesting the violence of the scene and the smashed preconceptions of those present.

The capping-phrase quality of the following poem is readily apparent:

> When Te-shan was leaving the Yangtze, he summoned Kao-t'ing. Kao-t'ing left Heng-ch'ü.
>
> > Te-shan's invitation is
> > one two three four five six seven
> > and eight nine ten,
> > Kao-t'ing's departure is
> > ten nine eight seven six five four
> > and three two one.[47]

Even if one lacks further information about the incident in the head-note, the poem is a light-hearted expression of the "thusness" prized by Zen. Comings and goings—just as they are—abundantly manifest Buddha-nature, so they are also not-comings and not-goings. According to the full story, Te-shan summoned Kao-t'ing by gesturing with a fan; Kao-t'ing thereupon had an enlightenment experience, and that is why Kao-t'ing left Heng-ch'ü.[48]

Zen, Language, and Zen Language

In the *Gateless Barrier,* Wu-men skillfully frames a long-standing conundrum:

> If you understand the first word of Zen
> you will know the last word.
> The last word or the first word—
> "it" is not a word.[49]

Zen tradition reserves its highest praise for masters who combined deep realization with verbal fluency. Daitō is among those so honored. We have seen how energetically he used language in the service of spiritual liberation: delivering Dharma talks, engaging students in Zen debate, exchanging correspondence, copying manuscripts, creating koans, quoting or composing capping phrases, and writing poetry. One of the first manuscripts in Daitō's hand is his transcription of the *Transmission of the Lamp.* It testifies to his belief that Dharma transmission has a verbal dimension as well as a nonverbal one, and it shows him hard at work learning the conventions of his discursive community. In his reverent colophon Daitō referred simultaneously to the patriarchal lineage and to the text that recorded it: "This is indeed the spiritual activity of a thousand sages, the life-artery of the heroic patriarchs."[50]

Daitō's eloquent Zen begins, paradoxically, with a recognition of the limitations of language, a cardinal tenet of Buddhism in general and Zen in particular. One of the most troublesome properties of language, according to the Buddhist critique, is its implicit acceptance of the dualistic view of self-and-other that is at the root of delusion. Nāgārjuna (second century c.e.) went to great lengths to demonstrate that if a statement is construed as a true representation of reality, it inevitably leads to self-contradiction, and the import of his analysis was embraced by all later schools of Buddhism. A hermeneutical claim is central to Ch'an's classic self-definition: "a separate transmission outside the teachings, not depending on words." Countless Ch'an/Zen anecdotes and images reiterate the point that the essential Zen experience cannot be adequately conveyed through a text: a famous painting depicts the Sixth Patriarch tearing up a sutra, Te-shan destroys his lecture notes, Ta-hui burns the *Blue Cliff Record,* and so on.

The theme of language's limits was prominent in Daitō's early training and later teaching. He had his first Zen insight when he overheard someone recite Pai-chang's verse about the ineffability of truth:

> Truth's naked radiance,
> cut off from the senses and the world,
> shines by itself—
> no words for it.[51]

Daitō's most memorable rejoinder in the Shōchū Debate was prompted by the question "What is Zen, which claims to be a separate transmission outside the teachings?" He answered with his mysterious flying millstone image—whatever Zen is, it cannot be explained verbally. In a short treatise called *Evening Discussion at Shōun-an (Shōunyawa)*, he confronts a fellow Zen teacher identified only as Kō, known for his reliance on the *Śūraṅgama Sutra* and certain doctrinal formulations. Daitō accuses Kō of trying to "get the meaning through words" and says, "I strongly reject that."[52]

With his own students, Daitō emphasized that those with the Dharma eye see things too momentous to be fitted into language. He favored the Zen adage "As soon as you call it something, you've already missed the mark," assigning it to his disciples as a koan.[53] Approaching the issue from a different direction, he made it clear that the least authentic course is to attempt to expound the Dharma without any personal experience of realization. In one of his vernacular sermons he relates a graphic story about a Chinese Dharma master named Yün-kuang who served Emperor Wu of Liang. Though Yün-kuang preached Buddhism with apparent eloquence, he had not awakened, and someone accused him of being "a species of animal." Emperor Wu sharply dismissed this charge, reports Daitō, but the next time the Emperor saw Yün-kuang teaching the Dharma, "Yün-kuang was a cow."[54]

The matter does not end, of course, with an acknowledgment of the pitfalls of language. Although Zen masters decry the power of words to perpetuate ignorance, they nonetheless use words to express their own enlightenment and to spur others on the path. Paradoxical as it may seem, Pai-chang's declaration that there are "no words for it" was set in verse, and the line communicated enough to Daitō, across gaps of time and culture, to spark a powerful insight. Rather than lapse into silence, which can also be one-sided, masters sought to make language fresh and full of impact. The *Blue Cliff Record* declares:

> The ancients weren't like people today with their spurious shallow talk; otherwise, how could they have used a single word or half a phrase for a whole lifetime? Therefore, when it came to supporting the teaching of the school and continuing the life of the buddhas, they would spit out a word or half a phrase which would spontaneously cut off the tongues of everyone on earth. There's no place for you to produce a train of thought, to make intellectual interpretations, or to grapple with principles.[55]

From a Buddhist standpoint, the problem faced by Zen masters can be expressed in terms of the (provisional) distinction between the ultimate and conventional realms. Enlightenment is ultimate, language is conventional. How can one speak from an ultimate level using conventional-level language? This dilemma was the wellspring of the diverse rhetorical strategies employed by the masters: ordinary language used in nonordinary ways, meaningless language, paradox, poetry, capping phrases, acting out, gestures, and silence. All these are the language of Zen.

Though the slogan "not depending on words" was accepted as classic Ch'an doctrine after the ninth centry, interpretations of it varied. Tsung-mi was among the first to treat the phrase as an expedient teaching device rather than a literal statement.[56] The grammatical ambiguity of the original wording permits another reading that expands the possibilities for eloquent Zen: "words that are not dependent." Such words are used freely, without attachment, and with an understanding that they are mere pointers to a reality that is itself nonsubstantial. Words may thus lead to bondage or liberation, depending on the spirit behind them, the manner in which they are used, and the receptivity of the listener. Yüan-wu accordingly made a heuristic distinction between two kinds of language:

> Examine the live word; don't examine the dead word. One who adheres utterly to the live word will not forget for an eternity of kalpas. One who adheres utterly to the dead word will never be able to save himself. If you want to take the patriarchs and buddhas as your masters, you must clearly choose the live word.[57]

In this context, silence does not have privileged status. Though it may appear to transcend conventional-level discourse, it too functions as a sign. In a letter to Hanazono's consort, Daitō asserted: "It [the Original Face] cannot be reached by words, it cannot be reached by silence."[58] A koan favored by Daitō further illumines this point:

> A monk asked Feng-hsüeh, "Both speech and silence are involved in separation and discrimination. How can we proceed without erring?" Feng-hsüeh said,
>
> > I'll always remember Chiang-nan in spring—
> > the partridges chirping, the flowers so fragrant.[59]

The master in the koan, Feng-hsüeh, does not quarrel with the monk's point that words and silence are equally subject to relative distinctions. Rather, the master makes a revealing move—he turns to poetry and describes a natural scene. Daitō not only presented this koan to his disciples; in at least one instance he cited it verbatim as his response to another koan.[60] In this way, the Zen discourse about the deficiencies of language and silence exhibits a rich intertextuality, however ironic or paradoxical that may be.

Some of the conclusions reached by Ch'an/Zen were reinforced by parallel developments in East Asian literary theory, especially in Japan. For poets, words were needed to express the ineffable heart/mind; for Zen practitioners, the world of form was the only point of access to the realm of emptiness. The dialectics of both traditions accordingly sanctioned the revelation of meaning in language and form. As David Pollack has noted:

> Earlier Japanese poetic thought held that heart and words, while obviously different, were inseparable aspects of the same unity. Zen metaphysics, too, insisted upon a simultaneous identity and distinction between Void and Color [emptiness and form]. If carried to its logical extreme, then, the equation implies that not only is meaning formless and form meaningless; meaning is also to be found in form itself, and form in meaning.[61]

Daitō composed a verse in Japanese that deftly addresses the interrelation of form, emptiness, and meaning. It is a response to a verse in the *Diamond Sutra* in which the Buddha states that those who try to see him through form or hear him through sound are searching in the wrong direction. The poem in the sutra says:

> If you try to see me through form
> or hear me through sound,
> nothing you see or hear
> is where I am.[62]

This is a koan (it was so used in Zen), since all we can see is form. Can Buddha-nature be seen through form or not? Daitō capped the *Diamond Sutra* verse with one of his own:

> No form, no sound—
> here I am;
> white clouds fringing the peaks,
> river cutting through the valley.[63]

Daitō's pithy verse solves a number of problems concurrently. In characteristic Zen fashion, he speaks in the Buddha's voice as well as his own. Becoming the Buddha beyond form and sound, he (paradoxically) reveals his true form. Buddha/Daitō can indeed be seen by those who have the eye: just look at the clouds over the mountain, or the river in the valley, or anywhere else. The poem exemplifies Daitō's participation in Zen's shift from the philosophical to the literary. In poetry he found a means to express the inexpressible; such poetry was also a "separate transmission outside the teachings."

Because Zen language is so distinctive and unconventional—and because language is so consequential in Zen—learning Zen and learning its language are intimately related. As Dale Wright has observed, "Some degree of fluency in this language would be prerequisite to experiencing what Zen is about."[64] By extension, mastery of Zen discourse is a key indication of mastery in Zen. However, to recognize that some aspects of Zen experience are linguistically mediated is not to assert that enlightenment is reducible to language. Enlightenment may be an awakening *from* language, at least in the sense that one is less bound by false assumptions about language's referential capacity. Enlightenment may also be an awakening *to* language, "a transformation of how one dwells in the linguistically shaped cultural world that is the practitioner's inheritance."[65]

Thus the matter comes around full circle. What begins with a denial of language's ability to express enlightenment ends with a dialectically opposite claim—that it is possible for realization and expression to converge. If so, we must add one further category to the list of distinctive Zen rhetorical strategies: ordinary language used in ordinary ways. "Even in ordinary conversation," wrote Daitō, "an awakened person speaks in the voice of the Dharma."[66] And yet such speaking is also a kind of nonspeaking. According to Yün-men,

> Even if he talks all day, in reality nothing cleaves to his lips and teeth, for he has actually not spoken a single word.[67]

11

DAITŌ'S IMPACT

I'll join Shakyamuni in retirement.
DAITŌ CAPPING PHRASE

DAITŌ PASSED AWAY on a cold afternoon in the winter of 1337. The earliest account of his death, in Shunsaku's *Exploits of National Master Daitō,* asserts that on the twenty-second day of the twelfth month, after nine months of an unnamed illness, the master knew that he would soon take his last breath. Despite his weakened condition and a crippled left leg, he resolved to die in the traditional full-lotus posture. When he wrenched both legs into position, he broke his left leg at the knee, and blood began to seep through his robe. At this point, according to Shunsaku, Daitō still had the strength and the composure to write a four-line death verse in Chinese. He finished the poem, dropped his brush, and passed away sitting upright.[1]

Here again we confront the ambiguous interface between biography and hagiography. Because the attributes of an exemplary death had previously been articulated in Ch'an/Zen, influencing Daitō and his biographers alike, distinctions between fact and legend remain elusive. The following prayer, attributed to Ch'an master Ta-hui, is still chanted daily in many Japanese Zen monasteries:

> I wish to die with a premonition of death the week beforehand, with little pain or affliction, abiding serenely in the proper state of mind. At the end I would like to discard this body freely and be reborn quickly into a Buddha-realm, surrounded by buddhas. I want to receive their sanction of authentic enlightenment and take form in the Dharma realm, so that I may save all beings everywhere.[2]

For a Ch'an or Zen master, an ideal death traditionally included such elements as the prior confirmation of a successor, a last testament, a final poem, and the ability to pass away in the zazen posture. Daitō's determination to emulate the deaths of his eminent predecessors was undoubtedly inspired by this ideal and by previous hagiography. Though we cannot know which points Shunsaku may have embellished to fit the paradigm more closely, his dramatic description seized the imagination of later generations of Zen practitioners. At Daitokuji a bloodstained robe believed to have been Daitō's is still brought forth on special occasions.

Three texts in Daitō's own hand, penned during his final days or final hours, are extant. One of the documents concerned the Dharma robe Daitō had inherited from Nanpo, and another confirmed Tettō Gikō as Daitō's successor at Daitokuji. The third text is the master's death poem:

> I cut aside all buddhas and patriarchs,
> my Mind-sword honed to a razor edge.
> Activity's wheel begins to turn—
> emptiness gnashes its teeth.[3]

Even in appearance this verse is impressive: sixteen bold characters are perfectly spaced in four vertical rows, on a sizable scroll one yard wide and fourteen inches high (figure 5). The terseness of the language conveys the master's concentrated power, and each line specifies some kind of prodigious motion—cutting, honing, turning, or gnashing. Daitō begins by declaring that he has no further need for the sages of the past (having experienced buddhahood himself). A further implication is that the usual distinction between "enlightened" and "ignorant" beings no longer concerns him. The "Mind-sword" of the second line is a free translation of "Blown-hair [Sword]," a reference to a legendary sword so sharp that a hair blown against it would be severed instantly. A symbol of the enlightened wisdom that cuts through delusion, this sword appears in the last line of Lin-chi's death poem: "After the Blown-hair Sword is used, it must be quickly honed."[4] Having just used the sword to cut aside all buddhas, Daitō too must keep it burnished—by abandoning even the notion that he has cut off buddhas.

"Activity's wheel," in line three, was cited by Daitō thirty years earlier in the poem that marked his satori, another momentous transition. Whenever this wheel turns, an entirely new world is experienced. The most powerful line of the poem is the final one, "emptiness gnashes its teeth." Daitō himself, teeth clenching in pain, is none other than emptiness. At the same time, death is about to swallow the master whole, and yet death may be gnashing its teeth in defeat if Daitō is truly free of fear and attachment. In this poem and in Shunsaku's account of Daitō's death, it may appear that the master failed to achieve Ta-hui's aim of

FIGURE 5. DAITŌ'S DEATH VERSE. COURTESY OF DAITOKUJI.

"abiding serenely in the proper state of mind." But an enlightened Zen master is expected to transcend death by becoming one with it—if this is achieved, gnashing teeth may not differ from a buddha's sublime smile.

This death poem is a provocative artifact of Daitō's eloquent Zen. Whether composed in his final moments or prepared in advance, it shows the master upholding the conventions of his religious tradition and his cultural milieu, in which most of life's consequential experiences were also topics for poetry and calligraphy. The persistent influence of China can be seen in Daitō's choice of language *(kanbun)* and his allusion to Ch'an master Lin-chi. Visually, Daitō's stanza does not convey any of the messy, uncontrollable, or agonizing aspects of death. Not only did he beautifully arrange and balance the sixteen characters of the poem; he even included the month, his personal mark *(kaō)*, and a brief farewell: "Take care, head monk and congregation."[5] Ideally, a Zen master's skill in versification matched the depth of his religious experience (and vice versa). For Daitō's heirs at least, this scroll is a crowning emblem of Daitō's eloquent Zen, in which death is transmuted not only through insight but also through poetry and calligraphy.

Daitō's Sphere of Influence

Most of Daitō's medieval and modern chroniclers depict him as a leader in the Zen world of his period, and they suggest that Daitokuji had become a grand establishment by the time of its founder's death. "Soon the temple compound was filled with lofty towers and imposing gates, and Daitokuji became a major monastery," biographer Kokai exults.[6] Contemporary scholar Ogisu Jundō contends that Daitō was recognized early in his career as one of the two leading masters of the day, called "the two gates of sweet dew." Ogisu goes on to assert that Daitokuji "achieved even greater prominence" during Daitō's final years, when the center of government shifted from Kamakura to Kyoto.[7] Such claims inflate Daitō's initial accomplishments in the public realm. When he died in 1337, Daitokuji was a middle-sized temple, and the abbot's sphere of influence was commensurately limited. Unlike some of his contemporaries, Daitō had little impact on the politics of his age. Once the Ashikaga generals triumphed, he was unable to repudiate his association with Emperor Go-Daigo or protect his temple from an impending reversal of fortune. In contrast, Musō managed to keep one step ahead of the defeats of his patrons, and as a close advisor of the victorious Ashikaga, he participated directly in national policy toward religious institutions.

Only one reported incident between Daitō and a national leader touches on political issues. When Emperor Go-Daigo's first revolt aborted in 1331, he was forced to flee to Kasagidera in the Nara hills. From his besieged position, the Emperor allegedly sent a messenger to Daitō to ask, "What is the great meaning of the Buddha-Dharma?" The master replied, "When two armies face each other, there is nothing else."[8] This exchange is so cryptic that we cannot judge whether Go-Daigo was seeking consolation, political support, or spiritual guidance. Ogisu (writing during World War II) gives Daitō's response a bellicose interpretation: "When two armies face each other, the deep meaning of the Buddha-Dharma is none other than confronting the enemy's arrows and attacking head-on."[9] However Daitō's comment was understood at the time, it probably had little impact on Go-Daigo's military plans or spiritual development.

The fragility of Daitō's political position is underscored by an ill-fated episode involving one of his closest disciples. Takuan's *Chronicle* gives the following account in an entry of 1337:

> At this time the former emperor [Go-Daigo] had established his court at Kanao in Yoshino. The Master [Daitō] dispatched head monk Ryōgi with a message for the former emperor. The military regime had set up barrier guards and strictly regulated travel. This was the period when National Master Musō of Tenryūji won many converts, and he had followers within the military regime. A barrier guard said to head monk Ryōgi, "If you pretend to be a disciple of National Master Musō, you will escape and be allowed to pass through the barrier." Ryōgi replied, "Just to save my life, how could I dishonor the robe and bowl [of a monk]?" In the end he extended his neck, and it met the guard's bright sword blade. White milk flowed onto the ground.[10]

Takuan does not indicate whether Ryōgi's death had any repercussions; instead he cites another self-sacrificing Buddhist who bled white milk. Even if Takuan's account cannot be verified, it conveys the intensity of the discord that attended the rise of Japanese Zen.

The establishment of Myōshinji in the last year of Daitō's life is another source of information about the nature of his influence. Cooperating closely with retired emperor Hanazono, Daitō arranged to have Kanzan Egen, a senior disciple, installed as Myōshinji's resident master. Although this development confirmed Daitō's stature as founding abbot of Daitokuji, it may also have been prompted by the friction between the two courts: Daitō needed to strengthen his link to Hanazono once his alliance with Go-Daigo had become a liability. Daitō's apparent success in establishing a second monastery ironically led to a split in his lineage within a few generations (an outcome he may even have foreseen).

Though Ogisu claims that Daitō was one of the two most famous masters of his day, an incident in Shunsaku's *Exploits* inadvertently reveals the bounds of Daitō's influence within the Zen world. Immediately after describing Daitō's death, Shunsaku states:

> Ch'an master Ta-chien [Ch'ing-cho] was then abbot of Nanzenji. When he heard someone recite the Master's [Daitō's] death poem, he was surprised. "I never imagined that such a clear-eyed Zen master was to be found in Japan!" he exclaimed. "I wanted to meet him while he lived, but everyone resisted and I was prevented from doing so. Now I have many regrets." He wished to attend the Master's funeral service, but he was unable to go because he was performing prayer rituals for the court. He sent a monk to ask the time of the service, and as soon as the monk returned, he made a public announcement. Thereupon he led the assembly to the front gate of Nanzenji, chanting sutras, and he sent two personal attendants to present some incense in memorium.[11]

The émigré Chinese master Ch'ing-cho Cheng-ch'eng (Ta-chien, 1274–1339) was abbot of a major monastery across town from Daitokuji. His inability to meet Daitō or attend Daitō's funeral probably stemmed from political considerations—a Nanzenji abbot could not risk the appearance of support for a temple closely identified with Go-Daigo, and Daitō's prestige was not sufficient to override the factionalism of the day. Moreover, Ch'ing-cho's surprise upon hearing Daitō's death poem—"I never imagined that such a clear-eyed Zen master was to be found in Japan!"—hardly conveys the impression that Daitō's accomplishments were widely recognized in Zen circles.

Still, Shunsaku's primary intention in citing a Ch'an master's praise was to exalt Daitō, and Ch'ing-cho's reaction is in accord with a principal theme of the present study: Daitō was indeed one of the first Japanese monks to reach the level of his eminent Chinese predecessors in his mastery of Zen and Zen expression. The unquestioned assumption that Ch'ing-cho would have been able to make such a judgment after hearing a poem of sixteen words is evidence of the conviction that Zen realization can be conveyed through language, and especially through poetry.

Another important index of Daitō's immediate impact is the state of Daitokuji during his last years. Though the historical materials are far from complete, they enable us to assess three related topics: the temple compound, provincial landholdings, and the monastic population. In 1333 Go-Daigo confirmed the Kyoto precincts of Daitokuji, an area slightly over twelve acres. Though this was more than enough land to support a large-scale monastery, only two important buildings are known to have been erected during Daitō's tenure as abbot. One was the Dharma hall, inaugurated in 1326, and the other was the abbot's residence, which the Tendai abbot Gen'e allegedly donated. Ordinarily, a hall or pagoda dedicated to the founder would be added soon after his death, but Daitō specifically forbade such a memorial: "After I have gone, place my bones in the abbot's quarters. Do not build a separate memorial pagoda. I have my reasons, and I trust you to honor this request."[12] Accordingly, no founder's hall was ever built, and Daitō's memorial alcove, called Unmon-an, is still located within the traditional abbot's residence. Daitō's successor, Tettō, added a Buddha hall and the first Daitokuji subtemple, Tokuzenji. Most of Daitokuji's early architecture was destroyed by fire in the mid-fifteenth century, and the origins of other structures such as the main gate or the monks' hall cannot be determined. Compared to the major monasteries of Kyoto and Kamakura (and to its own later magnificence), the Daitokuji of Daitō's day must have been a relatively humble temple, its uncluttered compound surrounded by farmers' fields and quiet woods.

At Daitō's death the provincial landholdings of Daitokuji were impressive, at least on paper. Six of its revenue-producing estates enjoyed full immunity from intervention by local officials. When Go-Daigo issued his spate of decrees during the Kenmu Restoration, he inflated the temple's official income to 7,600 *koku* (a measure of rice by volume), capable of supporting two thousand monks.[13] This figure approaches the wealth of the largest Gozan temples at the height of their prestige; for example, Tenryūji received about 8,000 *koku* from its taxable domains in 1386.[14] However, Daitokuji never actualized the potential windfall from its patrons' grants: when Go-Daigo fell from power the year before Daitō's death, the temple's fortunes plummeted, and it was unable to enforce its claims. Thirty-five years later, its official income had declined by more than 80 percent, to a mere 433 *koku*.[15]

Without reliable records it is difficult to estimate the monastic population of Daitokuji during Daitō's last years. The biographers supply no figures, though Kokai claims that "students gathered in great numbers to hear the Master's teaching," and "monks ran to the Master from all directions."[16] The presence of a respected and charismatic teacher plus the glamor of patronage from two emperors undoubtedly attracted many aspiring disciples. A number does appear in Go-Daigo's 1333 decree, when he praises Daitokuji's "thousand monks [who] live in peace," but that is language appropriate to proclamations.[17] At one point in the *Record of Daitō* a monk asks Daitō to address the "seventy Zen Buddhists" in attendance."[18] Though no registers of monks remain from Daitō's time, his heir Tettō was a conscientious record keeper. Around 1368 Tettō listed the names of the monks at Daitokuji and two of its subtemples: Daitokuji had 180 monks, Shōden-an had 24, and Tokuzenji had 14. Because the names of most of the subtemple monks are duplicated on Daitokuji's list, the actual total is 191 monks.[19] These figures also suggest the extent of the monastic congregation that Daitō led, since the dual loss of Daitō's presence and Go-Daigo's patronage may well have been offset by Tettō's reinforcement of the temple's central and provincial organization. A community of about two hundred monks would have placed Daitokuji in the middle rank of Zen institutions: there were countless smaller temples, but half a dozen well-established monasteries had one thousand to two thousand residents.[20] Musō is said to have administered the precepts to a throng of 2,500 disciples just before his death in 1351.[21]

Destiny of a Zen Patriarch

Daitō's destiny as a Zen patriarch is complex: he continued to act upon history, and history continued to act upon him. His impact after his death in many respects exceeds his influence during his lifetime, a phenomenon that owes much to the eventual triumph of his religious descendants over all other lines of Japanese Rinzai Zen. Daitō was elevated to patriarchal status by his heirs, who enhanced his image consciously and unconsciously.

The dying master left Daitokuji in the hands of Tettō Gikō, his disciple during the years of obscurity at Ungo-an and the head monk of Daitokuji since its inauguration. Tettō, an able and energetic administrator, served as abbot for thirty-one years. He persuaded several well-known nobles and warriors to become personal disciples and temple patrons, stabilizing Daitokuji during a period of political and economic adversity. Tettō was so fervent in the guidance of his monks that he once threatened to cut off his own tongue unless someone attained *kenshō* during a ninety-day training session. Midway through the term Gongai Sōchū (1315–1390) came to enlightenment, and Gongai later became Tettō's principal successor.[22]

The disciple Daitō selected to be the first abbot of Myōshinji, Kanzan Egen, had joined him in 1329, late in the Zen careers of both men (Kanzan was five years older than Daitō). Two decades earlier they had briefly been fellow students of Nanpo. Under Daitō's guidance, Kanzan achieved satori through Yün-men's "Barrier," the same koan that had precipitated Daitō's enlightenment. At Myōshinji, Kanzan's best-known patron and follower was former emperor Hanazono, who maintained a residence on the temple grounds until his death in 1348. No written records of Kanzan's teachings remain. The claim that "he never lectured"[23] may be based on fact, or his discourse record may have been destroyed by fire.

Kanzan had only one Dharma heir, Juō Sōhitsu (1296–1380). Yet it was Kanzan's branch, not Tettō's, that ensured the survival of Daitō's lineage. The *Ōtōkan* lineage that represents the mainstream of present-day Rinzai Zen takes its name from Daiō (Nanpo), Dai*tō,* and *Kan*zan. The term itself is relatively late and of uncertain origin; scholars trace it to a period that begins with Gudō (1577–1661) and ends with Hakuin (1686–1769). During these years of Myōshinji's ascendancy and its rivalry with Daitokuji, a spurious "Final Admonitions" was attributed to Kanzan, and he was called a reincarnation of Yün-men (as Daitō had been identified). Kanzan continues to be honored for certain koans he favored, for the austerity of his way of life, and for his devotion to his two masters, Nanpo and Daitō. According to a Rinzai Zen adage, Daitō "left the temple to Daitokuji but the school to Myōshinji."[24]

For nearly a century and a half after Daitō's death, Japanese Zen was dominated by the Gozan, or "Five Mountains," network. The temples within this system were divided into three tiers, and rankings were adjusted periodically to reflect shifts in patronage or prestige. During the first half of the fourteenth century, enrollments in Gozan temples increased sharply, and by the early fifteenth century the institution embraced about three hundred active monasteries. As Martin Collcutt has written,

> The *gozan* was certainly the most socially influential, economically powerful sector of medieval Zen. Moreover, the fully articulated *gozan* network spread from Kyoto and Kamakura throughout all the provinces of Japan, and *gozan* monasteries served as centers for the introduction and diffusion not only of Zen Buddhism but also of Chinese learning and culture, contributing inestimably to the enrichment of medieval intellectual and cultural life.[25]

For political and sectarian reasons, Daitokuji and Myōshinji were denied the benefits of Gozan affiliation. In 1334, before the ascension of the Ashikaga, Go-Daigo had placed Daitokuji at the apex of the Gozan, but it enjoyed this honor for only a few years. It did not appear again in the Gozan rankings until 1386, having fallen to the ninth position of the second tier (tenth and last was Ryōshōji, a Daitokuji branch temple). Daitokuji apparently retained this lowly status until 1431, when it withdrew completely from the Gozan system. Myōshinji, labeled as a *rinka* ("under the forest") temple, was consistently excluded from all three tiers.

In contrast to the prosperity of the major Gozan monasteries, Daitokuji thus endured relative austerity for at least a century after Daitō's death. It lost four of its six provincial estates between 1334 and 1371, and its annual income fell to a mere 6 percent of the revenue collected by leading temples such as Tenryūji.[26] Budgetary constraints affected nearly every aspect of life at Daitokuji, from the maintenance of monastery buildings to the conduct of ceremonies. Myōshinji, no wealthier than Daitokuji, suffered a severe political reversal in 1399, when its abbot was accused of conspiring with the rebel warrior Ōuchi Yoshihiro (1356–1399). The irate shogun, Ashikaga Yoshimitsu, confiscated all of Myōshinji's Kyoto and provincial lands, changed the temple's name, and dispersed its monks. Barely forty years after Kanzan's death, this branch of Daitō's lineage was almost snuffed out.

It was during this low ebb in the fortunes of Daitō's descendants that the Daitokuji monk Shunsaku Zenkō began to compile the first biography of the former master. He completed his *Exploits of National Master Daitō* in 1426. As we have seen, this work portrayed its subject as a spiritual hero whose life was marked by extraordinary events, and it decisively shaped posterity's image of the master. According to Shunsaku, miraculous portents accompanied Daitō's conception and birth, and he was precociously insightful as a child. Daitō consistently impressed his teachers, inviting comparisons with Ch'an master Yün-men and prompting predictions of future success. This first biography also emphasized Daitō's patronage by two emperors, highlighting their proclamations, their conversations with the master, and the titles they gave him. As abbot of Daitokuji, "the Master had the majesty of a king, and people hesitated to approach him."[27] Shunsaku's memorable account of Daitō's death, completing the Ch'an/Zen paradigm of sacred biography, reinforced Daitō's elevation to patriarchal status.

A generation later, Ikkyū Sōjun became the first of several influential masters to contribute significantly to Daitō's reputation. Ikkyū, a member of Tettō's line, felt that he alone grasped the true spirit of Daitō's Zen. He called himself "Daitō's descendant" during a period of intensified rivalry between the lineages of Musō, Enni, Tettō, and Kanzan. A prolific poet, Ikkyū answered each of Daitō's "three turning words" in verse, and he composed quatrains in praise of Daitō, Tettō, Nanpo, and Hsü-t'ang. When Daitokuji was threatened by political turmoil and fire around the time of the Ōnin War (1467–1477), Ikkyū personally protected Daitō's calligraphy and other treasured items. As we have seen, he criticized biographer Shunsaku for his preoccupation with Daitō's imperial connections:

Holding aloft this Great Lamp would illuminate heaven.
Imperial carriages jostled before the Dharma hall
but no one recorded his life of wind and water
for twenty years at the Gojō Bridge.[28]

Ikkyū was the first to stress the Gojō Bridge story and may even have initiated it. His uncommon perception of Daitō was promptly rejected by Yōsō Sōi, presiding abbot of Daitokuji, who declared, "What need is there to speak of cold and hunger in the records of our former master's life?"[29] Ikkyū and Yōsō openly clashed on many issues, so it is hard to gauge the seriousness of this particular disagreement about Daitō's status as insider or outsider. Ikkyū, who set himself apart from the religious institutions of his day, understandably linked Daitō's years of obscurity and hardship to the authenticity of Daitō's Zen.

With new support from ascendant warriors and prosperous merchants, Daitokuji began to recover during Ikkyū's lifetime. Its link with the imperial family survived, and the involvement of poets and tea masters soon made the temple a center of contemporary culture. In the sixteenth century the country was torn by internal wars that weakened the authority of the Ashikaga regime and the Gozan system it sponsored. By the time Japan was reunified in 1603, Daitokuji and Myōshinji were as wealthy and influential as any of the Gozan monasteries. Daitokuji was lavishly patronized by the second of Japan's "three unifiers," Toyotomi Hideyoshi (1536–1598), who regularly visited the temple to participate in tea ceremonies. Myōshinji, meanwhile, had found other sources of strength: exemplary fiscal management, a network of provincial branch temples, and increasing popularity among lay believers. Myōshinji gained control of at least fifty monasteries formerly affiliated with the Gozan, and it eventually became the headquarters of the largest branch of Rinzai Zen.

Daitō's descendants continued to honor his memory in their training, their ceremonies, and their writings. Takuan Sōhō, the 154th abbot of Daitokuji and one of the most influential masters of the seventeenth century, produced the second biography of Daitō, adding dates and new material to the earlier account by Shunsaku. The Kanbun era of 1661–1673 marked the peak of Daitokuji's prosperity. Not only was the main temple replete with architecturally distinguished gates and halls, but each of the twenty-four subtemples boasted its own configuration of elegant buildings and meticulous gardens. The abundant paintings, ceramics, tea utensils, altar figures, screens, and calligraphic scrolls that Daitokuji accumulated over the centuries are among Japan's most valued artistic treasures. The temple's Zen gardens epitomize the best of the genre, and its tea rooms are prized as the fountainhead of the Japanese tea ceremony.

The most influential assessment of Daitō was made by the eight-eenth-century Zen master Hakuin Ekaku, traditionally ranked beside Dōgen at the pinnacle of Japanese Zen. Hakuin is hailed for restoring the spiritual vitality of the Rinzai sect through his emphasis on rigorous monastic training, his organization of the koan system, and his reaffir-mation of *kenshō* as the focus of the Zen life. Like Ikkyū centuries earlier, Hakuin believed that he had a uniquely intimate understanding of Daitō. The accounts of Daitō's life as a beggar impressed Hakuin deeply, perhaps because he was somewhat of an outsider himself: Hakuin's small country temple was located far from the Kyoto head-quarters of his Myōshinji lineage.

A gifted painter with a bold and untutored style, Hakuin produced portraits of Daitō as a bearded and barefoot mendicant, his robe tat-tered but his gaze fiercely alive. The inscription on one of these por-traits (figure 2 in Chapter 3) alludes to the story of Daitō's discovery by Emperor Hanazono:

> Wearing a straw mat among the beggars,
> through his greed for sweet melons
> he's been taken alive.[30]

The second line of this verse also suggests the intensity of Daitō's spirit-ual aspiration, which led to his "capture" by the world of enlighten-ment. In other works Hakuin related the ideal of unworldliness, as represented by Daitō's poverty, to genuine Zen:

> None of the patriarchal teachers had any taste for fine imposing mon-astery halls and pavilions. They placed no value at all on the enthusi-astic acclaim of the crowd. They passed their days in rude cave dwell-ings, boiling vegetable roots in broken pots to sustain themselves. They were bent only on repaying their profound debt to the buddhas and patriarchs, and on passing some syllable of enlightened utterance along to trouble future generations.[31]

In this passage we can hear echoes of Daitō's "Final Admonitions," a text Hakuin often transcribed.

Hakuin did not hesitate to add new episodes to the Daitō legends in order to communicate his sense of the master's character and insight. In an autobiographical work called *Wild Ivy (Itsumadegusa)*, Hakuin tells a lively tale not found in earlier sources:

> And what about Myōchō's [Daitō's] life of self-denial on the banks of the Kamo River? Each night, in order to test the strength of his reli-gious purpose, he went to the neighborhood of the Shijō [Gojō] Bridge and sat in zazen on a seat of grass. At the time, the young ruf-fians of the capital were a particular menace. Gathering in groups of three or four, they would begin arguing the merits of the swords they

carried; then, to test their weapons, they would proceed to the broad banks of the Kamo River and dash around cutting down the hapless beggars and outcasts whom they found there. Great numbers fell victim to their blades.

A band of these scoundrels stole unperceived into the area near the Shijō Bridge and came upon Myōchō meditating on his grass seat. He seemed an ideal victim. "I'll strike the first blow with my long sword," one of them called out. "You can take your turns next." The villains pressed toward the seated figure, threatening him this way and that with raised weapons.

But Myōchō showed not the slightest sign of fear. He just sat, bolt upright, with a calm and blissful unconcern. Then one of the ruffians paused, looked long and hard at him, and all at once pressed his palms together in veneration. "Even if we did cause the death of this excellent priest, it wouldn't really prove the sharpness of our blades," he said. "And think what terrible karma such an act would bring upon us!" With that, they dropped their swords and fled.

Myōchō later wrote a poem:

Hardships still come
one upon another—
now I'll see if my mind
truly has cast off
this world.

The story which occasioned these lines should inspire people for a thousand years. Myōchō's establishment of the illustrious Daitokuji and the enduring brilliance of his radiant virtue are consequences of the hard, merciless perseverance of his practice.[32]

The text considered to be Hakuin's foremost work is an extensive interlinear commentary on the first two volumes of the *Record of Daitō*, fancifully entitled *Tales from the Land of Locust-Tree Tranquility (Kaiankoku-go)*. Hakuin acknowledged the difficulty of Daitō's *Record*, calling it "a huge mass of fiery flames," and he insisted that it could truly be fathomed only after one had resolved seven cardinal koans, including Yünmen's "Barrier" and Daitō's own "three turning words."[33] Hakuin commented on Daitō's *Record* using thousands of colorful capping phrases and richly allusive capping verses, freely mixing original material with quotations from the religious and secular literature of East Asia. The resulting work, immensely challenging for monks and scholars alike, is esteemed as one of the crowning achievements of Japanese Rinzai Zen: "To this day nothing has surpassed it," writes Yanagida Seizan.[34] For the past two hundred years Daitō has largely been perceived through the eyes of Hakuin, whose vivid imagery and self-assured commentary yielded the decisive interpretation of Daitō's life and teachings.

One further dimension of Daitō's patriarchal rank is his reputation as one of the outstanding calligraphers of Japan. In Zen, a work of calligraphy is regarded as an intimate expression of the writer's personality and awareness, analogous to a snapshot of the mind. Daitō's distinctive style fuses vigor and elegance. Connoisseurs, searching for a comparison, mention Huang T'ing-chien (1045–1105), an eminent Chinese calligrapher who preceded Daitō by two centuries. In Japan, most of Daitō's calligraphic pieces have been designated as "national treasures" or "important cultural properties," and his work is regularly featured in books, journals, and exhibitions.[35] Daitokuji's collection of Zen calligraphy, augmented by several of Daitō's successors, has been called "one of the finest in existence."[36] As a synthesis of Zen experience, language, and art, Daitō's calligraphy epitomizes his eloquent Zen.

Daitō and Contemporary Zen

Today Daitokuji is one of the fifteen headquarter temples of the Rinzai sect. Its nationwide organization embraces two active monasteries (in Kyoto and Fukuoka, Kyushu), about 200 branch temples, and over 50,000 adherents. In institutional terms, Daitokuji is surpassed by Myōshinji, which has reported 3,421 branch temples and 847,700 adherents.[37] Daitō's legacy survives not only in the monks' halls of Daitokuji and Myōshinji, but also in Rinzai monasteries throughout the country. Most Rinzai monks recite Daitō's "Final Admonitions" daily, before their master's Dharma lecture or at the end of the day. The importance of postenlightenment training is often associated with Daitō and the twenty years he allegedly spent among the beggars of Kyoto. Standard koan collections include Daitō's "three turning words," two encounter dialogues from his *Record*,[38] and the following conundrum:

> Daitō Kokushi is called the reincarnation of Yün-men, but they were separated by several hundred years. What was he doing all that time?[39]

The capping-phrase exercise has become an integral part of Rinzai monastic training, though there is little correlation between Daitō's phrases and those now in use. (Despite the pioneering role of Daitō's capping-phrase commentaries, they are known only by a few scholars and Daitokuji abbots.) In the current system, students working on koans consult the master in a private encounter known as *sanzen*. During intensive training periods *(sesshin)*, participants may be required to confront the master four or five times a day. When a practitioner has answered an assigned koan to the master's satisfaction, he or she must then express the spirit of that koan with a suitable phrase or verse taken from one of the standard capping-phrase collections. Though the capping phrases themselves are not secret, their application as koan answers is strictly guarded by the various Rinzai lineages.

In anticipation of the next encounter with the master, the student uses every spare moment to pore over pocket-sized editions of the capping-phrase anthologies, a task that must be handled discreetly in the monastery (where reading is discouraged). At each subsequent *sanzen* a different phrase or verse is offered until one of them wins the master's approval. Difficulties may be encountered at any point of the process: a koan that was solved with relative ease may be hard to cap, or an unusually obstinate koan, once solved, will be capped effortlessly. When multiple capping phrases are required for a given koan, the first few may be found quickly, but those that remain may seem to defy discovery. Unearthing a made-to-order phrase or verse usually elicits an "aha!" from the student that the teacher then validates. Ideally, an apt capping phrase will shed new light on the koan and/or stimulate new questions to be pondered. At times, however, the traditional answer expected by the master, once discovered, may strike the practitioner as inferior to previous choices that the master rejected.

In later stages of training, most koans are divided into parts, each of which requires an answer and (usually) a capping phrase. For example, the koan known as "Lin-chi's Four Classifications" divides naturally into four segments:

> To take away the man and not take away the surroundings.
> To take away the surroundings and not take away the man.
> To take away both the man and the surroundings.
> To take away neither the man nor the surroundings.[40]

When Daitō commented on this koan, he added only one capping phrase to each of the four lines (case 8 in the following chapter). At Daitokuji today, the capping-phrase exercise is more structured and more complex. For each line of this koan a monk must select six or seven capping phrases of various kinds, in a specified sequence. Then he must find one final phrase that caps the koan in its entirety. Other koans are divided and capped in a similar manner; an especially complicated one may require as many as fifty different phrases. Monks who remain in the monastery long enough to approach the end of the formal course of training also use capping phrases in written commentaries on koans. Often these essays are composed in *kanbun* and transcribed with a brush.

However tenuous the historical links between Daitō's use of capping phrases and the contemporary system, a comparison is revealing. Whereas Daitō created his own phrases or quoted material from a wide range of sources, practitioners are now limited to the phrases and verses that appear in the standard collections. Whereas Daitō varied his responses to a koan or a text each time he encountered it, tradition now specifies which answers are acceptable. Daitō actually marks a midpoint in the gradual formalization of the genre. While most of Yüan-wu's comments were inventive and colloquial, Daitō already exhibits the Japanese penchant for quoting other sources, especially if they have literary merit. The frequency of Chinese poetic couplets confirms this trend: Yüan-wu disregarded them, Daitō cited them occasionally, and the modern capping-phrase corpus is dominated by them.[41]

Within the Daitokuji compound, on the twenty-second day of each month, the current abbots of the twenty-four subtemples assemble for a memorial service in honor of their founder. The ceremony begins with the chanting of invocations and sutras in the Buddha hall, and then the abbots proceed to Daitō's memorial alcove in the traditional abbot's quarters. There they place flowers, green tea, and other offerings before a life-size wooden effigy of the master. In November of each year this service is performed publicly in the Dharma hall.[42] Those in attendance include a representative of the imperial family, prominent tea masters, dozens of abbots from other temples, and all the monks of Daitokuji and Myōshinji.

Fifty-year anniversaries of Daitō's death are commemorated with even greater pomp and solemnity. The week-long 650th anniversary, held in May 1983, drew over three thousand guests from around the country.[43] Daitō's effigy was moved to a towering dais in the brightly bannered Dharma hall, where scores of tonsured abbots in ornate robes performed nine separate memorial services. Emperor Shōwa (1901–1989) sent a personal donation and formally granted Daitō another posthumous title.[44] A new woodblock edition of the *Record of Daitō,* a replica of the 1621 printing, was distributed to selected guests. Two major publishing projects also commemorated the event: a three-volume collection of Daitokuji's calligraphic treasures and a multivolume compilation of the discourse records of Daitokuji's leading abbots.[45]

"Almost the Same Path!"

Soon after he attained enlightenment, Daitō rushed to his teacher Nanpo and exclaimed, "Almost the same path!"[46] That capping phrase can also be generalized to apply to the Japanese reception of Ch'an and to Daitō's place in the transmission process. "Almost the same path!" has the polysemous quality of most capping phrases, in part because the original *kanbun* lacks a stated subject or a clear referent for the word "same." As a consequence, the phrase continues to resonate meaningfully even in broader contexts.

When he experienced enlightenment, Daitō had been struggling with

Yün-men's answer, "Barrier," the kernel of the koan "Ts'ui-yen's Eyebrows." In that light, one way of expanding Daitō's original phrase would be as follows: "My path is almost the same as Yün-men's path." Daitō may also be pointing beyond Yün-men to the entire lineage of Ch'an masters, and since he is addressing Nanpo, his statement can also mean "My path is almost the same path as yours." (These variations are of course compatible.) The word "almost" introduces additional interpretive possibilities. If Daitō is refusing to place himself on the same level as his spiritual predecessors, "almost" could indicate humility. Or, it may actually signify its opposite—a claim by Daitō that his enlightenment is *exactly the same* as the enlightenment of Ch'an masters such as Yün-men. In Zen, "as soon as you call it something, you've already missed the mark," so if Daitō had said, "Exactly the same path!" he would only have been close.

Viewed from yet another angle, Daitō may be saying, "I almost took the same path as my predecessors. How fortunate that I did not!" In that case, he is asserting that one must find one's own way to realization; to follow Yün-men or any other predecessor is to go astray. Yün-men is Yün-men, and Daitō is Daitō; whatever the similarities between any two individuals, each has his or her own path. In its original context, therefore, Daitō's initial response to his own enlightenment may reflect a spirit of humility, confidence, independence, or even all three at once.

Moreover, each of these senses of "Almost the same path!" caps Daitō's life as well as his enlightenment. In terms of the spark of spiritual continuity that is believed to transcend differences of history and culture, Daitō may indeed have walked the way of his Buddhist forebears. Japanese Zen was not quite the same path as Chinese Ch'an—socially, institutionally, or doctrinally—yet it was a legitimate heir of the parent tradition, authentic and vital on its own terms. In the posture of humility suggested by "almost," Daitō consciously struggled to master the language and forms of Ch'an, aware that the roots of a Japanese Zen were not yet deep in his native soil. In a posture of confidence ("almost" as "exactly"), he treated the history of Ch'an as his own religious history, acknowledging himself as a worthy descendant of this unitary lineage. And in a posture of independence (avoiding the error of imitation), Daitō eloquently articulated his own vision of authentic Zen. Eventually, the path he forged became the main highway of the Japanese Rinzai tradition.

As for Daitō the man, after the passage of nearly seven centuries certain features will inevitably remain in shadow. We have seen how historical and religious truth are conjoined in the accounts of his life. Most of the traditional descriptions of Daitō encountered in these pages reveal as much about the prevailing ideal for Zen masters as they reveal about Daitō. Emperor Go-Daigo, who knew the master personally, nonetheless claimed that his "severe and awe-inspiring manner made it impossible for anyone to approach him."[47] Later portrayals by Daitoku-ji monks were even more grandiose: "His eyes scanned the universe, and his mouth swallowed buddhas and patriarchs. With thunderclap shouts and a rain of blows, he rattled the heavens and split the earth."[48] Assessments by modern scholars have been suggestive but spare. Daitō's impressive mastery of the Chinese language prompts Haga Kōshirō to call him a "genius."[49] Ogisu Jundō, citing Shunsaku's hagiographic description of the infant Daitō, argues that the master's character was "different from that of ordinary people even at birth."[50] Hirano Sōjō sees "two paradoxical aspects" of Daitō—his preference for seclusion and his eagerness to promote Daitokuji. Though this analysis is plausible, the career of Musō Soseki has been described in exactly the same terms.[51] Furuta Shōkin attempts a comparison of Daitō and Musō based on their calligraphy: "Musō's brushwork is pliable and conscientious, whereas Daitō's is vigorous and unaffected. . . . The two men were direct opposites."[52]

Some commentators have extrapolated from a well-known portrait of Daitō at age fifty-three (figure 6). In that work he is sitting cross-legged on a delicate Chinese chair, dressed in the formal robes of an abbot, his stocky body massively composed. The master's broad face is softened by rounded cheeks and rosy lips, and he is glancing off to his left. The inscription, by Daitō himself, challenges each viewer: "Who has been painted here on this new silk? Look!"[53] In the fifteenth century Ikkyū responded to this painting with admiration:

> Even his portrait shines openly,
> brilliant as a hundred million Sumerus.
> If Te-shan or Lin-chi were to enter here,
> they'd be fireflies before the sun.[54]

Viewing this same portrait centuries later, Hirano sees the look on Daitō's face as troubled, an expression that Hirano attributes to the competition between the master's two imperial patrons. To Furuta, however, the painting clearly conveys Daitō's indomitable will power.[55] If Daitō the man continues to elude capture, it may be for the best. As Shin'ei Sōetsu (1691–1775) wrote in a postscript to one of the master's early biographies,

> Why shoot the arrow
> after the robber has already left?
> The empty sky claps its hands
> and shouts "Enough!"[56]

FIGURE 6. PORTRAIT OF DAITŌ, 1334. COURTESY OF DAITOKUJI.

12

TRANSLATIONS

Selected Poems by Daitō

Sources for the following poems are indicated in the notes, according to the number at the left of the title. Titles have been added or modified for clarity.

1   Pilgrimage

The moon and the sun my sandals,
I'm journeying above heaven and earth.

2   Rain

No umbrella, getting soaked,
I'll just use the rain as my raincoat.

3   Leaving Kyushu

No footprints of mine are seen
wherever I wander:
on a tip of a hair I left the capital,
on three drum taps I am leaving Kyushu.

4   Shakyamuni Is Called

Śuddha-āvāsa, hands palm-to-palm, appears at the window.

> Full moon in the palace pond a gem
> though it's not yet autumn;
> this quiet night he knows the ripples have changed.
> From here he'll walk the path as if deluded,
> huge Dantaloka Mountain hard as iron.

5   Zazen

> How boring to sit idly on the floor,
> not meditating, not breaking through.
> Look at the horses racing along the Kamo River!
> That's zazen!

6   Through the Clouds

> Penetrating the clouds to the sky beyond,
> even on a rainy night I see the moon.

7   Enlightenment (I)

> I've broken through Cloud Barrier—
>   the living way is north south east and west.
> Evenings I rest, mornings I play,
>   no other no self.
> With each step a pure breeze rises.

8   Enlightenment (II)

> Cloud Barrier pierced, the old path's gone—
>   clear sky bright sun my true home.
> Activity's wheel turns freely beyond men.
> Golden Kāśyapa departs,
>   hands clasped on his chest.

9   Shakyamuni's Great Awakening

> One glance at the morning star, and the snow got even whiter.
> The look in his eye chills hair and bones.

If earth itself hadn't experienced this instant,
Old Shakyamuni never would have appeared.

10   Te-shan Summons Kao-t'ing

When Te-shan was leaving the Yangtze, he summoned Kao-t'ing. Kao-
t'ing left Heng-ch'ü.

> Te-shan's invitation is
>   one two three four five six seven
>   and eight nine ten,
> Kao-t'ing's departure is
>   ten nine eight seven six five four
>   and three two one.

11   Great Activity, Great Function

> If you clutch Mt. Sumeru and smash it to pieces,
> emptiness will break in two, three, four.
> If you swallow the great ocean then vomit it up,
> buddhas in the three worlds will flounder and drown.

12   Spring

> The spring hills are blue,
> the spring waters green,
> the spring clouds are scattered,
> the spring birds chirp ceaselessly.

13   What's Your Name?

Yang-shan asked San-sheng, "What is your name?" San-sheng said,
"Hui-chi." Yang-shan said, "Hui-chi? That's me." San-sheng said,
"My name is Hui-jan." Yang-shang laughed aloud.

Where did he go?

> Sun melts the early spring snow,
> willows and plum trees vie for the freshest smell.
> Every scene inspires innumerable poems,
> but I seek the lines of just one man, off on his own.

14   No Dharmas

P'an-shan instructed, "There are no dharmas in the three realms; where can mind be sought?"

Rain clears from distant peaks, dew glistens frostily.
Moonlight glazes the front of my ivied hut among the pines.
How can I tell you how I am, right now?
A swollen brook gushes in the valley darkened by clouds.

15   The Summit of Wonder Peak

Once when Pao-fu and Ch'ang-ch'ing were strolling in the mountains, Pao-fu pointed with his hand and said, "Right here is the summit of Wonder Peak." Ch'ang-ch'ing said, "Indeed it is, but what a shame!" Hsüeh-tou comments: "Today what's the purpose of strolling in the mountains with this fellow?" Hsüeh-tou again comments: "Hundreds of thousands of years hence, I don't say there will not be any, just that there will be few." Later this [original incident] was quoted to Ching-ch'ing, who said, "If it hadn't been for Mr. Sun [Ch'ang-ch'ing], then you would have seen skulls all over the fields."

The lone tip of Wonder Peak is beyond any climber's reach.
One can only see white clouds drifting this way and that.
Thick pine and cypress forests—how old could they be?
Still, in rare moments birds along the steep cliffs sing.

16   Buddhas

Nan-ch'üan said, "I don't know anything about buddhas in the three worlds."

If he had known buddhas exist
   in the three worlds,
suddenly no spring flowers,
no full moon in the fall.

17   An Ancient Buddha and a Bare Pillar

Yün-men said to the assembled monks, "The ancient Buddha is merging with the bare pillar. What level of activity is that?" Answering for the monks, he said, "When clouds gather on South Mountain, rain falls on North Mountain."

Ablaze in Buddha's light, what level of activity?
Few people know what lies behind clouds on South Mountain.
At dusk, woodcutters follow the path into the valley,
singing, "We're on our way home, on our way home."

18   Fox-words

"Delusion," "enlightenment"—
just fox-words fooling
Zen monks everywhere.

19   The Leaves of the Sutras

After the Buddha's passing, Kāśyapa announced to the assembled
monks, "The Buddha has now been cremated. His adamantine relic-
bones are not our concern. We must compile a record of the authentic
Dharma teachings so that they are not lost."

Cut in thirds, split in half, how can truth be expressed?
Can one see beyond white clouds with the naked eye?
The monks still have not come back from Mt. Kukkuṭapāda.
The leaves of the sutras merely stir a sad wind.

20   Snow in a Silver Bowl

A monk asked Pa-ling, "What is the school of Āryadeva?" Pa-ling said,
"Snow piled in a silver bowl."

The school of Āryadeva is so hard to analyze.
Snow piled up in a silver bowl—who could have said it
    better than that?
The same wind blows across earth, mountains, rivers;
it leaves all human and heavenly realms refreshed, pure.

21   Nan-ch'üan Cuts the Cat

Holding up a cat for everyone to see,
cutting it one, two, three—
a hammer head without a hole.

22   Huang Ch'ao's Sword

Yen-t'ou asked a monk, "Where have you come from?" The monk
said, "I've come from the Western Capital [Ch'ang-an]." Yen-t'ou

said, "After Huang Ch'ao left, were you able to get the sword?" The monk said, "I got it." Yen-t'ou extended his neck toward the monk and shouted. The monk said, "Your head has fallen, Master." Yen-t'ou laughed loudly. Later the monk called upon Hsüeh-feng. Hsüeh-feng asked, "Where have you come from?" The monk said, "From Yen-t'ou." Hsüeh-feng asked, "What did he say?" The monk told the preceding story. Hsüeh-feng hit him thirty times and drove him away.

> Once Huang Ch'ao has left, that sword is hard to find.
> Waving it around, the monk cut his own hands—pitiful!
> If he hadn't been hit thirty times with a gnarled staff
> the whole world would have been soaked with blood.

23   Chao-chou's Sandal

Chao-chou removed his sandal and put it on his head.

> Chao-chou crowns himself with a sandal—
> three, two, one, heaven becomes earth,
> earth becomes heaven.

24   The Kalpa Fire

A monk asked Ta-sui, "In the roar of the kalpa fire, the whole universe is destroyed. Tell me, is This destroyed?" Ta-sui said, "Destroyed." The monk said, "Then [This] will go along with [the destruction of the universe]?" Ta-sui said, "It goes along with it."

> It perishes in the kalpa fire and can't be recovered.
> This monk, going back and forth from distant Szechuan,
> sees the equality of a thousand worlds.
> That radiant old Buddha Ta-sui opens his mouth and laughs.

25   Recovery

> It's over, the "buddhas and patriarchs" disease
> that once gripped my chest.
> Now I'm just an ordinary man
> with a clean slate.

26   Tattered Sleeve

> So many years of begging,
> this robe's old and torn;

tattered sleeve chases a cloud.
Beyond the gate, just grass.

27   Facing Death

I cut aside all buddhas and patriarchs,
my Mind-sword honed to a razor edge.
Activity's wheel beings to turn—
emptiness gnashes its teeth.

28   Falling into Hell

Who is falling alive into hell?
Lin-chi shouts "Ho!"
Te-shan hits you!

29   Here I Am

No form, no sound—
here I am;
white clouds fringing the peaks,
river cutting through the valley.

Daitō's Capping-Phrase Commentaries: Twenty Cases

The following selections are from two of Daitō's written capping-phrase
commentaries: *One Hundred Twenty Cases (Hyakunijussoku)* and *Capping
Phrases on the Blue Cliff Record (Hekigan agyo)*.[30] The cases are presented in
order of increasing structural complexity. Case 1 is a single sentence
with a single capping phrase. Case 4 is the first instance of multiple capping phrases: Daitō gives three responses to one question. Interlinear
capping phrases begin with case 6, and the capping phrases in all
remaining cases are interlinear. Cases 9 through 15 are dialogues
between two persons; in case 16 the number of protagonists jumps to
four. Case 18 is a complicated koan with two capping phrases by
Hsüeh-tou already embedded in it. In case 20 a monk has two separate
dialogues with two different masters.

Three of the koans to follow played a role in Daitō's early Zen training. They are "A Dying Snake," "An Ox Passes Through the Window," and "Ts'ui-yen's Eyebrows [Yün-men's Barrier]." The first
koan in the *Blue Cliff Record* ("Emperor Wu Questions Bodhidharma")
and the first koan in the *Gateless Barrier* ("Chao-chou's Mu") are
included because of their importance in Ch'an/Zen. Daitō commented

on some material more than once, so various comparisons are possible. Cases 16 and 17 present two sets of capping phrases on the same koan. Case 5 and poem 14 (preceding section) deal with one koan; case 10 and poem 20 deal with another koan. For "The Kalpa Fire," two sets of capping phrases and one poem have been translated (cases 14 and 15, poem 24). Three responses to "The Summit of Wonder Peak" are also presented (cases 18 and 19, poem 15).

Not all of the cases are formal koans. For example, in cases 1, 3, and 8, Daitō excerpted material from the *Record of Lin-chi*. When Daitō does cite a koan, he may give the full version or a shortened one; for instance, he uses the long (and less familiar) version of "Chao-chou's Mu."

Daitō's capping phrases are italicized below. The note at the end of each case provides bibliographic information and a key to Appendix II, where characters for all of the capping phrases may be found. For clarity, the titles of some of the cases have been modified.

Case 1   Huang-po Strikes Lin-chi

Huang-po struck Lin-chi sixty times.
  The sun appears and the moon disappears. [31]

Case 2   A Dying Snake

An ancient said, "When you encounter a dying snake in the road, don't beat it to death. Carry it home in a bottomless basket."
  All right. [32]

Case 3   A Man on the Road

Lin-chi ascended the abbot's seat and said, "There is a man who is on the road but has never left home. And there is another man who has left his home but is not on the road."
  Where the white clouds are deep, a golden dragon dances. [33]

Case 4   An Ox Passes Through the Window

Wu-tsu [Fa-]yen said, "An ox passes through the window. His head, horns, and four legs all go through. But why can't the tail pass too?"
  One game, two victories.
  Under a peony, a kitten naps.
  Someone else would not have been able to trace the footprints. [34]

Case 5   No Dharmas

P'an-shan instructed, "There are no dharmas in the three realms; where can mind be sought?"

> *The sky cannot cover it, the earth cannot uphold it.*
> *No road to advance upon, no gate to retreat through.*
> *The iron ball has no seams.*
> *The sky is high in the southeast, the earth is low in the northwest.* [35]

Case 6   The Three Mysteries

The mystery within the essence.
> *Mt. Sumeru.*

The mystery within the phrase.
> *Ring of Iron Mountain.*

The mystery within the mystery.
> *The Eighth Sea.* [36]

Case 7   Tou-shuai's Three Turning Words

Tou-shuai gave three turning words: "You search through grasses and investigate profundities, in order to see your true nature. Right at this moment, where is your true nature?"

> *The moon is bright, the wind is pure.*

"If you've seen your true nature you are free from life-and-death. How will you be free in your final moments, as the light is failing?"

> *Pure wind, bright moon.*

"If you've freed yourself from life-and-death, you know where you will go. So when the four elements disperse, where will you go?"

> *Pure wind, bright moon.* [37]

Case 8   Lin-chi's Four Classifications

Lin-chi gave four classifications: "To take away the man and not take away the surroundings."

> *A poor man thinks about his unpaid debts.*

"To take away the surroundings and not take away the man."

> *The foreign monk [Bodhidharma] sits at Shao-lin.*

"To take away both the man and the surroundings."

> *The old mouse drags raw ginger.*

"To take away neither the man nor the surroundings."

> *General Li shoots a stone tiger with an arrow.* [38]

Case 9   Who Is the Master?

A monk asked Hsiang-lin, "Who is the master of the vast unculti-
vated rice field?"
   To put a nail in a tree.
Hsiang-lin said, "Look, look! The twelfth month is coming to
an end."
   To buy iron and receive gold. [39]

Case 10   Snow in a Silver Bowl

A monk asked Pa-ling, "What is the school of Āryadeva?"
   To beat the grass and see a snake.
   Gold is tested with fire.
Pa-ling said, "Snow piled in a silver bowl."
   A white horse enters the reed flowers.
   *Since long ago, a white cloud has been sleeping among the reed
      flowers.* [40]

Case 11   Chao-chou's Mu

A monk asked Chao-chou, "Does a dog have Buddha-nature
or not?"
   His tongue is already long.
Chao-chou said, *"Mu."*
   To buy iron and receive gold.
   Completely fills emptiness.
   To throw a holeless iron hammer head right at him.
The monk said, "Even creeping creatures all have Buddha-nature.
Why wouldn't a dog have Buddha-nature?"
   Why doesn't he get control of himself and leave?
Chao-chou said, "Because it has its karmic nature."
   The old thief has met complete defeat. [41]

Case 12   Wash Your Bowls

A monk said to Chao-chou, "I've just entered the monastery.
Please teach me."
   To open the mouth is to err.
Chao-chou asked, "Have you eaten your breakfast?"
   Spilled his guts and disgorged his heart.
The monk said, "Yes I have."
   To move the tongue is to slander.

Chao-chou said, "Then go and wash your bowls."
A double koan.
The monk gained insight.
The iron ball has no seams.[42]

Case 13   Emperor Wu Questions Bodhidharma

Emperor Wu of Liang asked the geat master Bodhidharma, "What
is the highest principle of the holy teachings?"
Didn't think he could ask.
Bodhidharma said, "Vast emptiness, nothing holy."
One slab of iron stretching ten thousand miles.
Thrust out right in front.
Stars in the sky, rivers on the earth.
The Emperor said, "Who is facing me?"
What a pity!
Bodhidharma replied, "I don't know."
Completely fills emptiness.
The moon is bright, the wind is pure.[43]

Case 14   The Kalpa Fire (I)

A monk asked Ta-sui, "In the roar of the kalpa fire, the whole uni-
verse is destroyed."
Spilled his guts and disgorged his heart.
"Tell me, is This destroyed?"
Why don't you go right away?
Ta-sui said, "Destroyed."
Spilled his guts and disgorged his heart.
The monk said, "Then [This] will go along with [the destruction of
the universe]?"
So pitiful and sad.
Ta-sui said, "It goes along with it."
A double koan.[44]

Case 15   The Kapla Fire (II)

A monk asked Ta-sui, "In the roar of the kalpa fire, the whole uni-
verse is destroyed. Tell me, is This destroyed?"
The exhausted fish is stuck in shallow water.
By asking, one is able to get it for the first time.
Ta-sui said, "Destroyed."
Knead it but it won't form a ball.

The monk said, "Then [This] will go along with [the destruction of the universe]?"

> *To stumble without knowing it.*
> *To delude oneself and follow after things.*

Ta-sui said, "It goes along with it."

> *Cannot be split apart.* [45]

Case 16   Ts'ui-yen's Eyebrows (I)

At the end of the summer retreat, Ts'ui-yen said to the assembly, "All summer long I've been talking to you. Look and see if my eyebrows are still there."

> *Where the white clouds are deep, a golden dragon dances.*
> *What public office is without secrecy?*
> > *What water is without fish?*
> *It's hard to bore a nine-curved hole into a jewel.*
> *Hundreds of birds hover over their chicks.*
> *To come out evenly.*

Pao-fu said, "In his heart the thief is afraid."

> *Though the Chien-ko Road is steep,*
> > *travelers are even more numerous at night.*
> *To arrest all with one warrant.*

Ch'ang-ch'ing said, "Grown."

> *The patterns of the mountain flowers resemble brocade;*
> > *the waters of the lakes are blue as indigo.*
> *Unable to leap out.*

Yün-men said, "Barrier."

> *The watchman steals at night.*
> *Sons cover up for their fathers.*
> *Reversing the error and getting it right.* [46]

Case 17   Ts'ui-yen's Eyebrows (II)

At the end of the summer retreat, Ts'ui-yen said to the assembly, "All summer long I've been talking to you. Look and see if my eyebrows are still there."

> *He hides his body but his shadow shows.*
> *There is an echo in his words.*

Pao-fu said, "In his heart the thief is afraid."

> *Those walking together certainly understand.*
> *His eyes look toward the southeast, but his heart is in the northwest.*

Ch'ang-ch'ing said, "Grown."

Pine [needles] are straight, thorns are crooked.

The color of pines is not old or new.

Yün-men said, "Barrier."

To decide the sentence according to the criminal's confession.

The shrimp cannot leap out of the wooden dipper.

To arrest all with one warrant.

Hsüeh-tou comments: "To lose one's money and suffer punishment."

To add error to error. [47]

Case 18   The Summit of Wonder Peak (I)

Once when Pao-fu and Ch'ang-ch'ing were strolling in the mountains, Pao-fu pointed with his hand and said, "Right here is the summit of Wonder Peak."

The measuring stick is in his hand.

A pair of flags struck by lightning.

Ch'ang-ch'ing said, "Indeed it is, but what a shame!"

In the same hole the soil does not differ.

Hsüeh-tou comments: "Today what's the purpose of strolling in the mountains with this fellow?"

The pine accompanies the sound of the wind.

One victory, two games.

Hsüeh-tou again comments: "Hundreds of thousands of years hence, I don't say there will not be any, just that there will be few."

Later this [original incident] was quoted to Ching-ch'ing, who said, "If it hadn't been for Mr. Sun [Ch'ang-ch'ing], then you would have seen skulls all over the fields."

To add error to error.

Hitting both with one blow. [48]

Case 19   The Summit of Wonder Peak (II)

Once when Pao-fu and Ch'ang-ch'ing were strolling in the mountains, Pao-fu pointed with his hand and said, "Right here is the summit of Wonder Peak."

Wind blows but does not enter, water washes but does not touch.

Ch'ang-ch'ing said, "Indeed it is, but what a shame!"

After a long journey you know your horse's strength;

*   after long years together you know another's mind.*

Hsüeh-tou comments: "Today what's the purpose of strolling in the mountains with this fellow?"

Above, no supports for climbing; below, self is extinguished.
Two stone statues whisper into each other's ears.

Hsüeh-tou again comments: "Hundreds of thousands of years hence, I don't say there will not be any, just that there will be few."

One hand lifts up, one hand presses down.
Half open, half closed.
A thousand soldiers are easy to get, but a single general is hard to find.

Later this [original incident] was quoted to Ching-ch'ing, who said, "If it hadn't been for Mr. Sun [Ch'ang-ch'ing], then you would have seen skulls all over the fields."

A close friend understands, but who else understands?
Few people nurture others, many people thwart others. [49]

Case 20   Huang Ch'ao's Sword

Yen-t'ou asked a monk, "Where have you come from?"

He reveals his dynamism in his words.

The monk said, "I've come from the Western Capital [Ch'ang-an]."

There is an echo in his words.

Yen-t'ou said, "After Huang Ch'ao left, were you able to get the sword?"

There are thorns in the soft mud.

The monk said, "I got it."

To stumble without knowing it.

Yen-t'ou extended his neck toward the monk and shouted.

The thief in the grass has met complete defeat.

The monk said, "Your head has fallen, Master."

Recklessly he inserts needles.

Yen-t'ou laughed loudly.

His tongue has bones.

Later the monk called upon Hsüeh-feng.

He loves fragrant grasses, and he can't stop [seeking them].

Hsüeh-feng asked, "Where have you come from?"

A weed-tipped fishing pole.

The monk said, "From Yen-t'ou."

Seeking it from others is forbidden.

Hsüeh-feng asked, "What did he say?"

Falling into the weeds and seeking someone.

The monk told the preceding story.

His losses are not slight.

Hsüeh-feng hit him thirty times and drove him away.

To insert the needle where it hurts. [50]

Gleanings from Daitō's Capping Phrases

Daitō quoted or composed 2,279 capping phrases in his three written capping-phrase commentaries.[51] Though he used the vast majority of these phrases only once, he also favored a core group: 24 phrases appear 10 or more times throughout the corpus. The phrase he repeated most often (27 times) was "One slab of iron stretching ten thousand miles." The 230 phrases translated and arranged here are a representative sample of the comments Daitō added to the Ch'an classics. For reference, the phrases are numbered in the right-hand column. Appendix II gives the Chinese characters for each phrase, and Appendix III leads to an index that provides the locations of each phrase in Daitō's three commentaries.

A real Zen master!

Unusual even amidst the unusual.

Don't call him a novice.

All right.

That's fine too.

Just so, just so.

I am not equal to you.

Mistake.

Wasted effort.

Blind.   (10)

To add error to error.

A fellow who is always playing with mudpies.

Such dullness kills people.

Already fallen to a secondary level.

He doesn't know the smell of his own shit.

To compare donkey dung with horse shit.

To lead someone into the weeds.

Falling into the weeds and seeking someone.

Shame on you!

Too crude!   (20)

Big words are easy to say.

One day he will have regrets.

Why doesn't he get control of himself and leave?

To stumble without knowing it.

To delude oneself and follow after things.

So pitiful and sad.

What a pity!

One hand lifts up, one hand presses down.

Half open, half closed.

One in front, one in back.   (30)

Like that, like that; not like that, not like that.

His eyes look toward the southeast, but his heart is in the
     northwest.

Straight as a *koto* string, bent as a hook.

The first arrow went in lightly, the second arrow went deep.

A double koan.

A triple koan.

I come back to this koan again.

Three thousand blows in the morning, eight hundred blows
     in the evening.

Three-foot stick, seven-foot staff.

Then he hit.   (40)

The drum beats, the bell rings.

To return one's sandal allowance to one's master.

With each step a pure wind rises.

A wild tiger sitting right on the path.

Watch your step!

Walking together on the Ch'ang-an Road, hand-in-hand.

Traveling the old road by twos and threes.

Those walking together certainly understand.

No road to advance upon, no gate to retreat through.

After a long journey you know your horse's strength;
    after long years together you know another's mind.   (50)

Someone else would not have been able to trace the footprints.

Though the Chien-ko Road is steep,
    travelers are even more numerous at night.

I withdraw three steps.

Let's go home.

The exhausted fish is stuck in shallow water.

The shrimp cannot leap out of the wooden dipper.

Unable to leap out.

His life hangs from a thread.

The obligation is so large it is difficult to requite.

Thrust out so suddenly it's hard to handle.   (60)

It's hard to save people from false Dharma.

It's hard to bore a nine-curved hole into a jewel.

Extremely difficult!

An opportunity hard to come by.

Not to begrudge one's life.

Seeking it from others is forbidden.

To test a person through words.

Close question, distant answer.

The answer is in the question.

If they hadn't trained together,
    how could he have discerned the real point?   (70)

The monk must know this moment for himself.

Great Master Yün-men has arrived here.

Chao-chou's practice at the age of eighty.

Practicing alongside Chao-chou.

How would Lin-chi and Te-shan meet each other?

Do not make a mistake because of Lin-chi.

Losing one's way and running into Bodhidharma.

The foreign monk [Bodhidharma] sits at Shao-lin.

Hsüeh-tou has opened only one eye.

Hsüeh-tou must understand that kind of talk. (80)

Hsüeh-tou alone [understands].

This is indeed Hsüeh-tou.

Do not make a mistake because of Hsüeh-tou.

To swallow Hsüeh-tou.

We cannot split Hsüeh-tou.

Hsüeh-tou has not yet gotten that far.

Where is Hsüeh-tou?

Master Shakyamuni's eyeballs pop out.

I'll join Shakyamuni in retirement.

Buddha's hand cannot be opened. (90)

The buddhas and patriarchs hold their breath.

Blue sky, bright sun.

The sun is close to setting.

The moon is bright, the wind is pure.

A double ring around the moon.

The sun appears and the moon disappears.

Pure wind, bright moon.

The wind blows and the grass bends.

Though the bamboo forest is dense, water flows
    through it freely.

Bamboo in the South, trees in the North. (100)

Stars in the sky, rivers on the earth.

Pine [needles] are straight, thorns are crooked.

The color of pines is not old or new.

The pine accompanies the sound of the wind.

When the clouds disperse, the cave becomes bright.

The patterns of the mountain flowers resemble brocade;
    the waters of the lakes are blue as indigo.

Under a peony, a kitten naps.

The old mouse drags raw ginger.

To lie flat in the tiger's mouth.

Hundreds of birds hover over their chicks.   (110)

The crane flies over a thousand feet of snow.

Eyes black as a crow.

To beat the grass and surprise a snake.

Seeing a rabbit, he releases the hawk.

A white horse enters the reed flowers.

The clever dog bites the man.

Birds fly, rabbits run.

The blue sky is not blue, the white clouds are not white.

Two stone statues whisper into each other's ears.

General Li shoots a stone tiger with an arrow.   (120)

Inside the pot, heaven and earth keep a different calendar.

The more it is hidden, the more it manifests.

To wash a clod of earth in the mud.

Rabbits and horses have horns, cows and sheep don't
    have horns.

Amidst the sound of running water, not to hear running water.

One slab of iron stretching ten thousand miles.

A drop of ink transmutes: two dragons appear.

Since long ago, a white cloud has been sleeping among the
    reed flowers.

An octagonal millstone flies through the air.

Where the white clouds are deep, a golden dragon dances. (130)

Many lies are not as effective as a few facts.

Small compassion is a hindrance to great compassion.

A bitter melon is bitter even to its roots;
   a sweet melon is sweet even to its stem.

The son inherits the occupation of the father.

Under a good general, one is certain to find brave soldiers.

A thousand soldiers are easy to get, but a single general is
   hard to find.

If you hear it incorrectly, you will mistake a bell for a
   cooking pot.

In the same hole the soil does not differ.

In a group of three people, one will be my teacher.

A poor man thinks about his unpaid debts.   (140)

One must drink wine among friends
   and recite poems before those who understand.

Ch'ang-an is a pleasant place, but it's difficult to live
   there long.

Virtue never stands alone.

With one experience comes one bit of knowledge.

Few people nurture others, many people thwart others.

The sky does not have four walls.

The watchman steals at night.

In his heart the thief is afraid.

The old thief has met complete defeat.

The thief in the grass has met complete defeat.   (150)

Sons cover up for their fathers.

To arrest all with one warrant.

To decide the sentence according to the criminal's confession.

When killing someone, make sure you see his blood.

One victory, two games.

One game, two victories.

Defeated.

He has lost.

His losses are not slight.

His tongue has bones.   (160)

His tongue has no bones.

His tongue is already long.

To move the tongue is to slander.

To open the mouth is to err.

His mouth is like a bowl of blood.

One, two, three.

A thousand.

One, two, three, four, five, six, seven.

Thirty-three people.

Six, five, four, three, two, one.   (170)

Seven times nine is sixty-three.

A mute eats bitter melons.

Gives me goose bumps.

To open one's eyes in a coffin.

One flake of snow above a blazing hearth.

There are thorns in the soft mud.

Blood flowing out.

To extract an arrow from the back of his head.

Knead it but it won't form a ball.

Recklessly he inserts needles.   (180)

To insert the needle where it hurts.

He loves fragrant grasses, and he can't stop [seeking them].

Sudhana enters Maitreya's palace.

He hides his body but his shadow shows.

Spilled his guts and disgorged his heart.

It plugs the ears of everyone on earth.

Iron wall, silver mountain.

Scoop up water, the moon lies in your hands;
    toy with a flower, its fragrance soaks your robe.

The sky cannot cover it, the earth cannot uphold it.

Who? (190)

Where did it go?

Is he there? Is he there?

What is the place?

What is the understanding?

What state of mind?

A close friend understands, but who else understands?

What public office is without secrecy?
    What water is without fish?

Of what use is an iron hammer head with no hole?

If a master arrives here, how will you respond?

Bodhidharma did not come to China,
    the Second Patriarch did not go to India. (200)

The iron ball has no seams.

The sky is high in the southeast, the earth is low in the
    northwest.

Mt. Sumeru.

Ring of Iron Mountain.

The Eighth Sea.

To put a nail in a tree.

To buy iron and receive gold.

To beat the grass and see a snake.

Gold is tested with fire.

Completely fills emptiness.   (210)

To throw a holeless hammer head right at him.

Didn't think he could ask.

Thrust out right in front.

Why don't you go right away?

By asking, one is able to get it for the first time.

Cannot be split apart.

To come out evenly.

Reversing the error and getting it right.

There is an echo and his words.

The measuring stick is in his hand.   (220)

A pair of flags struck by lightning.

Hitting both with one blow.

Wind blows but does not enter, water washes but does
    not touch.

Above, no supports for climbing; below, self is extinguished.

He reveals his dynamism in his words.

A weed-tipped fishing pole.

Please drink this cup of wine;
    beyond the Western outpost you'll find no friends.

A command that cannot be disobeyed.

There are just a lot of [ordinary] people.

Would Hsüeh-tou [stoop to] fight with you?   (230)

APPENDIX I
The Daitō Corpus

THE WORKS attributed to Daitō include scrolls in his own hand, teachings transcribed by disciples, poetry in Japanese and Chinese, commentaries, and correspondence. Most of these texts are in *kanbun,* though a few are in vernacular Japanese. The surviving versions of Daitō's writings or teachings are usually handwritten copies of earlier handwritten copies. As a result, a given work may have several redactions, sometimes with different titles, whereas other texts may have no title at all. Dating such materials is problematic. Few works are dated during Daitō's lifetime, with the exception of some of his own calligraphy. Often a date, say 1450, will first appear on a later transcription, yet that document of 1450 will survive only through an even later recension, which may or may not bear its own date. The authenticity of many works is therefore difficult to confirm. Though Daitō's calligraphy and discourse record can be attributed to him with relative certainty, it is more difficult to assess a long dialogue that sounds like fiction or a commentary that relies on several generations of oral transmission. Some of the works currently attributed to Daitō may in fact be his, or they may be partially his, or they may not be his at all. Because important new texts are still coming to light, the contours of the Daitō corpus continue to shift.

1. Record of National Master Daitō (Daitō Kokushi goroku)

Daitō Kokushi goroku is the authorized collection of Daitō's formal and informal discourses, beginning with the inauguration of Daitokuji in 1326 and ending in 1337, the year of the master's death. The full name of the text is expanded by Daitō's posthumous titles: *Ryūhō Kaisan Tokushi Kōzen Daitō Kōshō Shōtō Kokushi goroku (Record of the Imperially Favored National Master Kōzen Daitō Kōshō Shōtō, Founder of the Dragon Treasure Mountain [Daitokuji]).* One of the compilers was Daitō's disciple Kanzan Egen (1277–1360), who later founded Myōshinji.

Through the end of 1336 Daitō's talks follow the full monastic schedule, but only two undated talks are recorded for 1337. The *Record* also includes Daitō's forty-eight commentarial verses *(juko)*, the earliest Daitō biography, and his capping-phrase commentary on portions of the *Record of Hsüeh-tou* (see no. 4 below). Though the first woodblock edition of Daitō's *Record* is undated, it was published sometime between 1426 (the date of Daitō's biography) and 1467 (the first year of the Ōnin War, during which the original woodblocks were destroyed). A second edition appeared in 1621.

Today the *Record of Daitō* is most accessible in Takakusu Junjirō, ed., *Taishō shinshū daizōkyō* (Tokyo, 1924–1932), volume 81, pp. 191a–242c. A substantial portion of the *Record* has been rendered in modern Japanese and annotated by Hirano Sōjō in *Daitō,* volume 6 of *Nihon no Zen goroku* (Tokyo, 1978). More recently, Hirano has published a two-volume *Daitō Kokushi goroku* (Kyoto, 1986); volume 1 is a replica of the 1621 woodblock edition, and volume 2 presents the text in classical Japanese with notes.

2. Dharma Words of National Master Daitō (Daitō Kokushi hōgo)

Daitō Kokushi hōgo consists of two short sermons on Zen practice, one of which is addressed to Emperor Hanazono's consort, Senkō (d. 1360). Whereas Daitō's other principal works are written in *kanbun,* this text is written in Japanese. Several redactions exist; the oldest is a hand-copied manuscript from the Muromachi period, added to the *Shōichi kanahōgo (Dharma Words of Shōichi [Enni], in Japanese).* For a study of the text's background, see Sanae Kensei, "Yomogisawa Bunkobon *Shōichi kanahōgo* no kenkyū: I," in *Zenbunka kenkyūjo kiyō* 6: 265–294 (May 1974). Hirano Sōjō translates the text into modern Japanese in his *Daitō Zen no tankyū* (Tokyo, 1974), pp. 7–37.

3. Calligraphy

Many of Daitō's writings survive in his own hand. His two enlightenment poems, his correspondence with emperors Hanazono and Go-Daigo, his death verse, and his final testament have been reverently preserved at Daitokuji. Daitō's calligraphic copies of the *Transmission of the Lamp* and his glosses on the *Record of Ta-ch'uan* predate his move to Daitokuji. About ten of Daitō's letters to disciples are also extant; many are addressed to nuns, lay men, and lay women. The most comprehensive collection of Daitō's calligraphy is found in Maruoka Sōnan, ed., *Daitokuji bokuseki zenshū* (Tokyo, 1984), volume 1. Also useful is Tayama Hōnan, ed., *Daitokuji,* volume 11 of *Hihō* (Tokyo, 1968).

4. Essential Words for Careful Study (Sanshō goyō)

This work is Daitō's capping-phrase commentary on two volumes of the *Record of Hsüeh-tou (Hsüeh-tou lu).* Its full title is *Tokushi Kōzen Daitō Kokushi sanshō goyō.* Hsüeh-tou Ch'ung-hsien (980–1052) is best known as the first compiler of the *Blue Cliff Record. Sanshō goyō* was first published between 1426 and 1467 as part of the *Record of Daitō.* Nothing further is known about its date of composition, subsequent editor(s), or early history of transmission. No other recensions exist. Today this work is most accessible in the *Taishō daizōkyō* edition of Daitō's *Record* (volume 81, pp. 224c–242c).

5. One Hundred Twenty Cases (Hyakunijussoku)

In *Hyakunijussoku* Daitō added interlinear capping phrases to his own selection of koans and other material from Ch'an texts. Thirty-five of the 120 "cases" are koans from the *Blue Cliff Record,* and fourteen are koans from the *Gateless Barrier.* The collection begins with the two koans that were most crucial in Daitō's Zen training. The earliest extant edition of *Hyakunijussoku* (now in a private collection) dates from 1519; it is signed by Seian Sōi (1483–1562), the 93rd abbot of Daitokuji. Seian's transcription is flawed by minor errors: his numbering of the 120 cases does not tally with his table of contents, and he occasionally treats a portion of a case as a Daitō capping phrase. Tandō Shōshuku (1629?– 1713), the 226th abbot of Daitokuji, added a later colophon to this text.

Two other recensions are preserved by Reisen-in and Ryōkō-in temples. The Ryōkō-in text includes a postscript with a Zen dialogue between Daitō and a monk, dated the first month of Kenmu 4 [1337]. This encounter, not found in Daitō's *Record,* seems to be the master's last recorded discourse. Several other redactions, transmitted within the Myōshinji lineage, retain the *Hyakunijussoku* title, but their contents depart from Seian's text: they contain fewer than fifty koans, the capping phrases differ, and they include explanations in Japanese.

In 1944 D. T. Suzuki introduced *Hyakunijussoku* to the Japanese scholarly community in an essay entitled "Nihon Zen shisōshi no ichidanmen," reprinted in *Suzuki Daisetsu zenshū* (Tokyo, 1968), volume 4, pp. 5–37. In 1971 Hirano Sōjō published the first edited and corrected *Hyakunijussoku,* after comparing the three known recensions; see "Daitō Kokushi agyo no kenkyū: I," in *Zenbunka kenkyūjo kiyō* 3: 61–74 (October 1971). Hirano has also rendered the text in classical Japanese in *Daitō Zen no tankyū,* pp. 38–54.

6. Capping Phrases on the Blue Cliff Record (Hekigan agyo)

In *Hekigan agyo* Daitō supplied interlinear capping phrases to the hundred core koans of the *Blue Cliff Record.* (Hsüeh-tou's verses and Yüan-wu's glosses are omitted.) The text's full title is usually given as *Hekigan hyakusoku Daitō Kokushi agyo.* Thirty-five of the koans also appear in *Hyakunijussoku,* but the capping phrases on these duplicated koans differ in the two works. The text includes a pithy colophon, dated 1414 and signed by Kasō Sōdon (1352–1428), an early and influential Daitokuji abbot. It states in part:

> Fundamentally there is heavenly true nature, manifest before the separation of heaven and earth. . . . In the future, you must guard it carefully. Disseminate my Way and illuminate [true nature]. Consider this deeply, consider this deeply. Ōei 21 [1414], first month, 18th day. Humbly written by Old Kasō.

From the language of this colophon, we may infer that Kasō allowed one of his Dharma heirs to transcribe a copy of *Hekigan agyo,* and then Kasō added these words. Since a nearly identical colophon is appended to the discourse record of Kasō's successor, Yōsō Sōi (1378–1458), the disciple who made this copy of *Hekigan agyo* was probably Yōsō.

The three handwritten recensions that survive today are early Tokugawa-period copies of an older manuscript. They are housed in the archives of

Shinju-an (a Daitokuji subtemple), the library of Komazawa University, and Kōfukuji temple (the Kōfukuji text was rediscovered in 1968). In 1971 Hirano Sōjō published an edited version of *Hekigan agyo* based on these recensions; see "Daitō Kokushi agyo no kenkyū: I," in *Zenbunka kenkyūjo kiyō* 3: 47–58 (October 1971).

7. Untitled Capping-Phrase Anthology

In addition to the three capping-phrase works just cited, there is a fourth manuscript, which is not a commentary. Rather, it lists about nine hundred capping phrases, divided into thirty-six groups with headings such as "Praise," "Denunciation," and "Ridicule." The work is untitled, undated, and unsigned; irregularities on its first page suggest that an opening section is missing. Even if the attribution to Daitō cannot be verified conclusively, the manuscript is the earliest Japanese capping-phrase anthology that has come to light. Significantly, it predates Tōyō Eichō's influential *Kuzōshi* ([*Zen*] *Phrase Book*), which was compiled in the late fifteenth century but is known only through seventeenth-century recensions.

Gyokushū Sōhan (1599–1668), the 185th abbot of Daitokuji, appended the earliest colophon on the text, identifying the calligraphy as Daitō's: "These are the tracks of the running rabbit [brush strokes] of our patriarch National Master Daitō. Do not doubt them." Gyokushū's claim was reinforced by Tenshitsu Sōchiku (1604–1667), another Daitokuji abbot of the period. A final colophon was written by Chūhō Sō'u (1759–1838), abbot of the Daitokuji subtemple Hōshun-in. During the late nineteenth century one of the Hōshun-in abbots transferred the first portion of the text to the Kyoto National Museum, and it was not rediscovered until 1983, when museum curators were asked to search their archives for Daitō-related materials. In 1984 photographic reproductions of the Hōshun-in manuscript were made public in Maruoka's *Daitokuji bokuseki zenshū*, volume 1, pp. 60–68. Then the second portion of the text (from an unidentified collection) was brought to the attention of Hirano Sōjō, who published a full transcription of the reunited manuscript in "Den Daitō senkushū," *Zenbunka kenkyūjo kiyō* 15: 561–600 (December 1988).

8. *Evening Dialogue at Shōun-an (Shōunyawa)*

Shōunyawa purports to record a conversation between Daitō and an elder monk identified only as Kō. Its alternate titles are *Hasonshukuyawa* and *Ha'ichisonshukuyawa (Defeating a Priest in an Evening Talk)*. Initially, *Shōunyawa* was transmitted within the Ikkyū branch of Daitō's lineage. A redaction in the Ryōgen-in archives is dated 1457, and a similar manuscript in Shinju-an is also thought to date from the Muromachi period. Hirano Sōjō traces the text's development in "Daitō Kokushi *Hasonshukuyawa* no kenkyū," in Zenbunka kenkyūjo, *Zengaku ronkō* (Kyoto, 1977), pp. 343–349. He also translates the work into modern Japanese in *Daitō*, pp. 371–395.

9. *Light[hearted] Oxherding Poems (Yōgyukyōginka)*

Yōgyukyōginka includes about seventy brief poems in Japanese, most of them on Zen-related topics. The earliest of the three woodblock redactions, dating from

1678, was edited by the monk Dōkai (1628–1695). Because the quality of the material is uneven, some of the verses may be later additions to a core group of original poems by Daitō. A modern Japanese translation of this work is found in Hirano, *Daitō Zen no tankyū,* pp. 55–85.

10. The Spoken Meaning of The Blue Cliff Record (Hekigan kugi)

The ten-volume *Hekigan kugi* is a detailed commentary on the complete *Blue Cliff Record.* Some portions may have been transmitted orally before being recorded. Daitō is the principal commentator, but the work also includes annotation by other Daitokuji masters. Among those named, the latest is Shunpo Sōki (1408–1496). The earliest known recension is housed in Ryōkō-in; according to its ambiguous colophonic material, it was transcribed by hand in 1556 or 1560 by Sankansai or Sōji. *Hekigan kugi* remains virtually unknown outside Daitokuji. A later but undated woodblock redaction of the text, entitled *Hekiganshū koshō (Classic Notes on the Blue Cliff Record),* is stored in the library of Kyoto Fine Arts University. Also in ten volumes, it bears the inscription: "The secret notes of Daiō, Daitō, and Tettō, reprinted by woodblock."

APPENDIX II
Characters for Capping Phrases Cited

1. 作家作家
2. 異中異也
3. 莫謂新到
4. 応諾
5. 也是
6. 但惟但惟
7. 吾不如你
8. 錯
9. 閑葛藤
10. 瞎
11. 将錯就錯
12. 依然弄泥団漢
13. 鈍致殺人
14. 既落第二
15. 自屎不覚臭
16. 駅屎比馬糞
17. 教人入荒草裏去
18. 落草求人
19. 咄
20. 俗気俗気
21. 大言易出
22. 他日自悔
23. 何不自領去
24. 蹉過亦不知
25. 迷己逐物
26. 可痛可悲
27. 可惜許
28. 一手抬一手搦

29. 半開半合
30. 一向一背
31. 恁麼恁麼不恁麼不恁麼
32. 眼見東南心在西北
33. 直如絃曲如鉤
34. 前箭猶軽後箭深
35. 両重公案
36. 三重公案
37. 還我話頭来
38. 朝打三千暮打八百
39. 三尺竹篦七尺拄杖
40. 便打
41. 皷鳴鐘響
42. 与老師還草鞋銭
43. 步步清風起
44. 猛虎当路坐
45. 看脚下
46. 把手共行長安路
47. 両両三三旧路行
48. 同行者当知
49. 進無路退無門
50. 途遠知馬力
 年久知人心
51. 若是別人出蹄跡不得
52. 劍閣路雖嶮
 夜行人更多
53. 山僧退身三步
54. 帰去来也

214

55. 困魚止濼
56. 蝦跳不出斗
57. 跳不出
58. 命如懸系
59. 恩大難酬
60. 突出難弁
61. 邪法難扶
62. 珠穿九曲難
63. 大難大難
64. 時節難逢
65. 不惜身命
66. 切忌隨佗去
67. 以語試人
68. 近問遠答
69. 答在問処
70. 若是不同參
　　爭得弁端的
71. 衲僧家自須知時
72. 雲門大師来也
73. 趙州八十行脚
74. 与趙州同參
75. 林際德山如何祇対
76. 不誤為臨済
77. 迷逢達磨
78. 胡僧坐少林
79. 雪竇也只開得一隻眼
80. 雪竇也須解与麼説話
81. 但雪竇一箇
82. 将謂雪竇
83. 不誤為雪竇
84. 呑却雪竇
85. 雪竇無分
86. 雪竇未到
87. 雪竇在甚処
88. 釈迦老師眼睛突出
89. 与釈迦老子隱屈
90. 仏手劈不開
91. 仏祖呑気
92. 青天白日
93. 日勢稍晩
94. 月白風清
95. 月帶重輪
96. 日出月没
97. 清風明月
98. 風行草偃
99. 竹密不妨流水過
100. 南地竹北地木

101. 天上星地下水
102. 松直棘曲
103. 松無古今色
104. 松添風声
105. 雲出洞中明
106. 山花開似錦
　　澗水湛如藍
107. 牡丹花下睡猫児
108. 老鼠引生薑
109. 虎口裡横身
110. 百鳥為子屈
111. 鶴飛千尺雪
112. 眼睛烏律律
113. 打草驚蛇
114. 見兎放鷹
115. 白馬入芦花
116. 俊狗咬人
117. 鳥飛兎走
118. 青天不青白雲不白
119. 両箇石人相耳語
120. 李公射石虎
121. 壺中天地別有日月
122. 隱而弥露
123. 泥裡洗土塊
124. 兎馬有角牛羊無角
125. 流水声中不聞流水
126. 万里一条鉄
127. 一点水墨両処化竜
128. 白雲依旧宿芦花
129. 八角磨盤空裏走
130. 白雲深処金竜躍
131. 多虚不如少実
132. 小慈妨大慈
133. 苦瓜連根苦
　　甜瓜徹帶甜
134. 子受父業
135. 重将下必有勇夫
136. 千兵易得一将難求
137. 聴事不真喚鐘作甕
138. 同坑無異土
139. 三人中必有我師
140. 貧児思旧債
141. 酒逢知己飲
　　詩向会人吟
142. 長安雖楽難久居
143. 德兮不孤
144. 因一事長一智

145. 成人者少敗人者多
146. 天無四壁
147. 巡人犯夜
148. 作賊人心虛
149. 老賊大敗也
150. 草賊大敗
151. 子為父隱
152. 一状領過
153. 拃款結案
154. 殺人須見血
155. 一賽両彩
156. 一彩両賽
157. 敗也
158. 失
159. 敗欠不少
160. 舌頭有骨
161. 舌頭無骨
162. 舌頭己長
163. 動舌即乖
164. 開口即錯
165. 口似血盆
166. 一二三
167. 千
168. 一二三四五六七
169. 三十三人
170. 六五四三二一
171. 七九六十三
172. 啞子喫苦苽
173. 寒毛卓豎
174. 棺木裡瞠眼
175. 紅炉上一点雪
176. 爛泥裏有棘
177. 血滴滴地
178. 脳後抜箭
179. 捏不成団
180. 浪下針錐
181. 痛処下針錐
182. 恋芳草未得休
183. 善財入弥勒閣
184. 蔵身露影
185. 劈腹剜心
186. 塞断尽大地人耳根
187. 鉄壁銀山
188. 掬水月在手
       弄花香滿衣

189. 天蓋不能地載不起
190. 阿誰
191. 什麼去也
192. 有麼有麼
193. 是什麼所在
194. 是什麼消息
195. 是什麼境界
196. 知音知後亦誰知
197. 何官無私何水無魚
198. 無孔鉄鎚堪作甚麼用
199. 你衲僧家到者裏作麼生酬対
200. 達磨不来東土
       二祖不行西天
201. 鉄丸無縫罅
202. 天高東西地低西北
203. 須弥山
204. 鉄囲山
205. 第八海
206. 寸鉄入木
207. 買鉄得金
208. 打草見蛇
209. 金以火試
210. 逼塞虛空
211. 無孔鉄鎚当面擲
212. 将謂問不得
213. 当陽突出
214. 何不即便去
215. 問得始可得
216. 劈不開
217. 平出
218. 回邪打正
219. 言中有響
220. 秤尺在手
221. 双旗収電影
222. 一槌両当
223. 風吹不入水洒不着
224. 上無攀仰下絶己躬
225. 句裡呈機
226. 探竿影草
227. 勧君尽此一盃酒
       西出陽関無故人
228. 不犯之令
229. 只有人在
230. 雪竇豈争你底

APPENDIX III
Location of Capping Phrases Cited

Daitō's use of the capping phrases cited in this book can be traced with the aid of the following table and an index compiled by Hirano Sōjō. The left-hand numbers below refer to capping phrases; numeration corresponds to Chapter 12, where the phrases are translated, and Appendix II, where they appear in Sino-Japanese. The right-hand entries below refer to pages and columns of the Hirano index, which provides the locations of the capping phrases in Daitō's written commentaries. Hirano compared all known recensions of Daitō's *Hekigan agyo* and *Hyakunijussoku* as well as the *Taishō daizōkyō* edition of Daitō's *Sanshō goyō*. For Hirano's index, see "Daitō Kokushi agyo no kenkyū: II," in *Zenbunka kenkyūjo kiyō* 4 (June 1972), pp. 151–184. (An asterisk below indicates a phrase that appears in Daitō's works but was omitted from Hirano's index.)

1. 160c	16. 184a	31. 153b	46. 175c	61. 164a
2. 151c	17. 157c	32. 156b	47. 183c	62. 164c
3. 179c	18. 183a	33. 163c	48. 173b	63. 170c
4. 153c	19. 173c	34. 168c	49. 166c	64. 163b
5. 180a	20. 169c	35. 183b	50. 172c	65. 177b
6. 170c	21. 170b	36. 161c	51. 164b	66. 168a
7. 159c	22. 169c	37. 156a	52. 158c	67. 151b
8. 161b	23. 154b	38. 171c	53. 162a	68. 157c
9. 156a	24. 161a	39. *	54. 156c	69. 173a
10. 155b	25. 181b	40. 178c	55. 160c	70. 164b
11. 166b	26. 154a	41. 159b	56. 155a	71. 175b
12. 151c	27. 154a	42. 182b	57. 171c	72. 153c
13. 174a	28. 152b	43. 179a	58. 181a	73. 166c
14. 156b	29. 176a	44. 181b	59. 153c	74. 182b
15. 163a	30. 152a	45. 155c	60. 174a	75. 183c

76. 177a	107. 179a	138. 173b	169. 161c	200. 170c
77. 181b	108. 184b	139. 162a	170. 184b	201. 172a
78. 159b	109. 159b	140. 176c	171. 163c	202. 172b
79. 168b	110. 176c	141. 164c	172. 151a	203. 164c
80. 168b	111. 155b	142. 171b	173. 155c	204. 172a
81. 170c	112. 156b	143. 173c	174. 156a	205. 170c
82. 166b	113. 170a	144. 153a	175. 160b	206. 167b
83. 177a	114. 158c	145. 167c	176. 183a	207. 175c
84. 174a	115. 176a	146. 172c	177. 158b	208. 170a
85. 168b	116. 165b	147. 165b	178. 175b	209. 157c
86. 168a	117. *	148. 161a	179. 175b	210. 176c
87. 168b	118. 167c	149. 184b	180. 184b	211. 181a
88. 164a	119. 183b	150. 169b	181. 171c	212. 166b
89. 182b	120. 183a	151. 162b	182. 184a	213. 173a
90. 178a	121. 159b	152. 152b	183. 168c	214. 154b
91. 178a	122. 153b	153. 157b	184. 169c	215. 181c
92. 167c	123. 172a	154. 161c	185. 178c	216. 178b
93. 174c	124. 172c	155. 183b	186. 161b	217. 178b
94. 158c	125. 183b	156. 152a	187. 172a	218. *
95. 158c	126. 176b	157. 175c	188. 156c	219. 159a
96. 174c	127. 152c	158. 163c	189. 172b	220. 166b
97. 168a	128. 176a	159. 175c	190. 151a	221. 169a
98. 178a	129. 176a	160. 168b	191. 174b	222. 152c
99. 171a	130. 176a	161. 168b	192. 182a	223. 178a
100. 174b	131. 169c	162. 168b	193. 167c	224. 166c
101. 172b	132. 166a	163. 173b	194. 167c	225. 158a
102. 166a	133. 158a	164. 155b	195. 167c	226. 170c
103. 166a	134. 162b	165. 159c	196. 171a	227. 156a
104. 166a	135. 165a	166. 152c	197. 154b	228. 177b
105. 153c	136. 168c	167. 168b	198. 181a	229. 162c
106. 162a	137. 171c	168. 153b	199. 174c	230. 168a

NOTES

Abbreviations

DBZ   *Daitokuji bokuseki zenshū* 大德寺墨跡全集 (Complete calligraphy of Daitokuji). Ed. Maruoka Sōnan 丸岡宗男 et al. Vol. 1. Tokyo: Asahi Shinbunsha, 1984.

DZZ   *Dōgen Zenji zenshū* 道元禅師全集 (Complete works of Zen Master Dōgen). Ed. Ōkubo Dōshū 大久保道舟. Tokyo: Chikuma Shobō, 1969–1970.

TSD   *Taishō shinshū daizōkyō* 大正新修大蔵経 (Taishō era edition of the Buddhist canon). Ed. Takakusu Junjirō 高楠順次郎 et al. Tokyo: Daizō Shuppan, 1924–1932.

In citations that contain only the volume and page number(s), "vol." and "p." are omitted. Thus TSD, 81, 224, is TSD, vol. 81, p. 224.

1. Entering the World of Daitō

*Jacques Barzun, *On Writing, Editing, and Publishing,* p. 65.

**This epigraph refers to a portrait of Daitō dated Karyaku 2 [1327]; see DBZ, plate 35, p. 49. The inscription is slightly modified from Norman Waddell's translation in DBZ, p. 295.

1. Among those who give some credence to the beggar stories are D. T. Suzuki, Ogisu Jundō, Yanagida Seizan, Katō Shōshun, and Jon Covell. See Chapter 3, final section.

2. Kenpō Shidon (d. 1361), quoted in David Pollack, *The Fracture of Meaning: Japan's Synthesis of China from the Eighth through the Eighteenth Centuries,* p. 119.

3. Ogisu Jundō, "Daitō," p. 221.

4. It has become traditional at Daitokuji to commemorate Daitō's major death anniversaries several years early (e.g., in 1983 instead of 1987).

5. Isshū Miura and Ruth F. Sasaki, *Zen Dust,* p. 388.

6. Yanagida Seizan, *Rinzai no kafū*, p. 173.

7. Suzuki Daisetsu, "Nihon Zen shisōshi no ichidanmen," p. 19.

8. Ogisu Jundō, ed., *Zen to Nihon bunka no shōmondai*, p. 44.

9. Heinrich Dumoulin, *Zen Buddhism: A History*, p. 190.

10. The best treatments of Daitō's life are found in Ogisu Jundō, *Musō, Daitō*, pp. 135–218, and Yanagida Seizan, *Rinzai no kafū*, pp. 159–197. Both authors use a wide range of sources, though Ogisu uncritically accepts sectarian depictions of Daitō. Katō Shōshun evaluates the earliest accounts of Daitō's life in "Kakushū Daitō-den no idō ni tsuite." Hirano Sōjō is responsible for most of the modern scholarship on Daitō's written works. He renders Daitō's discourse record in classical Japanese, with notes, in *Daitō Kokushi goroku*, and he translates about half of this same text into modern Japanese in *Daitō*. His *Daitō Zen no tankyū* focuses on the master's brief vernacular texts. Hirano's index of Daitō's capping phrases appears in "Daitō Kokushi agyo no kenkyū: II."

The two best Western-language treatments of Daitō are only a few pages each. One is a brief biography in Miura and Sasaki, *Zen Dust*, pp. 231–234. The other is found in Dumoulin, *Zen Buddhism: A History*, pp. 185–190. Regrettably, the sketch of Daitō in Jon Carter Covell and Yamada Sōbin, *Zen at Daitoku-ji*, pp. 26–32, is marred by errors of fact and translation. D. T. Suzuki's *Manual of Zen Buddhism*, first published in 1935, includes a translation of Daitō's "Final Admonitions."

11. T. Griffith Foulk, "The 'Ch'an School' and Its Place in the Buddhist Monastic Tradition," pp. 91–92.

12. See Shibayama Zenkei, ed., *Zenrin kushū*, and Fujita Genro, ed., *Zudokko*.

13. In the West, capping phrases and verses have been selectively translated, though they rarely play a role in the koan training of Western Zen practitioners. Volume 1 of R. H. Blyth's *Haiku* contains 74 translated verses (pp. 10–23). In *Zen Dust*, Miura and Sasaki offer an "anthology" of 210 phrases (pp. 79–122). Numerous capping phrases are found in two works by Yoel Hoffmann: *Every End Exposed* and *The Sound of the One Hand*. The latter is a translation of a 1916 text critical of Japanese Rinzai Zen; out of context it may create a misleading impression of Zen training. Sōiku Shigematsu has published two books that offer freely translated selections from the Japanese capping-phrase anthologies used by Rinzai Zen practitioners: *A Zen Forest* and *A Zen Harvest*. Capping phrases and verses are also scattered throughout the English works of D. T. Suzuki.

14. *Hyakunijussoku (One Hundred Twenty Cases)*, in Suzuki Daisetsu, *Suzuki Daisetsu zenshū*, 4, 373–394.

15. Yanagida, *Rinzai no kafū*, p. 167.

16. Hirano Sōjō, "Daitō Kokushi agyo no kenkyū: I," pp. 47–58.

17. For further bibliographic information on this manuscript and the other works cited in this paragraph, see Appendix I: The Daitō Corpus.

18. See Katō Shōshun, "Kanzan Egen-den no shiryōhihan."

2. Japan in the Early Fourteenth Century

1. H. Paul Varley, trans., *A Chronicle of Gods and Sovereigns*, pp. 233–234.

2. Martin Collcutt, *Five Mountains: The Rinzai Zen Monastic Institution in Medieval Japan*, p. 71.

3. Helen Craig McCullough, trans., *The Taiheiki: A Chronicle of Medieval Japan*, p. xxxv.

4. In the *Taiheiki*, Akamatsu is introduced as follows: "Around that time in

the province of Harima, there was a matchless man of valor called the lay monk Akamatsu Jirō Enshin, an offspring of the line of Suefusa of junior third rank, who was a descendant in the sixth generation of the Prince of the Blood Guhei, the seventh son of Emperor Murakami. Enshin was a man of large ideas, such as would not willingly give place to others." McCullough, *Taiheiki,* pp. 162–163.

5. Ibid., p. 202.

6. H. Paul Varley, "Ashikaga Yoshimitsu and the World of Kitayama: Social Change and Shogunal Patronage in Early Muromachi Japan," p. 190.

7. Ibid., p. 188.

8. Donald Keene, trans., *Essays in Idleness: The Tsurezuregusa of Kenkō,* p. 23.

9. Ibid., p. 28.

10. McCullough, *Taiheiki,* p. 18.

11. Ibid., p. xxv.

12. Robert E. Morrell, *Sand and Pebbles (Shasekishū),* p. 120.

13. McCullough, *Taiheiki,* p. 18.

14. Ibid., p. 318.

15. Ibid., p. 12.

16. Ibid., p. 91.

17. Keene, *Essays in Idleness,* p. 25.

18. William R. LaFleur, trans., *Mirror for the Moon,* p. 45 (slightly modified).

19. Philip Kapleau, *The Three Pillars of Zen,* p. 187.

20. Varley, *A Chronicle of Gods and Sovereigns,* p. 26n.

21. McCullough, *Taiheiki,* p. 15.

22. Varley, *A Chronicle of Gods and Sovereigns,* p. 237.

23. Morrell, *Sand and Pebbles,* p. 135.

24. Keene, *Essays in Idleness,* p. 69.

25. H. Paul Varley, *Imperial Restoration in Medieval Japan,* p. 76.

26. Keene, *Essays in Idleness,* p. 90.

27. Trevor Leggett, *The Warrior Koans: Early Zen in Japan,* p. 128.

28. Tayama Hōnan, ed., *Daitokuji,* plates 253 and 307, pp. 255, 288.

29. McCullough, *Taiheiki,* p. 365.

30. Ivan Morris, *The Nobility of Failure: Tragic Heroes in the History of Japan,* p. 110.

31. Collcutt summarizes scholarly interpretations of the Kenmu Restoration in *Five Mountains,* pp. 96–97; Andrew Goble sympathetically assesses Go-Daigo's achievements at greater length in "Go-Daigo and the Kemmu Restoration."

32. TSD, 81, 223b.

33. Kenkō's involvement with Nanpo and later with Daitokuji is documented in Yasuraoka Kōsaku, "Kenkō no tonsei seikatsu to *Tsurezuregusa* no seiritsu."

3. Daitō's Early Zen Training

1. The original manuscript of this biography is not extant. The earliest version of it is found in the *Record of Daitō,* printed by woodblock between 1426 and 1467. Today the most accessible edition is in TSD, 81, 222b–224c.

2. Takuan's biography of Daitō was not published until 1984, when Yanagida Seizan transcribed the original manuscript and translated it into classical Japanese. See DBZ, pp. 266–278.

3. Brief biographies of Daitō are found in the following works: (a) *Fusō Zenrin sōbōden (Biographies of the Treasured Zen Monks of Japan),* 1675, edited by

Kōsen Seikyō (1633–1695); (b) *Enpō dentōroku (Enpō [Era] Record of the Transmission of the Lamp)*, 1678, edited by Mangen Shiban (1626–1710); (c) *Daitokuji hennen ryakki (Brief Chronology of Daitokuji)*, c. 1685, edited by Tenrin Sōkotsu (1626–1697); (d) *Daitō Kokushi gyōgōki (Accomplishments of National Master Daitō)*, 1686, also edited by Tenrin Sōkotsu; (e) *Tentaku tōinroku (Tentaku[ji] Record of the Eastern Lineage)*, 1696, edited by Tenrin's disciple Kakuin Gitei; and (f) *Honchō kōsōden (Biographies of the Eminent Monks of Japan)*, 1701, also edited by Mangen Shiban. Three of these works are found in Nanjo Bunyū et al., *Dai Nihon Bukkyō zensho:* (a) in vol. 109, pp. 228–230; (b) in vol. 108, pp. 275–277; and (f) in vol. 102, pp. 358–361. Two are found in Daiki Sōyū, ed., *Ryūhōzan Daitokuji-shi,* vol. 1: (c) on pp. 125–136, and (d) on pp. 73–80. Ryūkoku University Library has (e) as text 2964-20.

4. Kokai's text is extant, housed in the Daitokuji subtemple Shinju-an. Its full title includes Daitō's posthumous titles (at that time): *Daitoku Kaisan Kōzen Daitō Kōshō Shōtō Daiji Unkyōshin Kōkan Jōmyō Kokushi nenpu (Chronicle of National Master Kōzen Daitō Kōshō Shōtō Daiji Unkyōshin Kōkan Jōmyō, Founder of Daitokuji)*. In 1933 this text was edited by Okuda Shōzō and published as the *Kōzen Daitō Kokushi nenpu*. For Daitō's additional posthumous titles and their variant pronunciations, see Chapter 11, note 44.

5. An alternative explanation of the Daitō-Akamatsu relationship is that Akamatsu was Daitō's nephew, the son of Daitō's elder sister (Daiki, *Ryūhōzan Daitokuji-shi*, p. 126).

6. TSD, 81, 222b.

7. DBZ, p. 267.

8. Helen Craig McCullough, *The Taiheiki*, p. 318.

9. Ogisu Jundō, *Nihon chūsei Zenshū-shi*, p. 232.

10. DBZ, p. 267.

11. TSD, 47, 506c; Ruth F. Sasaki, trans., *The Record of Lin-chi*, p. 62.

12. A koan based on the words of Chia-shan Shan-hui (805–991), later quoted in the *Transmission of the Lamp (Ching-te ch'uan-teng lu)*, ch. 20. See TSD, 51, 362a.

13. TSD, 81, 222c.

14. Ibid.

15. Ibid.

16. Hirano Sōjō has suggested that "Shūhō Myōchō" alludes to case 23 of the *Blue Cliff Record*, "The Summit of Wonder Peak." In Japanese, "Wonder Peak" is *Myōhō*. These two characters appear in Daitō's monastic name, albeit in reverse order and in separate words. See Hirano Sōjō, *Daitō*, p. 319.

17. TSD, 80, 484c.

18. Pai-chang's verse is recorded in the *Transmission of the Lamp (Ching-te ch'uan-teng lu)*, ch. 9, in TSD, 51, 268a.

19. TSD, 81, 222c.

20. See TSD, 47, 497b; Sasaki, *Record of Lin-chi*, p. 7.

21. "Nanpo" will be used rather than "Daiō" to avoid possible confusion between Daiō and Daitō. Jōmyō can also be read as Jōmin.

22. DBZ, p. 268.

23. TSD, 81, 222c–223a.

24. Philip Yampolsky, trans., *The Platform Sutra of the Sixth Patriarch*, pp. 127–128.

25. TSD, 48, 297c; Zenkei Shibayama, *Zen Comments on the Mumonkan*, p. 272. The koan can also be translated "an ox passes *by* the window."

26. TSD, 81, 223a.

27. Okuda Shōzō, *Kōzen Daitō Kokushi nenpu,* p. 10.
28. TSD, 81, 223a.
29. TSD, 48, 148b; Thomas Cleary and J. C. Cleary, trans., *The Blue Cliff Record,* p. 53.
30. TSD, 81, 223a.
31. Ibid.
32. TSD, 81, 191a.
33. TSD, 80, 485a.
34. TSD, 81, 223a.
35. Akizuki Ryōmin, *Zen nyūmon,* p. 160.
36. James H. Sanford, *Zen-man Ikkyū,* p. 60.
37. TSD, 81, 223a–223b; DBZ, p. 56.
38. TSD, 81, 223b; DBZ, p. 56.
39. TSD, 8, 826b. Compare Edward Conze, trans., *The Short Prajñāpāramitā Texts,* p. 171.
40. *Ching-te ch'uan-teng lu,* ch. 28, in TSD, 51, 246a.
41. Takashi James Kodera, *Dogen's Formative Years in China,* pp. 122, 233.
42. *Ching-te ch'uan-teng lu,* ch. 28, in TSD, 51, 444.
43. Cleary and Cleary, *Blue Cliff Record,* p. 20.
44. TSD, 81, 191a.
45. Okuda, *Kozen Daitō Kokushi nenpu,* p. 23.
46. Isshū Miura and Ruth F. Sasaki, *Zen Dust,* p. 233.
47. Katō Shū'ichi and Yanagida Seizan, *Ikkyū,* p. 73. Translation adapted from Sanford, *Zen-man Ikkyū,* p. 99.
48. Yanagida Seizan and Katō Shōshun, *Hakuin,* p. 128.
49. Miura and Sasaki, *Zen Dust,* p. 140 (modified slightly).
50. Yamada Yoshio et al., *Konjaku monogatari shū,* p. 189.
51. The name Eisai may also be pronounced Yōsai. Since the former is more familiar to Western readers, it will be used here.
52. D. T. Suzuki, *Japanese Spirituality,* p. 198.
53. Jon Carter Covell, *Zen's Core: Ikkyu's Freedom,* pp. 98–99.
54. Ogisu Jundō, *Musō, Daitō,* p. 153; Yanagida and Katō, *Hakuin,* p. 128.
55. TSD, 81, 223b.
56. D. T. Suzuki skirts this issue with the statement: "In spite of his many years as a wandering beggar he was very learned, and this turned out to be very helpful later when he became a distinguished abbot" (Suzuki, *Japanese Spirituality,* p. 198).
57. Translated by Norman Waddell in DBZ, p. 295. The first page of Daitō's transcription is reproduced in DBZ, p. 59; the postscript is reproduced in DBZ, p. 60.
58. DBZ, plate 48, pp. 72–79.
59. DBZ, plate 47, pp. 69, 71.

4. The Foundations of Japanese Zen

1. Elements of T'ang Buddhism identified as "Ch'an" had been tentatively introduced to Japan five centuries earlier, without success. The Japanese pilgrim Dōshō (629–700) went to China in 653, and after his return he is said to have taught Ch'an meditation. The Chinese monk Tao-hsüan (702–760) transmitted a Northern School lineage of Ch'an. I-k'ung arrived in Kyoto in the mid-ninth century and expounded Ch'an to Emperor Saga (786–842), but he failed to win adherents and he returned to China after a few years. Of greater impact were the Ch'an teachings brought back to Japan by Saichō (767–822).

"Ch'an" meditation, a component of the T'ien-t'ai practice Saichō found in China, was also incorporated into Japanese Tendai.

2. *Genkō Shakusho,* ch. 6, in Bussho Kankōkai, *Dai Nihon Bukkyō zenshū,* p. 75.

3. In his *Five Mountains,* Martin Collcutt identifies three stages of early Japanese Zen: a "syncretic phase," a "period of consolidation," and "a stage of metropolitan Zen" (pp. 28–30 and passim). The term "syncretic" is potentially misleading if it implies that a "pure" Sung Ch'an was forcibly mixed with the non-Zen Buddhist schools of Japan, because Sung Ch'an shared important elements with the other Buddhist schools of China and Japan.

4. *Genkō Shakusho,* cited in Bernard Faure, "The Daruma-shū, Dōgen, and Sōtō Zen," p. 29.

5. Faure, "The Daruma-shū, Dōgen, and Sōtō Zen," pp. 25–55; Heinrich Dumoulin, *Zen Buddhism: A History,* pp. 69–70.

6. The most comprehensive English-language treatment of the Gozan is Collcutt's *Five Mountains: The Rinzai Zen Monastic Institution in Medieval Japan.* See also Dumoulin, *Zen Buddhism: A History,* 151–183; and Akamatsu Toshihide and Philip Yampolsky, "Muromachi Zen and the Gozan System," pp. 313–329.

7. Kenneth Kraft, trans., "Musō Kokushi's *Dialogues in a Dream,*" pp. 84–85.

8. Collcutt, *Five Mountains,* p. 172.

9. David Pollack, *Zen Poems of the Five Mountains,* p. 157.

10. Trevor Leggett, *Zen and the Ways,* p. 41.

11. Ibid., p. 250.

12. Kageki Hideo, *Gozanshi-shi no kenkyū,* p. 121.

13. Kamimura Kankō, ed., *Gozan bungaku zenshū,* 3, 70.

14. Haga Kōshirō, *Chūsei Zenrin no gakumon oyobi bungaku ni kansuru kenkyū,* p. 159.

15. Yanagida Seizan and Umehara Takeshi, *Mu no tankyū,* p. 196.

16. T. Griffith Foulk, "The Zen Institution in Modern Japan," p. 157.

17. Ogisu Jundō, *Nihon chūsei Zenshū-shi,* pp. 11–24.

18. Faure, "The Daruma-shū, Dōgen, and Sōtō Zen," p. 54.

19. Since the T'ang dynasty the balance of power had shifted periodically among the different lines of Ch'an. A Sung period classification identified five leading "Houses." They were named after their founders: Ts'ao-tung (Ts'ao-shan and Tung-shan), Fa-yen, Yün-men, Kuei-yang (Kuei-shan and Yang-shan), and Lin-chi. In the eleventh century Lin-chi's heirs split into the Yang-ch'i and Huang-lung branches, which were added to the Five Houses to create the "Seven Schools" of Ch'an.

The Huang-lung line spread within the central provinces of Hunan and Kiangsi; it became the most influential branch of Ch'an during the Northern Sung period (960–1127). The descendants of Yang-ch'i dominated the Ch'an world of the Southern Sung period (1127–1279) and helped bring Ch'an into the cultural mainstream. The best-known representatives of Yang-ch'i Ch'an are Yüan-wu K'o-ch'in (1063–1135) and his disciple Ta-hui Tsung-kao (1089–1163). In the early thirteenth century the Yang-ch'i branch split into the P'o-an and Sung-yüan lines, named for P'o-an Tsu-hsien (1136–1211) and Sung-yüan Ch'ung-yüeh (1139–1209). P'o-an Ch'an maintained primacy over Sung-yüan Ch'an throughout the thirteenth century.

20. *Genkō Shakusho,* ch. 7, in Bussho Kankōkai, *Dai Nihon Bukkyō zenshū,* 101, 85.

21. *Kōzen gokokuron (Promulgation of Zen as a Defense of the Nation),* in TSD, vol. 80, pp. 10c, 11b, and passim.

22. T. Griffith Foulk, "The 'Ch'an School' and Its Place in the Buddhist Monastic Tradition," pp. 91–92 and passim.

23. TSD, 80, 127a–127b.

24. Dumoulin, *Zen Buddhism: A History,* 61–62.

25. Carl Bielefeldt, "Recarving the Dragon: History and Dogma in the Study of Dōgen," p. 35.

26. TSD, vol. 48, p. 387b; vol. 51, p. 291b. See also Isshū Miura and Ruth F. Sasaki, *Zen Dust,* pp. 153–154.

27. TSD, 48, 139c.

28. TSD, 47, 503c; Ruth F. Sasaki, trans., *The Record of Lin-chi,* pp. 43–44.

29. Robert E. Buswell, Jr., "The 'Short-cut' Approach of *K'an-hua* Meditation: The Evolution of a Practical Subitism in Chinese Ch'an Buddhism," p. 345.

30. Ibid., p. 349.

31. TSD, 48, 292c. There is no satisfactory way to translate Chao-chou's answer. A literal rendering ("No") ignores the interpretation that the term has traditionally been given in Ch'an/Zen. A philosophical rendering (such as "absolute Nothingness") is misleading in other ways (see Thomas Dean, "Masao Abe's Zen and Western Thought," pp. 73–74). The original Chinese pronunciation of Chao-chou's reply is *wu,* pronounced *mu* in Japanese. Although the use of *mu* here violates conventions of scholarly consistency (Chao-chou didn't speak Japanese), Westerners are most familiar with this pronunciation.

32. TSD, 48, 298a.

33. TSD, 47, 504a; Sasaki, *Record of Lin-chi,* p. 46.

34. TSD, 47, 504a; Sasaki, *Record of Lin-chi,* p. 45.

35. Edward Conze, *Buddhist Wisdom Books,* p. 63; Trevor Leggett, *The Warrior Koans,* p. 167 (modified).

36. Leggett, *Warrior Koans,* p. 131 (modified).

37. Ibid., pp. 129–130 (modified).

38. Ibid., p. 130.

39. Ibid., pp. 42, 103–104, 112–113, and passim.

40. Ibid., p. 1.

41. Bielefeldt, "Recarving the Dragon," p. 38.

42. Leggett, *Warrior Koans,* pp. 24–26; TSD, 80, 87c.

43. Leggett, *Zen and the Ways,* p. 67 (modified slightly).

44. Collcutt, *Five Mountains,* p. 72.

5. Daitō Ascendant at Daitokuji

1. DBZ, p. 268; TSD, 81, 223b.

2. David Pollack, *Zen Poems of the Five Mountains,* p. 64.

3. David Pollack, *The Fracture of Meaning,* p. 119.

4. Daitō's earliest biographers vary considerably in attempting to date the move to Murasakino. In Shunsaku's *Exploits* the move is undated; in Takuan's *Chronicle* it is 1315; in two biographies it is 1319; in one it is "after 1321"; and in two others it is 1326. Katō Shōshun weighs the evidence in "Kakushū Daitō-den no idō ni tsuite," p. 83.

5. Okuda Shōzō, *Kōzen Daitō Kokushi nenpu,* p. 27.

6. Tayama Hōnan, ed., *Daitokuji,* plate 280, p. 274.

7. The text of Hanazono's proclamation is given in Ogisu Jundō, *Musō, Daitō,* p. 164. Go-Daigo's decree is reproduced in Tayama, *Daitokuji,* plate 308, p. 288. Both documents, written by the emperors themselves, are extant.

8. Hanazono's diary has been reprinted in a number of works. Two are used interchangeably in this study: Nakatsuka Eijirō, ed., *Shinkishū;* and Ōta Zen, ed., *Shiryō sanshū: Hanazono Tennō shinki.*

9. Nakatsuka, *Shinkishū,* 2, 424. Shunsaku reports two Daitō-Hanazono meetings, and Takuan dates them as 1316, but the date given by Takuan is apparently seven years too early.

10. See Andrew Goble, "Truth, Contradiction and Harmony in Medieval Japan: Emperor Hanazono (1297–1348) and Buddhism."

11. Ōta, *Shiryō sanshū,* 2, 10; Goble, "Truth, Contradiction and Harmony in Medieval Japan," p. 28.

12. Nakatsuka, *Shinkishū,* 2, 250. Some writers have mistakenly assumed that Hanazono's references to Gatsurin were references to Daitō.

13. Ōta, *Shiryō sanshū,* 2, 162; Goble, "Truth, Contradiction and Harmony in Medieval Japan," p. 43.

14. Iwahashi Koyata, *Hanazono Tennō,* pp. 147–151.

15. TSD, 81, 223b–223c.

16. Ōta, *Shiryō sanshū,* 2, 279; Goble, "Truth, Contradiction and Harmony in Medieval Japan," p. 35.

17. According to Takuan, the first meeting between Daitō and Go-Daigo took place in 1319 (DBZ, p. 272), but the available evidence suggests that this date is about five years too early.

18. TSD, 48, 154a; Thomas Cleary and J. C. Cleary, trans., *The Blue Cliff Record,* p. 89.

19. Shunsaku does not refer to the debate by name or date (TSD, 81, 223b); Takuan dates it 1323 (DBZ, p. 272); Kokai dates it 1324 (Okuda, *Kōzen Daitō Kokushi nenpu,* p. 20). The 1325 date currently accepted gives credence to the report in the diary of Emperor Hanazono (Nakatsuka, *Shinkishū,* 2, 539). Because of the uncertainty of the date, the debate is sometimes called the "Genkō Debate," after the era that preceded the Shōchū period.

20. The following account of the debate is drawn from Takuan's *Chronicle* (DBZ, p. 272) and Kokai's edition of the *Chronicle* (Okuda, *Kōzen Daitō Kokushi nenpu,* p. 20).

21. The phrase is attributed to Yang I (968–1024). For its citation in the *Blue Cliff Record,* see TSD, 48, 183a; or Cleary and Cleary, *Blue Cliff Record,* p. 327. An earlier use of the phrase in Japan is found in the writings of Lan-ch'i Tao-lung (Trevor Leggett, *Zen and the Ways,* p. 61).

22. Daigan Matsunaga and Alicia Matsunaga, *Foundation of Japanese Buddhism,* 1, 156.

23. TSD, 48, 181c; Cleary and Cleary, *Blue Cliff Record,* p. 318.

24. TSD, 48, 169a; Cleary and Cleary, *Blue Cliff Record,* p. 187.

25. Shunsaku recounts this additional exchange (undated) but does not mention the Shōchū Debate (TSD, 81, 223b). Takuan recounts the Shōchū Debate but does not mention the additional exchange (DBZ, p. 272). Kokai includes both dialogues, dating the additional exchange a year before the Shōchū Debate (Okuda, *Kōzen Daitō Kokushi nenpu,* pp. 19–20).

26. TSD, 81, 223b. Compare D. C. Lau, trans., *Mencius,* pp. 139–140.

27. Kenneth Kraft, trans., "Musō Kokushi's *Dialogues in a Dream,*" p. 93.

28. TSD, 81, 223b.

29. DBZ, p. 273.

30. *Ch'an-men kuei-shih,* in TSD, 51, 251a.

31. The *kaidō* quotations in this paragraph and the next are from TSD, 81, 191a.

32. See, for example, Ruth F. Sasaki, trans., *The Record of Lin-chi*, p. 1. Ironically, Lin-chi's disparagement of "customary etiquette" later became a formula used in *kaidō* ceremonies.

33. TSD, 81, 191c.

34. In 1325, at age fifty-one, Musō took over Nanzenji. In 1327 he became abbot of Jōchiji and then Zuisenji. In 1329 he headed Engakuji, and in 1332 he headed Rinsenji. In 1334 he headed Nanzenji again, in 1336 he headed Rinsenji again, and in 1339 he went to Saihōji. In 1340 Musō founded his own major monastery, Tenryūji, but he left Tenryūji in 1346 and went to Ungo-an, where he died at age seventy-seven.

35. TSD, 81, 206c.

36. TSD, 81, 209c.

37. DBZ, plate 51, p. 82.

38. To compile the most inclusive list of Go-Daigo's proclamations regarding Daitokuji, one must consult two sources: *Daitokuji monjo*, in *Dai Nihon komonjo, iewake* 17, vol. 1; and *Dai Nihon shiryō*, vol. 6, nos. 1, 2. Andrew Goble gives the dates of over twenty decrees concerning the temple's landholdings (especially for the Tomono, Takaie, Urakami, and Miyake estates) in "Go-Daigo and the Kemmu Restoration," pp. 328–329, nn. 66, 68.

39. Tayama, *Daitokuji*, plate 253, p. 255.

40. Ibid., plate 306, p. 287.

41. Ibid., plate 278, p. 273.

42. Ibid., plate 307, p. 288.

43. Ibid., plate 309, p. 289.

44. Okuda, *Kōzen Daitō Kokushi nenpu*, pp. 30–31.

45. TSD, 81, 216c.

46. Okuda, *Kōzen Daitō Kokushi nenpu*, p. 18.

47. TSD, 81, 223b.

48. Okuda, *Kōzen Daitō Kokushi nenpu*, p. 32.

49. TSD, 81, 214c. Chapter 25 of the *Lotus Sutra* states: "To those who can be conveyed to deliverance by the body of the general of the gods he preaches Dharma by displaying the body of the general of the gods" (Leon Hurvitz, trans., *Scripture of the Lotus Blossom of the Fine Dharma*, p. 314).

50. TSD, 81, 217c.

51. Tayama, *Daitokuji*, plate 305, p. 287. The directives by emperors Go-Daigo and Hanazono establishing Daitokuji's single-line succession set it apart from most of its peer monasteries. In theory, this privilege was intended to preserve Daitō's style of Zen, though the ensuing lack of access to talented monks from other lineages was at times a disadvantage for the monastery. Today the injunction is interpreted loosely: most of Daitokuji's recent abbots have belonged to the Myōshinji line of Daitō's heir Kanzan. In recognition of their abiding link with the imperial family, the priests of Daitokuji still chant sutras for the "two courts" three times a month.

52. The granting of Daitō's earliest titles cannot be dated with precision. A 1912 history of Daitokuji states that Hanazono awarded "Kōzen Daitō" after his first formal interview with the master and that Go-Daigo awarded "Shōtō" after his meeting with Daitō at the palace (Hirano Sōjō, *Ryūhōzan Daitokuzenji seifu*, pp. 88–89). Isshū Miura and Ruth F. Sasaki claim that 1334 was the year that Hanazono conferred "Kōzen Daitō" and Go-Daigo conferred "Kōshō Shōtō" (*Zen Dust*, p. 234). According to the documentary evidence, however, these estimates seem too early.

53. *Bakuryō hinmoku kaisetsu*, p. 28.

54. In 1322 Go-Daigo and Hanazono were involved in a mild dispute over land, and in 1324 Hanazono was displeased by Go-Daigo's behavior in the aftermath of the antishogunal plot. See Goble, "Go-Daigo and the Kemmu Restoration," pp. 90–93, 99.

55. Nakatsuka, *Shinkishū*, vol. 2, pp. 350, 414; H. Paul Varley, *Imperial Restoration in Medieval Japan,* p. 69.

56. Nakatsuka, *Shinkishū*, 2, 576.

57. Hirano Sōjō, *Daitō*, pp. 32, 38.

6. Enlightenment and Authenticity

1. Adapted from Katō Ryūhō, "Rinzaishū ni okeru zendō no seikatsu," pp. 81–82. The wandering monk is traditionally identified as the Ch'an master Hsüeh-feng I-ts'un (822–908) in his youth.

2. John C. Maraldo, "Is There Historical Consciousness within Ch'an?" p. 159.

3. Yanagida Seizan, *Rinzai roku*, p. 104; Ruth F. Sasaki, trans., *The Record of Lin-chi*, p. 14.

4. *Bendōwa*, in DZZ, 1, 734–735. Translation follows Norman Waddell and Abe Masao, "Dōgen's *Bendōwa*," p. 140.

5. TSD 48, 193a; Thomas Cleary and J. C. Cleary, trans., *The Blue Cliff Record*, p. 395.

6. *Shōbōgenzō Genjō kōan* (*Treasury of the True Dharma Eye, Realized Koan* fascicle), in DZZ, 1, 7.

7. DZZ, 1, 7. Two scholars who make a point of translating *shō* as "authenticate" are Thomas P. Kasulis, in *Zen Action/Zen Person*, p. 87, and Francis H. Cook, in "Dōgen's View of Authentic Selfhood," p. 133.

8. One of several scholars who translate *shō* as "enlighten" is Thomas Cleary in *Shōbōgenzō: Zen Essays by Dōgen*, p. 32.

9. *Bendōwa*, in DZZ, 1, 729.

10. Carl Bielefeldt, *Dōgen's Manuals of Zen Meditation*, p. 130.

11. *Butsudō*, in DZZ, 1, 386; Carl Bielefeldt, "Recarving the Dragon," p. 32.

12. Daigan Matsunaga and Alicia Matsunaga, *Foundation of Japanese Buddhism*, 2, 187.

13. Hee-jin Kim, *Dōgen Kigen—Mystical Realist*, p. 231.

14. Heinrich Dumoulin, *Zen Buddhism: A History*, p. 36.

15. Yanagida Seizan, *Rinzai no kafū*, p. 167.

16. Bernard Faure, "The Daruma-shū, Dōgen, and Sōtō Zen," p. 54.

17. Cleary and Cleary, *Blue Cliff Record*, p. 154.

18. D. T. Suzuki, *Zen and Japanese Culture*, p. 6.

19. John R. McRae, *The Northern School and the Formation of Early Ch'an Buddhism*, p. 123 (modified slightly).

20. Philip Yampolsky, trans., *The Platform Sutra*, p. 150.

21. Though attributed to Bodhidharma, this stanza first appeared as a set formula in *A Collection from the Gardens of the Patriarchs* (*Tsu-t'ing shih-yüan*), dated 1108. See Isshū Miura and Ruth F. Sasaki, *Zen Dust*, pp. 229–230.

22. In contemporary Japanese Zen, *kenshō* usually indicates the first experience of enlightenment (however shallow), a meaning that is narrower than earlier uses of the term in Ch'an/Zen.

23. Philip Kapleau, *The Three Pillars of Zen*, p. 194.

24. Miyauchi Sotai et al., *Kokuyaku Zengaku taisei*, 23, 9. Translation follows Thomas Cleary, trans., *The Original Face: An Anthology of Rinzai Zen*, pp. 29–30.

25. Cleary, *Shōbōgenzō*, p. 49 (modified slightly).
26. Neal Donner, "Effort and Intuition: The Sudden and the Gradual Reconsidered," p. 10.
27. Kenneth Kraft, trans., "Musō Kokushi's *Dialogues in a Dream*," pp. 90–91.
28. Kapleau, *Three Pillars of Zen*, p. 186.
29. Miyauchi, *Kokuyaku Zengaku taisei*, 23, 16.
30. Ibid., 23, 5.
31. Kapleau, *Three Pillars of Zen*, p. 177.
32. Cleary, *Shōbōgenzō*, p. 53.
33. Thomas Cleary, trans., *Timeless Spring: A Sōtō Zen Anthology*, pp. 113–114.
34. Kapleau, *Three Pillars of Zen*, p. 170.
35. Martin Collcutt, *Five Mountains*, p. 160.
36. Kim, *Dōgen Kigen*, pp. 69, 331.
37. *Shōbōgenzō Shizen biku (The Monk of Four Meditations)*, in DZZ, 1, 708.
38. Suzuki, *Zen and Japanese Culture*, p. 218.
39. See Shunryu Suzuki, *Zen Mind, Beginner's Mind*, p. 73.
40. Bielefeldt, "Recarving the Dragon," p. 37.
41. Personal correspondence from Sōgen Hori (May 1989).
42. Cleary, *The Original Face*, p. 27 (slightly modified).

7. Clarifying the Essentials of Zen

1. See, for example, Bernard Faure, "The Daruma-shū, Dōgen, and Sōtō Zen," pp. 52–55.
2. *Kōzen gokokuron*, in TSD, 80, 7b–7c; Faure, "The Daruma-shū, Dōgen, and Sōtō Zen," p. 40.
3. This statement may be truer for Japanese Zen than for Ch'an in China. The difficulties encountered by scholars who attempt to define Ch'an in terms of its meditation practices are summarized by T. Griffith Foulk in "The 'Ch'an School' and Its Place in the Buddhist Monastic Tradition," pp. 225–235.
4. John R. McRae, *The Northern School and the Formation of Early Ch'an Buddhism*, p. 130. The text attributed to Hung-jen was compiled by his disciples.
5. Martin Collcutt, *Five Mountains*, p. 160.
6. See Bernard Faure, "The Concept of One-Practice Samādhi in Early Ch'an," pp. 99–128; and Foulk, "The 'Ch'an School' and Its Place," pp. 116–130.
7. Ruth F. Sasaki, trans., *The Record of Lin-chi*, pp. 19, 54.
8. Kagamishima Genryū et al., *Yakuchū Zen'en shingi*, pp. 279–284.
9. Eisai, *Kōzen gokokuron*, in TSD, 80, 12a; Dōgen, *Fukan zazengi*, in DZZ, 2, 4; Lan-ch'i, *Zazenron*, in Miyauchi Sotai et al., *Kokuyaku Zengaku taisei*, 23, 25; Enni, *Shōichi Kokushi hōgo (Dharma Words of National Master Shōichi)*, in Raiba Takudō, ed., *Zenshū seiten*, p. 752.
10. Lan-ch'i was praised by Musō. See Kenneth Kraft, trans., "Musō Kokushi's *Dialogues in a Dream*," p. 84.
11. Collcutt, *Five Mountains*, pp. 159–160.
12. *Zazenron*, in Thomas Cleary, trans., *The Original Face*, pp. 21–22.
13. DZZ, 1, 737. Compare Norman Waddell and Abe Masao, trans., "Dōgen's *Bendōwa*," p. 144.
14. Carl Bielefeldt, *Dōgen's Manuals of Zen Meditation*, p. 169.
15. *Zazenron*, in Miyauchi, *Kokuyaku Zengaku taisei*, 23, 6; Cleary, *The Original Face*, p. 25.
16. Cleary, *The Original Face*, p. 76.

17. Waddell and Abe, "Dōgen's *Bendōwa,*" p. 139.
18. Hee-jin Kim, *Dōgen Kigen—Mystical Realist,* p. 74; Bielefeldt, *Dōgen's Manuals of Zen Meditation,* p. 125.
19. Kim, *Dōgen Kigen,* p. 75.
20. TSD, 48, 292c–293a; Philip Kapleau, *The Three Pillars of Zen,* p. 76.
21. McRae, *The Northern School,* p. 85.
22. Isshū Miura and Ruth F. Sasaki, *Zen Dust,* p. 255.
23. This account, recorded by Tsung-mi, was first brought to Japan by Saichō. Yanagida Seizan, *Daruma,* pp. 59–60.
24. *Transmission of the Lamp,* in Yanagida, *Daruma,* pp. 61–62. In reference to this story, Dōgen titled one of his *Shōbōgenzō* fascicles "Obtaining the Marrow Through Bowing" *(Raihai tokuzui).*
25. Philip Yampolsky, trans., *The Platform Sutra of the Sixth Patriarch,* p. 133.
26. Ruth F. Sasaki, trans., *The Record of Lin-chi,* p. 56.
27. Foulk, "The 'Ch'an School' and Its Place," pp. 72–73, 129.
28. Tayama Hōnan, ed., *Daitokuji,* plate 271, p. 268.
29. Kyoto National Museum, *Zen no bijutsu,* plate 28, p. 60.
30. *Shōbōgenzō Shisho (Documents of Succession),* in DZZ, 1, 338–339.
31. DBZ, plate 10, p. 20, translated by Norman Waddell, in DBZ, p. 300.
32. Yanagida Seizan, *Ikkyū: Kyōunshū no sekai,* p. 172.
33. *Hōkyōki* 31, in DZZ, 2, 384.
34. These and other robes from the period were exhibited by the Kyoto National Museum in 1981 and catalogued in its publication *Zen no bijutsu,* pp. 73–80.
35. Faure, "The Daruma-shū, Dōgen, and Sōtō Zen," pp. 35–38. See also Philip Yampolsky, "The Development of Japanese Zen," p. 142.
36. James H. Sanford, *Zen-man Ikkyū,* p. 51. Even if apocryphal, this account seems to capture Ikkyū's attitude toward seals of enlightenment.
37. Collcutt, *Five Mountains,* p. 153.
38. *Hōkyōki* 32, in DZZ, 2, 383, translated in Foulk, "The 'Ch'an School' and Its Place," p. 65 (modified slightly).
39. Eisai wrote *Essentials for Monks (Shukke taikō)* in 1195. Dōgen composed regulations throughout his teaching career, such as his *Precepts for the Head Cook (Tenzo kyōkun,* 1237). In 1278 Lan-ch'i created codes for two different temples, Jōrakuji and Kenchōji, and in 1339 Musō wrote his *Rinsenji Code (Rinsen kakun).*
40. Yuho Yokoi, trans., *Regulations for Monastic Life by Eihei Dogen,* pp. 30–31 (modified).
41. T. Griffith Foulk, "The Zen Institution in Modern Japan," p. 169.
42. D. T. Suzuki, *Manual of Zen Buddhism,* pp. 146–147 (modified slightly).
43. Cleary, *The Original Face,* p. 78.
44. Waddell and Abe, "Dōgen's *Bendōwa,*" pp. 148, 149.
45. *Shōbōgenzō Sanjushichihon-bodaibunpō (Thirty-seven Virtues of Bodhisattvahood),* in DZZ, 1, 511–513.
46. *Shōbōgenzō Shukke kudoku (Merits of Monkhood),* in DZZ, 1, 608.
47. Foulk, "The 'Ch'an School' and Its Place," p. 82.
48. Yampolsky, "The Development of Japanese Zen," p. 143.
49. Shibayama Zenkei, ed., *Zenrin kushū,* p. 267.
50. *Hōkyōki* 32, in DZZ, 2, 383.
51. Suzuki, *Manual of Zen Buddhism,* p. 46.
52. Foulk, "The 'Ch'an School' and Its Place," p. 90.
53. Collcutt, *Five Mountains,* pp. 188–189.
54. TSD, 80, 94b.

55. Collcutt, *Five Mountains,* p. 154.
56. Waddell and Abe, "Dōgen's *Bendōwa,*" p. 144.
57. Scholars cannot determine with certainty which master built the earliest Sung-style monks' hall. One problem is that the eagerness of the Zen pioneers (or their heirs) to claim credit for the first monks' hall in Japan may have led to distortions in the historical records. In addition, variant structures like Eisai's monks' hall at Kenninji, which incorporated Tendai and Shingon elements, are difficult to assess. Hee-jin Kim claims that the Kōshōji monks' hall, built by Dōgen in 1236, was the first (*Dōgen Kigen,* p. 251); Yokoyama Hideya quotes Dōgen (without citing a source) to the effect that the Eiheiji monks' hall of 1244 was the first (*Zen no kenchiku,* p. 177).
58. Collcutt, *Five Mountains,* p. 193.
59. *Ching-te ch'uan-teng lu,* ch. 28, in TSD, 51, 444.
60. Miura and Sasaki, *Zen Dust,* p. 250.
61. Cited by Dōgen in *Zuimonki (Gleanings)* 5:14, in DZZ, 2, 477.
62. Sasaki, *Record of Lin-chi,* p. 22.
63. Ibid., pp. 41, 49.
64. TSD, 82, 380a.
65. *Rinsen kakun,* cited in Collcutt, *Five Mountains,* pp. 153, 160.
66. *Shōbōgenzō Gyōji (Continuous Practice)* 2, in DZZ, 1, 153.
67. *Zuimonki* 5:14, in DZZ, 2, 477.
68. Haga Kōshirō et al., "Japanese Zen," p. 82. Other depictions of Dōgen as a seeker of seclusion are found in Kim, *Dōgen Kigen,* p. 228, and George Sansom, *A History of Japan to 1334,* pp. 429–430.
69. Furuta Shōkin, *Nihon Bukkyō shisō-shi no shōmondai,* pp. 154–155; Carl Bielefeldt, "Recarving the Dragon," pp. 40–41.
70. Furuta Shōkin, *Bassui,* p. 273.
71. Cited in Ogisu Jundō, *Nihon chūsei Zenshū-shi,* p. 95.
72. Haga, "Japanese Zen," p. 91 (modified slightly).
73. Sanford, *Zen-man Ikkyū,* p. 48.
74. Thomas P. Kasulis, "The Incomparable Philosopher: Dōgen on How to Read the *Shōbōgenzō,*" p. 93.
75. Faure, "The Daruma-shū, Dōgen, and Sōtō Zen," p. 53.

8. Daitō's Zen: The Primacy of Awakening

1. Scroll dated Kenmu 3 [1336], in DBZ, plate 73, p. 113, translated by Norman Waddell in DBZ, p. 291.
2. *Daitō Kokushi hōgo (Dharma Words of National Master Daitō),* in Raiba Takudō, *Zenshū seiten,* p. 744.
3. TSD, 81, 192a.
4. Scroll dated Gentoku 2 [1332], in DBZ, plate 72, p. 112, translated by Norman Waddell in DBZ, p. 290.
5. Raiba, *Zenshū seiten,* p. 741.
6. Ibid., pp. 748, 740.
7. Ibid., p. 749.
8. Scroll dated Kenmu 4 [1337], in DBZ, plate 64, p. 105, translated by Norman Waddell in DBZ, p. 293.
9. Raiba, *Zenshū seiten,* p. 740.
10. Ibid., pp. 745–746.
11. DBZ, p. 271. Daitō also discusses *kenshō* at some length in *Shōunyawa (Evening Dialogue at Shōun-an),* which purports to record a conversation between Daitō and another teacher. See Hirano Sōjō, *Daitō,* pp. 377, 379, 390.

12. Raiba, *Zenshū seiten*, p. 743.
13. Ibid., pp. 743–751.
14. Hirano Sōjō, *Daitō Zen no tankyū*, p. 61.
15. DBZ, pp. 274, 275. Though the first textual evidence for Daitō's "Final Admonitions" is found in Takuan's biography of 1617, there are references to the work in earlier texts, such as the first biography of Daitō in 1426 (TSD, 81, 224a–224b) and the poetry of Ikkyū. Scholars accordingly accept the traditional attribution to Daitō.
16. DBZ, p. 275.
17. Raiba, *Zenshū seiten*, p. 743.
18. Ibid., p. 743.
19. Ibid., p. 745.
20. DBZ, p. 274.
21. DBZ, p. 27.
22. Raiba, *Zenshū seiten*, p. 739.
23. Ibid., p. 749.
24. Ibid., p. 744.
25. Ibid., p. 739.
26. Ibid., p. 746.
27. Ibid., p. 746.
28. Ibid., p. 749.
29. Hirano, *Daitō Zen no tankyū*, p. 63.
30. Raiba, *Zenshū seiten*, p. 748.
31. TSD, 81, 224a.
32. TSD, 81, 209a.
33. Raiba, *Zenshū seiten*, p. 743.
34. Colophon to Daitō's transcription of the *Transmission of the Lamp*, translated by Norman Waddell in DBZ, p. 295.
35. Scroll dated Kenmu 3 [1336], in DBZ, plate 73, p. 113, translated by Norman Waddell in DBZ, p. 291.
36. Okuda Shōzō, *Kōzen Daitō Kokushi nenpu*, pp. 37–38.
37. Scroll dated Kenmu 4 [1337], in DBZ, plate 65, p. 106, translated by Norman Waddell in DBZ, p. 292 (slightly modified).
38. Scroll dated Karyaku 4 [1329], in DBZ, plate 52, p. 84, translated by Norman Waddell in DBZ, p. 294.
39. Scroll dated Kenmu 4 [1337], in DBZ, plate 66, p. 107, translated by Norman Waddell in DBZ, p. 292 (slightly modified).
40. Scroll dated Shōchū 2 [1325], in DBZ, plate 50, p. 81, translated by Norman Waddell in DBZ, p. 295.
41. Hirano Sōjō, *Ryūhōzan Daitokuji seifu*, p. 6.
42. Yanagida Seizan, *Rinzai no kafū*, pp. 176–177.
43. Ogisu Jundō, *Nihon chūsei Zenshū-shi*, p. 232.
44. Raiba, *Zenshū seiten*, p. 750.
45. Ibid., p. 740.
46. Ibid., p. 742.
47. Ibid., p. 750.
48. Okuda, *Kōzen Daitō Kokushi nenpu*, p. 22; decree by Emperor Go-Daigo, in Tayama Hōnan, ed., *Daitokuji*, plate 253, p. 255.
49. TSD, 81, 191a.
50. TSD, 81, 199b.
51. Raiba, *Zenshū seiten*, p. 748.
52. DBZ, p. 275.

53. Daitō's first biographer gives a brief description of the master's teaching style (TSD, 81, 224b), but the portrait is so idealized and the language so formulaic that it reveals little.

54. Inscription for a portrait dated Karyaku 2 [1327], in DBZ, plate 35, p. 49, translated by Norman Waddell in DBZ, p. 295 (slightly modified).

55. Portrait inscription by Emperor Go-Daigo, DBZ, plate 39, p. 53; portions of this translation follow Norman Waddell, DBZ, p. 296.

56. DBZ, plate 51, p. 83, translated by Norman Waddell in DBZ, p. 294 (slightly modified).

57. See, for example, Takeuchi Yoshinori, "The Philosophy of Nishida," in Frederick Franck, ed., *The Buddha Eye,* p. 194.

58. Ōta Zen, ed., *Shiryō sanshū: Hanazono Tennō shinki,* vol. 3, pp. 12, 25; Andrew Goble, "Truth, Contradiction and Harmony in Medieval Japan," p. 45.

59. DBZ, p. 272.

60. Undated scroll, DBZ, plate 70, p. 110, translated by Norman Waddell in DBZ, p. 292.

61. Undated scroll in Morita Shiryū, ed., *Bokubi,* no. 165, plate 16, pp. 26–27.

62. Kenneth Kraft, trans., "Musō Kokushi's *Dialogues in a Dream,*" p. 93.

9. Capping-Phrase Commentary in the Works of Daitō

1. TSD, 47, 614b.

2. Thomas Cleary and J. C. Cleary, trans., *The Blue Cliff Record,* p. 59 (modified slightly).

3. Trevor Leggett, *The Warrior Koans,* pp. 69–71 and passim.

4. John R. McRae, "Ch'an Commentaries on the *Heart Sūtra:* Preliminary Inferences on the Permutation of Chinese Buddhism," p. 99.

5. These five terms from the *Blue Cliff Record* appear in the following cases, respectively: case 4 (TSD, 48, 143b), case 17 (TSD, 48, 157b), case 8 (TSD, 48, 148b), case 83 (TSD, 48, 209a), and case 86 (TSD, 48, 211b).

6. See Tsuchiya Etsudō, ed., *Zenrin segoshū.*

7. Personal correspondence from Sōgen Hori (May 1989).

8. *Webster's New International Dictionary,* p. 395.

9. Yanagida Seizan, *Rinzai no kafū,* p. 175.

10. Shibayama Zenkei, ed., *Zenrin kushū,* p. 189.

11. Jon Carter Covell and Yamada Sōbin, *Zen at Daitoku-ji,* p. 28.

12. Shibayama, *Zenrin kushū,* p. 72.

13. TSD, 47, 505b; Ruth F. Sasaki, trans., *The Record of Lin-chi,* p. 54.

14. Sasaki, *Record of Lin-chi,* p. 86.

15. All the capping phrases in the following selection appear again in Chapter 12. There they are given a number that leads to their characters (Appendix II) and their sources (Appendix III). The phrases cited here are 135, 137; 107, 165, 46, 104; 6, 7; 19, 15, 23; 64; 24, 45; 41, 38; 187, 49, 55, 56; 52; 44; 109; 77; 105; 188; 130, 196; 86, 88; 189, 126, 118; 179, 172; 119; 181, 161, and 1; respectively.

16. Hirano Sōjō, "Daitō Kokushi agyo no kenkyū: I," p. 64.

17. Daitō's *One Hundred Twenty Cases* is discussed in Appendix I.

18. Hirano, "Daitō Kokushi agyo no kenkyū: I," p. 62. The full version of the text, with Daitō's capping phrases, continues in the following manner:

The monk said, "Even creeping creatures all have Buddha-nature. Why wouldn't a dog have Buddha-nature?"

Why doesn't he get control of himself and leave?
Chao-chou said, "Because it has its karmic nature."
The old thief has met complete defeat.

19. See Chapter 4, note 31.
20. TSD, 81, 191b.
21. Cleary and Cleary, *Blue Cliff Record,* p. 302.
22. Ibid., p. 301.
23. TSD, 81, 224c.
24. TSD, 47, 673c.
25. TSD, vol. 81, pp. 196a, 200a, 203b, 206a, 212a, 216c, 217c.
26. Phrases 79, 86, and 83 in Chapter 12.

10. *"His Tongue Has No Bones"*

1. Cited in Robert M. Gimello, "Wen-tzu Ch'an and K'an-hua Ch'an: Buddhism in the Transition from Northern to Southern Sung Literati Culture," p. 3.
2. Ibid., pp. 13–14 and passim. See also Robert M. Gimello, "Poetry and the *Kung-an* in Ch'an Practice," pp. 9–10; and Robert E. Buswell, Jr., "The 'Short-cut' Approach of *K'an-hua* Meditation," p. 345.
3. An early Japanese reference to *moji Zen* is cited in Haga Kōshirō, *Chūsei Zenrin no gakumon oyobi bungaku ni kansuru kenkyū,* p. 253. Another pertinent Ch'an/Zen term is *gonsen* (Ch. *yen-ch'üan*), "the investigation of words." Through *gonsen,* one may achieve an insightful understanding of language and an ability to use words skillfully. Whereas *moji Zen* had broad application, *gonsen* was a technical term related to koan practice.
4. *The Shorter Oxford English Dictionary,* 2, 641.
5. Yanagida Seizan, "Japanese Zen and the Turning of the Seasons," p. 21.
6. Burton Watson, "Zen Poetry," p. 115.
7. Ibid., p. 111; Shibayama Zenkei, ed., *Gōko fugetsu shū,* p. 46. Another translation is offered by David Pollack in *Zen Poems of the Five Mountains,* p. 7.
8. This text, known as the *Tai-pieh (Daibetsu)* of Hsü-t'ang, is included in his discourse record: TSD, 47, 1024b–1034b.
9. TSD, 80, 7b–7c. Portions of this rendering follow a translation by Philip Yampolsky, cited in Bernard Faure, "The Daruma-shū, Dōgen, and Sōtō Zen," pp. 39–40.
10. TSD, 80, 10c.
11. TSD, 80, 11b.
12. Faure, "The Daruma-shū, Dōgen, and Sōtō Zen," p. 42.
13. *Shōbōgenzō Bukkyō (Buddhist Teachings),* in DZZ, 1, 308; *Shōbōgenzō Bukkyō (Buddhist Sutras),* in DZZ, 1, 405.
14. DZZ, 1, 741; Norman Waddell and Abe Masao, trans., "Dōgen's Ben-dōwa," p. 149.
15. Cited in Tamamura Takeji, *Musō Kokushi,* p. 129.
16. Nakatsuka Eijirō, ed., *Shinkishū,* 2, 576.
17. Kenneth Kraft, trans., "Musō Kokushi's *Dialogues in a Dream,*" p. 92. Here the character *zen* refers to *dhyāna* meditation as well as the Zen school, just as *kyō* refers simultaneously to the teachings, the doctrinal schools, and the sutras.
18. See Stephen D. Miller, "Religious Boundaries in Aesthetic Domains: A Study of Buddhist Poetry *(Shakkyō-ka)* in the Late Heian and Early Kamakura Periods."

19. Cited in Gary L. Ebersole, "The Buddhist Ritual Use of Linked Poetry in Medieval Japan," p. 61.

20. Ibid., pp. 50–71.

21. Donald Keene, "The Comic Tradition in Renga," pp. 243–244.

22. Ibid., p. 244.

23. David Pollack, *The Fracture of Meaning*, p. 125.

24. Yanagida, "Japanese Zen and the Turning of the Seasons," p. 20.

25. Cited in Pollack, *The Fracture of Meaning*, p. 116.

26. Haga, *Chūsei Zenrin no gakumon*, pp. 245–256.

27. Ibid., p. 250.

28. Cited in Watson, "Zen Poetry," p. 115.

29. Cited in Pollack, *The Fracture of Meaning*, p. 123.

30. TSD, 80, 503c; Pollack, *The Fracture of Meaning*, p. 129.

31. Andrew Goble, "Truth, Contradiction and Harmony in Medieval Japan," pp. 48–49; Haga, *Chūsei Zenrin no gakumon*, p. 396.

32. Haga, *Chūsei Zenrin no gakumon*, pp. 395, 397.

33. Goble, "Truth, Contradiction and Harmony in Medieval Japan," p. 52.

34. TSD, 81, 554a, translated by Norman Waddell (unpublished manuscript; slightly modified).

35. TSD, 81, 559b, translated by Norman Waddell (unpublished manuscript; slightly modified).

36. TSD, 81, 218a.

37. TSD, 81, 554c.

38. *Yōgyukyōginka*, in Hirano Sōjō, *Daitō Zen no tankyū*, p. 73. Further information about *Yōgyukyōginka* is found in Appendix I.

39. *Yōgyukyōginka*, in Hirano, *Daitō Zen no tankyū*, p. 60.

40. TSD, 81, 213c.

41. Hsüeh-tou's verse is quoted in the *Record of Daitō*. See TSD, 81, 213b. See also Yanagida, "Japanese Zen and the Turning of the Seasons," p. 29.

42. TSD, 81, 213c; Yanagida, "Japanese Zen and the Turning of the Seasons," p. 30.

43. *Yōgyukyōginka*, in Hirano, *Daitō Zen no tankyū*, p. 68.

44. Chapter 12 includes several instances in which Daitō commented on the same koan using capping phrases and poems (in different works). Compare poem 14 and case 5; poem 20 and case 10; poem 15 and cases 18, 19; and poem 24 and cases 14, 15.

45. For example, see poem 13 in Chapter 12.

46. *Yōgyukyōginka*, in Hirano, *Daitō Zen no tankyū*, p. 75.

47. Ibid., p. 72.

48. *Ching-te ch'uan-teng lu*, ch. 16, in TSD, 51, 328b.

49. Shibayama Zenkei, *Zen Comments on the Mumonkan*, p. 101.

50. DBZ, p. 60, translated by Norman Waddell in DBZ, p. 295.

51. *Ching-te ch'uan-teng lu*, ch. 9, in TSD, 51, 268a.

52. Hirano Sōjō, *Daitō*, p. 379.

53. DBZ, plate 55, p. 87.

54. Raiba Takudō, *Zenshū seiten*, p. 746.

55. Thomas Cleary and J. C. Cleary, trans., *The Blue Cliff Record*, p. 33.

56. T. Griffith Foulk, "The 'Ch'an School' and Its Place in the Buddhist Monastic Tradition," p. 228.

57. Robert E. Buswell, Jr., "The 'Short-cut' Approach of *K'an-hua* Meditation," p. 336.

58. Raiba, *Zenshū seiten*, pp. 749–750.
59. *Gateless Barrier (Wu-men-kuan)*, case 24, in TSD, 48, 296a.
60. TSD, 81, 197b.
61. Pollack, *The Fracture of Meaning*, p. 131.
62. Edward Conze, *Buddhist Wisdom Books*, p. 63; Trevor Leggett, *The Warrior Koans*, p. 167 (modified).
63. *Yōgyukyōginka*, in Hirano, *Daitō Zen no tankyū*, p. 64.
64. Dale S. Wright, "Rethinking Transcendence: The Role of Language in Zen Experience," p. 13.
65. Ibid., p. 21.
66. Raiba, *Zenshū seiten*, p. 746.
67. John C. H. Wu, *The Golden Age of Zen*, p. 214.

11. Daitō's Impact

1. TSD, 81, 224a.
2. Raiba Takudō, *Zenshū seiten*, p. 1179.
3. DBZ, plates 67 and 68, pp. 108–109.
4. TSD, 51, 291a. This death poem is found in the Sung edition of the *Transmission of the Lamp* but not in the *Record of Lin-chi*. For another use of "the sword that splits a wind-blown hair," see Robert E. Buswell, Jr., "The 'Shortcut' Approach of *K'an-hua* Meditation," p. 335.
5. DBZ, p. 109.
6. Okuda Shōzō, *Kōzen Daitō Kokushi nenpu*, p. 22.
7. Ogisu Jundō, *Musō, Daitō*, p. 170. Ogisu identifies Ch'ing-cho Cheng-ch'eng (Ta-chien, 1274–1339) as the period's other influential master.
8. Reported in Takuan's *Chronicle*, DBZ, p. 275a.
9. Ogisu, *Musō, Daitō*, p. 169.
10. DBZ, p. 276c.
11. TSD, 81, 224a–224b. The slab of incense offered by Ch'ing-cho is preserved at Daitokuji.
12. TSD, 81, 224a.
13. Ogisu, *Musō, Daitō*, p. 171. One *koku* is equivalent to 44.8 gallons or 180 liters. Approximately 3.5 *koku* were said to support a monk for one year.
14. Martin Collcutt, *Five Mountains*, p. 265.
15. Ibid., p. 269.
16. Okuda, *Kōzen Daitō Kokushi nenpu*, pp. 14, 38.
17. Tayama Hōnan, ed., *Daitokuji*, plate 253, p. 255.
18. TSD, 81, 217a.
19. Takenuki Genshō, "Rinka ni okeru kyōdan keiei ni tsuite," pp. 132–133.
20. Collcutt, *Five Mountains*, pp. 222–224.
21. Tamamura Takeji, *Musō Kokushi*, p. 83.
22. Hirano Sōjō, *Daitō Zen no tankyū*, p. 154.
23. Isshū Miura and Ruth F. Sasaki, *Zen Dust*, p. 326.
24. Heinrich Dumoulin, *Zen Buddhism: A History*, p. 191.
25. Collcutt, *Five Mountains*, p. xviii.
26. Ibid., p. 269.
27. TSD, 81, 223b.
28. Katō Shū'ichi and Yanagida Seizan, *Ikkyū*, p. 73. Translation adapted from James H. Sanford, *Zen-man Ikkyū*, p. 99.
29. Ariyoshi Sawako and Kobori Nanrei, *Kojijunrei: Daitokuji*, p. 108. Compare Sanford, *Zen-man Ikkyū*, p. 99.
30. Translation follows Miura and Sasaki, *Zen Dust*, p. 140.

31. TSD, 81, 558c. Translated by Norman Waddell (unpublished manuscript).

32. Norman Waddell, trans., "Wild Ivy *(Itsumadegusa):* The Spiritual Autobiography of Hakuin Ekaku (II)," pp. 132–133, slightly modified. The poem Hakuin attributes to Daitō does not appear elsewhere in Daitō's writings.

33. TSD, vol. 81, pp. 558c, 579a.

34. Yanagida Seizan and Katō Shōshun, *Hakuin*, p. 93.

35. See, for example, Maruoka Sōnan, ed., *Daitokuji bokuseki zenshū;* Kyoto National Museum, *Zen no bijutsu;* Nakada Yujirō, ed., *Shodō geijutsu* 17; Morita Shiryū, ed., *Bokubi* 165.

36. Jan Fontein and Money L. Hickman, *Zen Painting and Calligraphy*, p. xliv.

37. T. Griffith Foulk, "The Zen Institution in Modern Japan," p. 158. These figures are based on a religious census taken in 1984.

38. Kajitani Sōnin, *Shūmon kattōshū*, pp. 231, 321, 375.

39. Akizuki Ryōmin, *Zen nyūmon*, p. 160.

40. TSD, 47, 497a; Ruth F. Sasaki, trans., *The Record of Lin-chi*, p. 6.

41. Hakuin's idiosyncratic capping phrases are the exception that proves the rule. He may have consciously resisted the increasing formalization of the genre.

42. Daitō's death is commemorated in November even though he died in the "twelfth month." This schedule reduces proximity with Kanzan's death anniversary (commemorated on December 12 at Myōshinji) and avoids the bitter cold of the unheated Dharma hall in late December.

43. During the Tokugawa era, one of the fifty-year anniversaries was held four years early to accommodate an abbot close to death, and that change determined the pattern of the ensuing fifty-year cycles.

44. The title granted by Emperor Shōwa (following a formal recommendation by the head abbot of Daitokuji) was "Reiki Inshō." Fifty years earlier Emperor Shōwa had given Daitō the title "Genkaku Kōen." The practice of granting "National Master" *(Kokushi)* titles to Daitō, initiated by emperors Go-Daigo and Hanazono, was renewed in 1686. It has yielded a title with over thirty characters: "Kōzen Daitō Kōshō Shōtō Daiji Unkyōshin Kōkan Jōmyō Enman Jōkō Daichi Shōkai Genkaku Kōen Reiki Inshō Kokushi" (see Glossary). When this title is chanted by the monks of Daitokuji, they use a variant pronunciation: "Kinzen Daiten Kōshō Shinten Daizu Inkyōshin Wankan Jōmin Enmon Jinkō Daishi Shinkai Engaku Ōen Rinki Inshō Kokushi."

45. The first volume of *Daitokuji bokuseki zenshū*, edited by Maruoka Sōnan, appeared in 1984; the first volume of *Daitokuji Zengoroku shūsei*, edited by Daitokuji, appeared in 1989.

46. TSD, 81, 223a. Daitō recorded this phrase on the scroll containing his enlightenment verses (DBZ, plate 43, p. 56).

47. DBZ, plate 39, p. 53.

48. A description by Kokai, editor of Takuan's *Chronicle* (Okuda, *Kōzen Daitō Kokushi nenpu*, p. 38).

49. Haga Kōshirō et al., "Japanese Zen," p. 97.

50. Ogisu, *Musō, Daitō*, p. 196.

51. Hirano Sōjō, *Ikkyū Sōjun*, pp. 60–61. For discussions of Musō's character, see Furuta Shōkin, *Zensō no shōji*, p. 186; Tsuji Zennosuke, *Buke jidai to Zensō*, p. 103.

52. Furuta Shōkin, "Kaisetsu," p. 169.

53. DBZ, plate 38, p. 52.

54. Sanford, *Zen-man Ikkyū*, p. 144 (modified slightly).

55. Hirano Sōjō, *Daitō,* p. 32; Furuta, "Kaisetsu," p. 169.
56. Okuda, *Kōzen Daitō Kokushi nenpu,* p. 51.

12. Translations

1. *Yōgyukyōginka,* in Hirano Sōjō, *Daitō Zen no tankyū,* p. 59.
2. Ibid., p. 60.
3. TSD, 81, 209c.
4. TSD, 81, 218a.
5. *Yōgyukyōginka,* in Hirano, *Daitō Zen no tankyū,* p. 63.
6. Ibid., p. 59.
7. TSD, 81, 223a; DBZ, p. 56.
8. TSD, 81, 223a; DBZ, p. 56.
9. TSD, 81, 192a.
10. *Yōgyukyōginka,* in Hirano, *Daitō Zen no tankyū,* p. 72.
11. Ibid., p. 65.
12. TSD, 81, 213c; Yanagida Seizan, "Japanese Zen and the Turning of the Seasons," p. 29.
13. TSD, 81, 218c.
14. Ibid., p. 218b.
15. Ibid., p. 218b.
16. *Yōgyukyōginka,* in Hirano, *Daitō Zen no tankyū,* p. 73.
17. TSD, 81, 218b–218c.
18. *Yōgyukyōginka,* in Hirano, *Daitō Zen no tankyū,* p. 61.
19. TSD, 81, 218a.
20. Ibid., p. 218b.
21. *Yōgyukyōginka,* in Hirano, *Daitō Zen no tankyū,* p. 75.
22. TSD, 81, 218b.
23. *Yōgyukyōginka,* in Hirano, *Daitō Zen no tankyū,* p. 75.
24. TSD, 81, 218a.
25. *Yōgyukyōginka,* in Hirano, *Daitō Zen no tankyū,* p. 68.
26. TSD, 81, 199b.
27. DBZ, plates 67 and 68, pp. 108–109.
28. *Yōgyukyōginka,* in Hirano, *Daitō Zen no tankyū,* p. 74.
29. Ibid., p. 64.
30. Bibliographic information on these two works is found in Appendix I.
31. *Hyakunijussoku,* case 23, in Hirano Sōjō, "Daitō Kokushi agyo no kenkyū: I," p. 64. Chinese source: *Record of Lin-chi* (TSD, 47, 504c; Ruth F. Sasaki, trans., *The Record of Lin-chi,* p. 50). Phrase 96 in Appendix II.
32. *Hyakunijussoku,* case 118, in Hirano, "Daitō Kokushi agyo: I," p. 74. Chinese source: *Transmission of the Lamp* (TSD, 51, 362a). Phrase 4 in Appendix II.
33. *Hyakunijussoku,* case 26, in Hirano, "Daitō Kokushi agyo: I," p. 64. Chinese source: *Record of Lin-chi* (TSD, 47, 497a; Sasaki, *Record of Lin-chi,* p. 5). Phrase 130 in Appendix II.
34. *Hyakunijussoku,* case 1, in Hirano, "Daitō Kokushi agyo: I," p. 61. Chinese source: *Gateless Barrier* (TSD, 48, 297c; Katsuki Sekida, *Two Zen Classics,* p. 112). Phrases 56, 107, and 51, respectively, in Appendix II.
35. *Hekigan agyo,* case 37, in Hirano, "Daitō Kokushi agyo: I," p. 51. Chinese source: *Blue Cliff Record,* case 37 (TSD, 48, 175a; Thomas Cleary and J. C. Cleary, trans., *The Blue Cliff Record,* p. 274). Phrases 189, 49, 201, 202 in Appendix II.
36. *Hyakunijussoku,* case 101, in Hirano, "Daitō Kokushi agyo: I," p. 72. Chinese source: *Blue Cliff Record,* case 15, Yüan-wu's commentary (TSD, 48,

155c; Cleary and Cleary, *Blue Cliff Record,* p. 101). Phrases 203–205 in Appendix II.

37. *Hyakunijussoku,* case 21, in Hirano, "Daitō Kokushi agyo: I," p. 64. Chinese source: *Gateless Barrier,* case 47 (TSD, 48, 298c; Sekida, *Two Zen Classics,* p. 131). Phrases 94, 97, 97 in Appendix II.

38. *Hyakunijussoku,* case 99, in Hirano, "Daitō Kokushi agyo: I," p. 72. Chinese source: *Record of Lin-chi* (TSD, 47, 497a; Sasaki, *Record of Lin-chi,* p. 6). Phrases 140, 78, 108, 120 in Appendix II.

39. *Hyakunijussoku,* case 31, in Hirano, "Daitō Kokushi agyo: I," p. 65. Chinese source: *Record of Hsü-t'ang* (TSD, 47, 986c). Phrases 206, 207 in Appendix II.

40. *Hekigan agyo,* case 13, in Hirano, "Daitō Kokushi agyo: I," p. 49. Chinese source: *Blue Cliff Record,* case 13 (TSD, 48, 153c; Cleary and Cleary, *Blue Cliff Record,* p. 88). Phrases 208, 209, 115, 128 in Appendix II.

41. *Hyakunijussoku,* case 6, in Hirano, "Daitō Kokushi agyo: I," p. 62. A shorter version of this koan is the first case of the *Gateless Barrier;* the longer version is found in the *Record of Equanimity (Ts'ung-jung lu),* case 18 (TSD, 48, 238b). Phrases 162, 207, 210, 211, 23, 149 in Appendix II.

42. *Hyakunijussoku,* case 48, in Hirano, "Daitō Kokushi agyo: I," p. 67. Chinese source: *Gateless Barrier,* case 7 (TSD, 48, 293c; Sekida, *Two Zen Classics,* p. 44). Phrases 164, 185, 163, 35, 201 in Appendix II.

43. *Hyakunijussoku,* case 67, in Hirano, "Daitō Kokushi agyo: I," p. 69. Chinese source: *Blue Cliff Record,* case 1 (TSD, 48, 140a; Cleary and Cleary, *Blue Cliff Record,* p. 1). Phrases 212, 126, 213, 101, 27, 210, 94 in Appendix II.

44. *Hyakunijussoku,* case 108, in Hirano, "Daitō Kokushi agyo: I," p. 73. Chinese source: *Blue Cliff Record,* case 29 (TSD, 48, 169a; Cleary and Cleary, *Blue Cliff Record,* p. 187). Phrases 185, 214, 185, 26, 35 in Appendix II.

45. *Hekigan agyo,* case 29, in Hirano, "Daitō Kokushi agyo: I," p. 50. For *Blue Cliff Record* source, see preceding note. Phrases 55, 215, 179, 24, 25, 216 in Appendix II.

46. *Hyakunijussoku,* case 2, in Hirano, "Daitō Kokushi agyo: I," p. 61. Chinese source: *Blue Cliff Record,* case 8 (TSD, 48, 148b; Cleary and Cleary, *Blue Cliff Record,* p. 53). Phrases 130, 197, 62, 110, 217, 52, 152, 106, 57, 147, 151, 218 in Appendix II.

47. *Hekigan agyo,* case 8, in Hirano, "Daitō Kokushi agyo: I," p. 48. For *Blue Cliff Record* source, see preceding note. Phrases 184, 219, 48, 32, 102, 103, 153, 56, 152, 11 in Appendix II.

48. *Hyakunijussoku,* case 74, in Hirano, "Daitō Kokushi agyo: I," p. 70. Chinese source: *Blue Cliff Record,* case 23 (TSD, 48, 164a; Cleary and Cleary, *Blue Cliff Record,* p. 154). Phrases 220, 221, 138, 104, 155, 11, 222 in Appendix II.

49. *Hekigan agyo,* case 23, in Hirano, "Daitō Kokushi agyo: I," p. 50. For *Blue Cliff Record* source, see preceding note. Phrases 223, 50, 224, 119, 28, 29, 136, 196, 145 in Appendix II.

50. *Hyakunijussoku,* case 66, in Hirano, "Daitō Kokushi agyo: I," p. 55. Chinese source: *Blue Cliff Record,* case 66 (TSD, 48, 196b; Cleary and Cleary, *Blue Cliff Record,* p. 419). Phrases 225, 219, 176, 24, 150, 180, 160, 182, 226, 66, 18, 159, 181 in Appendix II.

51. The capping phrases in this section are drawn from Daitō's three written commentaries: *Essential Words for Careful Study (Sanshō goyō), One Hundred Twenty Cases (Hyakunijussoku),* and *Capping Phrases on The Blue Cliff Record (Hekigan agyo).* The first of these works is part of the *Record of Daitō.*

GLOSSARY

Adashino 化野
Agui 安居院
agyo 下語
Akamatsu Jirō Enshin 赤松二郎円心
Akamatsu Norimura 赤松則村
Akamatsu Norisuke 赤松則祐
Amida 阿弥陀
anokutara sanmyaku sanbodai 阿耨多羅三
　藐三菩提
Anzan 安山
Ashikaga Takauji 足利尊氏
Ashikaga Yoshimitsu 足利義満
Asuka 明日香

Bankei 盤珪
Bassui Tokushō 抜隊得勝
Bendōwa 辦道話
Betsugen Enshi 別源円旨
betsugo 別語
Biwa 琵琶
Bukkoku Kokushi 仏国国師
busshin'in 仏心印
butsuden 仏殿
Byakugō-in 白毫院

chaku 着
Ch'an 禅
ch'an 禅

Ch'ang-an 長安
Ch'ang-ch'ing 長慶
Chang Ming-yüan 張明遠
Ch'an-men kuei-shih 禅門規式
Ch'an-yüan ch'ing-kuei 禅苑清規
Chao-chou Ts'ung-shen 趙州従諗
Chekiang 浙江
Chiang-nan 江南
Chiao 教
chiao 教
chiao-ch'an i-chih 教禅一致
chiao-wai pieh-ch'uan 教外別伝
Chia-shan Shan-hui 夾山善会
chien-hsing 見性
Chien-ko 剣閣
Ching-ch'ing 鏡清
Ch'ing-cho Cheng-ch'eng 清拙正澄
ch'ing-kuei 清規
Ching-shan 径山
Ching-te ch'uan-teng lu 景徳伝燈録
Ching-tz'u 淨滋
chinsō 頂相
Chishō 地性
Chou 周
cho-yü 著語
chōzetsu no ijin 超絶の異人
Ch'üan 全
ch'uan 伝

241

Chuang-tzu 荘子
Chüeh-fan Hui-hung 覚範慧洪
Chūgan Engetsu 忠巌円月
Chūhō En'i 仲芳円伊
Chūhō Sō'u 宙宝宗宇
Chü-ti 俱胝

Daibetsu 代別
daigo 代語
Daijōji 大乗寺
Dainichi Nōnin 大日能忍
Daiō Kokushi 大応国師
Daisen-in 大仙院
Daisetsu Sonō 大拙祖能
daishi 大死
Daitō 大燈
Daitō Kokushi goroku 大燈国師語録
Daitō Kokushi gyōgōki 大燈国師行業記
Daitō Kokushi gyōjō 大燈国師行状
Daitō Kokushi hōgo 大燈国師法語
Daitokuji 大徳寺
Daitokuji hennen ryakki 大徳寺編年略記
*Daitoku Kaisan Kōzen Daitō Kōshō Shōtō
    Daiji Unkyōshin Kōkan Jōmyō
    Kokushi nenpu* 大徳開山興禅大燈
    高照正燈大慈雲匡真弘鑑常明国
    師年譜
Dazaifu 太宰府
den 伝
denbōin 伝法印
dharani 陀羅尼
Dōgen Kigen 道元希玄
Dōkai 道海
Dōshō 道昭

Echizen 越前
Eiheiji 永平寺
engaku 円覚
Engakuji 円覚寺
Enkyōji 円鏡寺
Enni Ben'en 円爾辨円
Enpō dentōroku 延宝伝灯録
Enshin 円心

Fa-ju 法如
Fa-yen 法眼
Fen-chou Wu-yeh 汾州無業

Feng-hsüeh 風穴
Fen-yang Shan-chao 汾陽善照
Fo-chao Te-kuang 仏照徳光
Fugen 普賢
Fukan zazengi 普勧坐禅儀
Fukuoka 福岡
Funaoka 船岡
Fusō Zenrin sōbōden 扶桑禅林僧宝伝

Gatsurin Dōkō 月林道皎
Gazan 峨山
gedatsu 解脱
Gen'e 玄恵
Genkaku Kōen 玄覚浩淵
Genkō 元亨
Genkō Shakusho 元亨釈書
Gentoku 元徳
Gifu 岐阜
Giju Gikkodoku-on 祇樹給孤獨園
Gion 祇園
gō 号
Go-Daigo 後醍醐
Gojō 五条
Go-Murakami 後村上
Gongai Sōchū 言外宗忠
gonsen 言詮
goroku 語録
Go-Uda 後宇多
Gozan bungaku 五山文学
Gudō 愚堂
Guhei 具平
Gyokushū Sōhan 玉舟宗璠

ha 派
Ha'ichisonshukuyawa 破一尊宿夜話
Hakata 博多
Hakuin Ekaku 台隠慧鶴
Hanazono 花園
Han Yü 韓愈
hara-kiri 腹切り
Harima 播磨
Hasonshukuyawa 破尊宿夜話
hattō 法堂
Heian 平安
heigo 平語
Heike 平家
Hekigan agyo 碧巌下語

Hekigan hyakusoku Daitō Kokushi agyo
　碧巌百則大燈国師下語
Hekigan kugi 碧巌句義
Hekiganshū koshō 碧巌集古鈔
Heng-ch'ü 横趨
Hiei 比叡
Higashiyama 東山
Himeji 姫路
Hitachi 常磐
hitsudan 筆談
ho 喝
hōe 法衣
hōgo 法語
hōjō 方丈
Hōjō Masako 北条政子
Hōjō Sadatoki 北条貞時
Hōjō Tokimune 北条時宗
Hōjō Tokiyori 北条時頼
Hōkyōki 宝慶記
honbun no hito 本分の人
honbun no shūshi 本分の宗師
Honchō kōsōden 本朝高僧伝
Hōnen 法然
hongo 本語
hō no manako 法の眼
honrai 本来
Hōrinji 宝林寺
Hōshun-in 芳春院
Hsiang 象
Hsiang-lin 香林
Hsiang-yen 香巌
Hsia-t'ang Hui-yüan 瞎道慧遠
hsia-yü 下語
Hsien-ch'un 咸淳
Hsing-shan 杏山
Hsüan-i 玄義
Hsüeh-feng I-ts'un 雪峰義存
Hsüeh-tou Ch'ung-hsien 雪竇重顕
Hsüeh-tou lu 雪竇録
Hsü Hun 許渾
Hsü-t'ang Chih-yü 虚堂智愚
Huang Chao 黄巣
Huang-lung Ch'an 黄竜禅
Huang-po Hsi-yün 黄檗希運
Huang T'ing-chien 黄庭堅
hua-t'ou 話頭
Hua-yen 華巌

Hui-k'o 恵可
Hui-neng 恵能
Hunan 湖南
Hung-chih Cheng-chüeh 宏智正覚
Hung-jen 弘忍
Hyakunijussoku 百二十則
Hyōgo 兵庫
hyōjun 標準

Ibaraki 茨城
i-chuan-yü 一転語
Ikkyū Sōjun 一休宗純
I-k'ung 義空
imina 諱
inkajō 印可状
Isei 揖西
I-shan I-ning 一山一寧
Itsumadegusa 壁生草
ittengo 一転語

jaku 著
jakugo 著語
Jakushitsu Genkō 寂室元光
Jien 慈円
jijuyūzanmai 自受用三昧
Jinnō shōtōki 神皇正統記
jishō 自証
jōbutsu 成仏
Jōchiji 常智寺
jōdō 成道
Jōdo Shinshū 浄土真宗
Jōmin 紹明
Jōrakuji 常楽寺
Jufukuji 寿福寺
juko 頌古
jun'ichi no buppō 沌一の仏法
Junna 淳和
Juō Sōhitsu 授翁宗弼

kafū 家風
Kaiankokugo 槐安国語
kaidō 開堂
kaigen 開眼
kaisan 開山
Kaishin 戒信
kaku 覚

Kakua 覚阿
Kakuin Gitei 覚印義諦
Kakukai 覚海
Kakunyo 覚如
Kamakura 鎌倉
kami 神
kamikaze 神風
Kamo 加茂
kan 関
kana 仮名
Kanao 賀名生
Kanazawa 金沢
Kanbun 寛文
kanbun 漢文
k'an-hua 看話
Kannon 観音
Kanzan Egen 関山慧玄
Kaō 嘉応
kaō 花押
Kao-t'ing 高亭
Kariteimo 訶梨帝母
Karyaku 嘉暦
Kasagidera 笠置寺
Kasō Sōdon 華叟宗曇
katsu 喝
Keizan 瑩山
Kenchōji 建長寺
Kenmu 建武
Kenninji 建仁寺
Kenpō Shidon 乾峰士曇
kenshō 見性
kesa 袈裟
Ki 紀
Kiangsi 江西
Kii 紀伊
Kinugasa 衣笠
Kitabatake Chikafusa 北畠親房
Kitayama 北山
Kō 光
Kōan 弘安
kōan 公案
Kōfukuji 興福寺
Kōhō Kennichi 高峰顕日
koji o kyūmei-su 已事を究明す
Kokai Sōnyo 巨海宗如
Kokan Shiren 虎関師錬

koku 石
kokushi (provincial governor) 国司
kokushi (national master) 国師
Komazawa 駒沢
Kōmyō 光明
Kongō Dōji 金剛童子
Konjaku monogatari 今昔物語
Kosei 虎聖
Kōsen Seikyō 高泉性激
Kōshō-hōrinji 興聖宝林寺
Kōshōji 興聖寺
Kōshō Shōtō Kokushi 高照正燈国師
koto 琴
Kōtokuji 興徳寺
Kōya 高野
Kōzen Daitō Kōshō Shōtō Daiji
    Unkyōshin Kōkan Jōmyō
    Enman Jōkō Daichi Shōkai
    Genkaku Kōen Reiki Inshō
    Kokushi 興禅大燈高照正燈大滋
    雲匡真弘鑑常明圓満淨光大知性
    海玄覚浩淵霊暉永照国師
Kōzen gokokuron 興禅護国論
Kuei-shan 潙山
Kūkai 空海
Kumano 熊野
kung-an 公案
kuri 庫裏
kusunoki 楠
Kusunoki Masashige 楠正成
Kuzōshi 句雙紙
kyō 教
kyōge betsuden 教外別伝
Kyōgoku Tamekane 京極為兼
kyōzen itchi 教禅一致

Lan-ch'i Tao-lung 蘭溪道隆
Lao-tzu 老子
Li 李
Liang 梁
Lin-chi 臨済
Lin-chi lu 臨済録
Ling-yin-ssu 霊隠寺
Ling-yun 霊雲
Li tai fa pao chi 歴代法宝記
Liu-tsu t'an ching 六祖壇経

Lü 律

Lung-ya Chü-tun 龍牙居遁

maeku 前句

makuwa-uri 真桑瓜

Mangen Shiban 卍元師蛮

Manjuji 万寿寺

mappō 末法

matsudai 末代

Ma-tsu Tao-i 馬祖道一

Miidera 三井寺

Ming 明

Ming-chi Ch'u-chün 明極楚俊

Mino 美濃

Miyake 三宅

moji Zen 文字禅

mondō 問答

Monju 文殊

Morinaga 護良

Mu 無

mu 無

Mujū Ichien 無住一円

Murakami 村上

Murasakino 紫野

murie no tokoro ni mukatte 無理会の処に
　　向かって

Muromachi 室町

mushi dokugo 無師独悟

Musō Soseki 夢窓疎石

Myōan Eisai 明庵栄西

Myōchō 妙超

Myōgyō 妙暁

Myōhō 妙峯

Myōshinji 妙心寺

Nan-ch'üan P'u-yüan 南泉普願

Nanpo Jōmyō 南浦紹明

Nanshōbō 南証房

Nan-yüan Hui-yung 南院慧顒

Nanzenji 南禅寺

Nara 奈良

nenbutsu 念仏

nenro 拈弄

Nichiren 日蓮

Nihon Daruma 日本達摩

nijūnen chōyō 二十年長養

Nishida Kitarō 西田幾太郎

Nishitani Keiji 西谷啓治

Nitta Yoshisada 新田義貞

Niwase 庭瀬

nyūdō 入道

Ōei 応永

Oki 隠岐

omote no go 表の語

Ōnin 応仁

Ōtōkan 応燈関

Ōtomo Yorihisa 大友頼尚

Ōuchi Yoshihiro 大内義弘

Oyake 小宅

Pai-chang Huai-hai 百丈懐海

Pa-ling 巴陵

P'ang Yün 龐蘊

P'an-shan 盤山

Pao-fu 保福

pieh-yü 別語

Pi-yen lu 碧巌録

P'o-an Tsu-hsien 破庵祖先

Po-yün chi 白雲集

P'u-hua 普化

Reiki Inshō 霊暉永照

Reisen-in 霊泉院

renga 連歌

rinka 林下

Rinsenji 臨川寺

Rinsen kakun 臨川家訓

Rinzai Zen 臨済禅

Rokuhara 六波羅

Ryō 了

Ryōgen-in 竜源院

Ryōgi 了義

Ryōkō-in 竜光院

ryōsai issai 両釆一賽

Ryōshōji 竜祥寺

ryū 流

Ryūhō 竜宝

*Ryūhō Kaisan Tokushi Kōzen Daitō
　　Kōshō Shōtō Kokushi goroku* 竜宝開
　　山特賜興禅大燈高照正燈国師
　　語録

Saga 嗟峨
Saichō 最澄
Saigyō 西行
Saihōji 西芳寺
Sakai 堺
samurai 侍
sanmon 山門 (三門)
San-sheng Hui-jan 三聖慧然
Sanshō goyō 参詳語要
santengo 三転語
sanzen 参禅
satori 悟り
sego 世語
sei 省
Seian Sōi 清庵宗意
sei ari 省あり
Seiryōden 清涼殿
Senkō 宣光
Senshinshi 洗心子
sesshin 接心
Sesson Yūbai 雪村友梅
setsuwa bungaku 説話文学
Shakkyō-ka 釈教歌
Shao-lin 少林
shari 舎利
Sharisandan 舎利讃嘆
Shen-hsiu 神秀
Shih-ying Shih-ts'un 釈英実存
Shijō 四条
shikantaza 只管打坐
shin 真
Shinchi Kakushin 心地覚心
Shin'ei Sōetsu 心瑛宗悦
shingi (pure regulations) 清規
shingi (truth/falsity) 真偽
Shingon 真言
shinjitsu no buppō 真実の仏法
shinjō 真乗
Shinju-an 真珠庵
Shinran 親鸞
shinshō 真証
shinshō no kenge 真正の見解
Shinshū-an 心宗庵
shisho 嗣書
shō (true, authentic) 正
shō (authenticate, enlighten, prove) 証
shōbō 正法

Shōbōgenzō 正法眼藏
  Bukkyō (Buddhist teachings) 仏教
  Bukkyō (Buddhist sutras) 仏経
  Butsudō 仏道
  Genjō kōan 現成公案
  Gyōji 行持
  Jishō zanmai 自証三昧
  Raihai tokuzui 礼拝得髓
  Sanjushichihon-bodaibunpō 三十七品
    菩提分法
  Senjō 洗浄
  Shisho 嗣書
  Shizen biku 四禅比丘
  Shukke kudoku 出家功德
Shōchū 正中
shōden 正伝
Shōden-an 正伝庵
shōgaku 正覚
Shōichi kanahōgo 聖一仮名法語
shōjū 正宗
Shōkū 性空
shōmon 正門
Shōrinji 少林寺
Shosha 書写
shōtaichōyō 聖胎長養
Shōtaku 清沢
Shōun-an 祥雲庵
Shōunyawa 祥雲夜話
Shōwa (1312–1317) 正和
Shōwa (1926–1989) 昭和
shū 宗
shugo 守護
Shūhō Kokushi 宗峰国師
Shūhō Myōchō 宗峰妙超
shukke 出家
Shukke taikō 出家大綱
Shun 舜
Shunpo Sōki 春浦宗熙
Shunsaku Zenkō 春作禅興
so 祖
Sōden Dōkai 桑田道海
sōdō 僧堂
Sōfukuji 崇福寺
Sōgen 宗元
sōgo 総語
Sōin 宗印
Sōji 宗二

Sōju 宗寿
Sōnin 宗忍
Sōren 宗廉
Sōrin 宗琳
Sōtetsu 宗徹
Sōtō 曹洞
Sozan 祖山
Suefusa 季房
Suga 管
Sun 孫
Sung 宋
Sung-yüan Ch'ung-yüeh 松源崇岳
Szechuan 四川

Ta-chien 大鷲
Ta-ch'uan P'u-chi 大川普済
Ta-chüeh 大覚
Tadamasa 忠正
Ta-hui Tsung-kao 大慧宗杲
tai 体
taigo tettei 大悟徹底
Taiheiki 太平記
Tai-pieh 代別
tai-yü 代語
Takaie 高家
Takuan Sōhō 沢庵宗彭
Tandō Shōshuku 端堂紹繍
T'ang 唐
Tango 丹後
Tan-hsia 丹霞
Tao 道
Tao-hsüan 道璿
Tao-yüan 道源
Ta-sui 大隋
Tatsuno 竜野
Tendai 天台
Tenmon 天文
Tennōji 天王寺
Tenrin Sōkotsu 天倫宗忽
Tenryūji 天龍寺
Tenshitsu Sōchiku 天室宗竺
Tentakuji 天沢寺
Tentaku tōinroku 天沢東胤録
Tenzo kyōkun 典座教訓
Te-shan 徳山
Tettō Gikō 徹翁義亨
T'ien-t'ai 天台

T'ien-t'ung Ju-ching 天童如浄
Tōfukuji 東福寺
Tōji 東寺
Tōkō-an 韜光庵
Tokugawa 徳川
Tokuji 徳治
Tokushi Kōzen Daitō Kokushi sanshō goyō
　特賜興禅大燈国師参詳語要
Tokuzenji 徳禅寺
Tomono 伴野
tonseisha 遁世者
Toribeyama 鳥辺山
Tou-shuai 兜卒
Toyama 遠山
Tōyō Eichō 東陽英朝
Toyotomi Hideyoshi 豊臣秀吉
Ts'ao-hsi 曹渓
Ts'ao-shan 曹山
Ts'ao-tung 曹洞
Tso-ch'an i 坐禅儀
Ts'ui-feng 翠峯
Ts'ui-yen Ling-ts'an 翠巌令参
tsukeku 付句
tsung 宗
Tsung-ching lu 宗鏡録
Ts'ung-jung lu 従容録
Tsung-mi 宗密
Tsūō Kyōen 通翁鏡円
Tsurezuregusa 徒然草
Tsu-t'ang chi 祖堂集
Tsu-t'ing shih-yüan 祖庭事苑
Tung-ling Yung-yü 東稜永璵
Tung-ming Hui-jih 東明慧日

Uchiyama 内山
Ungo-an 雲居庵
Unmon-an 雲門庵
Unrin-in 雲林院
Urakami Kamon 浦上掃部
ura no go 裏の語
Usuba 臼庭
Ususama 烏蒭沙摩

waka 和歌
Wang Wei 王維
watō 話頭
wen-tzu Ch'an 文字禅

Wu 武
wu 無
Wu-chun Shih-fan 無準師範
Wu-hsüeh Tsu-yüan 無学祖元
Wu-men Hui-k'ai 無門懷海
Wu-men-kuan 無門関
Wu-t'ai 五台
Wu-tsu Fa-yen 五祖法演

Yamana Tokiuji 山名時氏
Yang-ch'i 楊岐
Yang I 楊億
Yang-shan Hui-chi 仰山慧寂
Yao-shan 藥山
yen-ch'üan 言詮
Yen-t'ou 嚴頭
Yōgyukyōginka 養牛軽吟歌
Yomogisa 蓬左
Yōsai 栄西
Yoshida Kenkō 吉田兼好
Yoshino 吉野
Yōsō Sōi 養叟宗頤

yū 用
Yüan 元
Yüan-wu K'o-ch'in 円悟克勤
yuikai 遺戒
Yung-chia 永嘉
Yün-kuang 雲光
Yün-men Wen-yen 雲門文偃
Yūtokuji 祐德寺

zazen 坐禅
Zazengi 坐禅儀
Zazenron 坐禅論
Zekkai Chūshin 絶海中津
Zen 禅
zengo 前語
Zenrin kushū 禅林句集
Zenrin segoshū 禅林世語集
zōbō 像法
Zudokko 塗毒鼓
Zuimonki 随聞記
Zuisenji 瑞泉寺

BIBLIOGRAPHY

Akamatsu Toshihide and Philip Yampolsky. "Muromachi Zen and the Gozan System." In John Whitney Hall and Toyoda Takeshi, eds., *Japan in the Muromachi Age*. Berkeley: University of California Press, 1977.

Akizuki Ryōmin 秋月龍珉. *Zen nyūmon* 禅入門 (Introduction to Zen). Tokyo: Chōbunsha, 1979.

Ariyoshi Sawako 有吉佐和子 and Kobori Nanrei 小堀南嶺. *Koji junrei: Daitokuji* 古寺巡礼・大徳寺 (Pilgrimages to old temples: Daitokuji). Tokyo: Tanbunsha, 1977.

Bakuryō hinmoku kaisetsu 曝涼品目解説 (Catalogue of aired scrolls). Kyoto: Daitokuji, 1982.

Barzun, Jacques. *On Writing, Editing, and Publishing*. Chicago: Chicago University Press, 1986.

Bielefeldt, Carl. "Recarving the Dragon: History and Dogma in the Study of Dōgen." In William R. LaFleur, ed., *Dōgen Studies*. Honolulu: University of Hawaii Press, 1985.

———. *Dōgen's Manuals of Zen Meditation*. Berkeley: University of California Press, 1988.

Blyth, R. H. *Haiku*. Vol. 1. Tokyo: Hokuseido, 1949.

Bussho Kankōkai 仏書刊行会. *Dai Nihon Bukkyō zenshū* 大日本仏教全集 (Complete works of Japanese Buddhism). Rev. ed., vol. 101. Tokyo: Meicho Fukyūkai, 1979.

Buswell, Robert E., Jr. "The 'Short-cut' Approach of *K'an-hua* Meditation: The Evolution of a Practical Subitism in Chinese Ch'an Buddhism." In Peter N. Gregory, ed., *Sudden and Gradual: Approaches to Enlightenment in Chinese Thought*. Honolulu: University of Hawaii Press, 1987.

Cleary, Thomas, trans. *The Original Face: An Anthology of Rinzai Zen*. New York: Grove Press, 1978.

————, trans. *Timeless Spring: A Sōtō Zen Anthology.* New York: Weatherhill, 1980.

————, trans. *Shōbōgenzō: Zen Essays by Dōgen.* Honolulu: University of Hawaii Press, 1986.

Cleary, Thomas, and J. C. Cleary, trans. *The Blue Cliff Record.* Boulder: Prajñā Press, 1978.

Collcutt, Martin. *Five Mountains: The Rinzai Zen Monastic Institution in Medieval Japan.* Cambridge: Harvard University Press, 1981.

Conze, Edward. *Buddhist Wisdom Books.* New York: Harper & Row, 1972.

————, trans. *The Short Prajñāpāramitā Texts.* London: Luzac & Co., 1973.

Cook, Francis H. "Dōgen's View of Authentic Selfhood." In William R. LaFleur, ed., *Dōgen Studies.* Honolulu: University of Hawaii Press, 1985.

Covell, Jon Carter. *Zen's Core: Ikkyu's Freedom.* Seoul: Hollym Corp., 1980.

Covell, Jon Carter, and Yamada Sōbin. *Zen at Daitoku-ji.* Tokyo: Kodansha International, 1974.

Daiki Sōyū 大亀宗雄, ed. *Ryūhōzan Daitokuji-shi* 龍寶山大德寺誌 (History of Ryūhōzan Daitokuji). Kyoto: Daitokuji, 1929.

Dai Nihon komonjo 大日本古文書 (Historical documents of Japan). *Iewake* 家分 (section) 17, vol. 1. Tokyo: Tokyo Imperial University, 1943.

Dai Nihon shiryō 大日本史料 (Historical materials of Japan). Vol. 6., nos. 1, 2. Tokyo: Tōkyō Daigaku Shiryō Hensanjo, 1901–1904.

Daitō Kokushi 大燈国師 (attributed). Untitled capping-phrase anthology. Calligraphic ms., no date.

Daitokuji 大德寺. *Daitokuji Zengoroku shūsei* 大德寺禅語録集成 (Zen discourse records of Daitokuji). Vol. 1. Kyoto: Hōzōkan, 1989.

Dean, Thomas. "Masao Abe's Zen and Western Thought." *The Eastern Buddhist* 22.2: 48–77 (Autumn 1989).

Donner, Neal. "Effort and Intuition: The Sudden and Gradual Reconsidered." *The Ten Directions* 2.3: 7–11 (October 1981).

Dumoulin, Heinrich. *Zen Buddhism: A History.* Vol. 2, *Japan.* New York: Macmillan, 1990.

Ebersole, Gary L. "The Buddhist Ritual Use of Linked Poetry in Medieval Japan." *The Eastern Buddhist* 16.2: 50–71 (Autumn 1983).

Faure, Bernard. "The Concept of One-Practice Samādhi in Early Ch'an." In Peter N. Gregory, ed., *Traditions of Meditation in Chinese Buddhism.* Honolulu: University of Hawaii Press, 1986.

————. "The Daruma-shū, Dōgen, and Sōtō Zen." *Monumenta Nipponica* 42.1: 25–55 (Spring 1987).

Fontein, Jan, and Money L. Hickman. *Zen Painting and Calligraphy.* Boston: Boston Museum of Fine Arts, 1970.

Foulk, T. Griffith. "The 'Ch'an School' and Its Place in the Buddhist Monastic Tradition." Ph.D. dissertation, University of Michigan, 1987.

————. "The Zen Institution in Modern Japan." In Kenneth Kraft, ed., *Zen: Tradition and Transition.* New York: Grove Press, 1988.

Franck, Frederick, ed. *The Buddha Eye.* New York: Crossroad, 1982.

Fujita Genro 藤田玄路, ed. *Zudokko* 塗毒鼓 (Poison-painted Drum). Kyoto: Kennin Sōdō, 1980.

Furuta Shōkin 古田紹欽. *Nihon Bukkyō shisō-shi no shōmondai* 日本仏教思想史の諸問題 (Problems in the intellectual history of Japanese Buddhism). Tokyo: Shunjusha, 1964.

————. *Zensō no shōji* 禅僧の生死 (Lives of Zen monks). Tokyo: Shunjusha, 1971.

————. "Kaisetsu" 解説 (Explanation). In Nakada Yujirō 中田勇次郎, ed., *Shodō geijutsu* 書道芸術 (Calligraphic arts), vol. 17. Tokyo: Chūō Kōronsha, 1975.

————. *Bassui* 抜隊 (Bassui). *Nihon no Zen goroku* 日本の禅語録 (Zen discourse records of Japan). Vol. 11. Tokyo: Kōdansha, 1979.

Gimello, Robert M. "Poetry and the *Kung-an* in Ch'an Practice." *The Ten Directions* 7.1: 9–11 (Spring/Summer 1986).

————. "Wen-tzu Ch'an and K'an-hua Ch'an: Buddhism in the Transition from Northern to Southern Sung Literati Culture." Unpublished paper, 1991.

Goble, Andrew. "Go-Daigo and the Kemmu Restoration." Ph.D. dissertation, Stanford University, 1987.

————. "Truth, Contradiction and Harmony in Medieval Japan: Emperor Hanazono (1297–1348) and Buddhism." *Journal of the International Association of Buddhist Studies* 12.1: 21–63 (1989).

Gregory, Peter N., ed. *Traditions of Meditation in Chinese Buddhism*. Honolulu: University of Hawaii Press, 1986.

————, ed. *Sudden and Gradual: Approaches to Enlightenment in Chinese Thought*. Honolulu: University of Hawaii Press, 1987.

Haga Kōshirō 芳賀幸四郎. *Chūsei Zenrin no gakumon oyobi bungaku ni kansuru kenkyū* 中世禅林の学問および文学に関する研究 (Research concerning medieval Zen scholarship and literature). Kyoto: Shibunkaku, 1981.

Haga Kōshirō et al. "Japanese Zen." *The Eastern Buddhist* 10.2: 76–101 (Spring 1977).

Hall, John Whitney, and Toyoda Takeshi, eds. *Japan in the Muromachi Age*. Berkeley: University of California Press, 1977.

Hekiganshū koshō 碧巌集古鈔 (Classic notes on the *Blue Cliff Record*). 10 vols. Woodblock ms., no date.

Hirano Sōjō 平野宗浄. "Daitō Kokushi agyo no kenkyū: I" 大燈国師下語の研究: I (Research on Daitō Kokushi's capping phrases: I). *Zenbunka kenkyūjo kiyō* 禅文化研究所紀要 (Annual report from the Institute for Zen Studies) 3: 43–74 (October 1971).

————. "Daitō Kokushi agyo no kenkyū: II." *Zenbunka kenkyūjo kiyō* 4: 141–186 (June 1972).

————. *Daitō Zen no tankyū* 大燈禅の探求 (In search of Daitō's Zen). Tokyo: Kyōiku Shinchōsha, 1974.

————. "Daitō Kokushi *Hasonshukuyawa* no kenkyū" 大燈国師破尊宿夜話の研究 (Research on Daitō Kokushi's *Defeating a Priest in an Evening Talk*). In Zenbunka kenkyūjo 禅文化研究所, *Zengaku ronkō* 禅学論攷 (Discourses in Zen studies). Kyoto: Shibunkaku, 1977.

————. *Daitō* 大燈 (Daitō). *Nihon no Zen goroku*, vol. 6. Tokyo: Kōdansha, 1978.

————. *Ikkyū Sōjun* 一休宗純 (Ikkyū Sōjun). Tokyo: Meicho Fukyūkai, 1981.

————. *Daitō Kokushi goroku* 大燈国師語録 (Record of Daitō Kokushi). 2 vols. Kyoto: Shibunkaku, 1986.

————. "Den Daitō senkushū" 伝大燈撰句集 (An anthology of selected phrases attributed to Daitō). *Zenbunka kenkyūjo kiyō* 15: 561–600 (December 1988).

————, ed. *Ryūhōzan Daitokuzenji seifu* 龍寶山大德禅寺世譜 (Genealogy of Ryūhōzan Daitokuji). Rev. ed. Kyoto: Shibunkaku, 1979.

Hoffmann, Yoel. *Every End Exposed*. Brookline, Mass.: Autumn Press, 1977.

————. *The Sound of the One Hand*. Rev. ed. New York: Bantam Books, 1977.

Hurvitz, Leon, trans. *Scripture of the Lotus Blossom of the Fine Dharma*. New York: Columbia University Press, 1976.

Iwahashi Koyata 岩橋小弥太. *Hanazono Tennō* 花園天皇 (Emperor Hanazono). Tokyo: Yoshikawa Kobunkan, 1962.

Kagamishima Genryū 鏡島元隆 et al. *Yakuchū Zen'en shingi* 訳註禅苑清規 (Pure regulations of Zen monasteries, annotated). Tokyo: Sōtōshū Shūmuchō, 1979.

Kageki Hideo 蔭木英雄. *Gozanshi-shi no kenkyū* 五山詩史の研究 (Research on the history of Five Mountains poetry). Tokyo: Kasama Shoin, 1977.

Kajitani Sōnin 梶谷宗忍. *Shūmon kattōshū* 宗門葛藤集 (Collected koans of the [Zen] sect). Kyoto: Hōzōkan, 1982.

Kamimura Kankō 上村觀光, ed. *Gozan bungaku zenshū* 五山文学全集 (Complete literature of the Five Mountains). Vol. 3. Tokyo: Gozan Bungaku Zenshū Kankōkai, 1936.

Kapleau, Philip. *The Three Pillars of Zen*. Rev. ed. Garden City, N.Y.: Anchor Press/Doubleday, 1980.

Kasulis, Thomas P. *Zen Action/Zen Person*. Honolulu: University of Hawaii Press, 1981.

————. "The Incomparable Philosopher: Dōgen on How to Read the *Shōbōgenzō*." In William R. LaFleur, ed., *Dōgen Studies*. Honolulu: University of Hawaii Press, 1985.

Katō Ryūhō 加藤隆芳. "Rinzaishū ni okeru zendō no seikatsu" 臨済宗における禅堂の生活 (Life in Rinzai Zen meditation halls). In Nishitani Keiji 西谷啓治, ed., *Zen no jissen* 禅の実践 (Zen practice). *Kōza Zen* 講座禅 (Symposium on Zen). Vol. 2. Tokyo. Chikuma Shobō, 1967.

Katō Shōshun 加藤正俊. "Kanzan Egen-den no shiryōhihan" 関山慧玄伝の史料批判 (Critique of materials on the biography of Kanzan Egen). *Zenbunka kenkyūjo kiyō* 4: 1–30 (June 1972).

————. "Kakushū Daitō-den no idō ni tsuite" 各種大燈伝の異同に就いて (Differences among various biographies of Daitō). *Zenbunka kenkyūjo kiyō* 7: 77–90 (September 1975).

Katō Shū'ichi 加藤周一 and Yanagida Seizan 柳田聖山. *Ikkyū* 一休 (Ikkyū). *Nihon no Zen goroku*, vol. 12. Tokyo: Kōdansha, 1978.

Keene, Donald. "The Comic Tradition in Renga." In John Whitney Hall and Toyoda Takeshi, eds., *Japan in the Muromachi Age*. Berkeley: University of California Press, 1977.

————, trans. *Essays in Idleness: The Tsurezuregusa of Kenkō*. New York: Columbia University Press, 1967.

Kim, Hee-jin. *Dōgen Kigen—Mystical Realist.* Tucson: University of Arizona Press, 1980.

Kodera, Takashi James. *Dogen's Formative Years in China.* Boulder: Prajñā Press, 1980.

Kraft, Kenneth, trans. "Musō Kokushi's *Dialogues in a Dream.*" *The Eastern Buddhist* 14.1: 75–93 (Spring 1981).

———, ed. *Zen: Tradition and Transition.* New York: Grove Press, 1988.

Kyoto National Museum. *Zen no bijutsu* 禅の美術 (Zen art). Kyoto: Ōtsuka Kōgei, 1981.

LaFleur, William R., trans. *Mirror for the Moon.* New York: New Directions, 1978.

———, ed. *Dōgen Studies.* Honolulu: University of Hawaii Press, 1985.

Lau, D. C., trans. *Mencius.* Middlesex: Penguin Books, 1970.

Leggett, Trevor. *Zen and the Ways.* Boulder: Shambhala, 1978.

———. *The Warrior Koans: Early Zen in Japan.* London: Routledge & Kegan Paul, 1985.

Maraldo, John C. "Is There Historical Consciousness within Ch'an?" *Japanese Journal of Religious Studies* 12.2: 141–171 (1985).

Maruoka Sōnan 丸岡宗男 et al. *Daitokuji bokuseki zenshū* 大德寺墨蹟全集 (Complete calligraphy of Daitokuji). Vol. 1. Tokyo: Asahi Shinbunsha, 1984.

Matsunaga, Daigan, and Alicia Matsunaga. *Foundation of Japanese Buddhism.* 2 vols. Los Angeles: Buddhist Books International, 1974–1976.

McCullough, Helen Craig, trans. *The Taiheiki: A Chronicle of Medieval Japan.* Tokyo: Charles E. Tuttle, 1979.

McRae, John R. *The Northern School and the Formation of Early Ch'an Buddhism.* Honolulu: University of Hawaii Press, 1986.

———. "Ch'an Commentaries on the *Heart Sūtra*: Preliminary Inferences on the Permutation of Chinese Buddhism." *Journal of the International Association of Buddhist Studies* 11.2: 85–115 (1988).

Miller, Stephen D. "Religious Boundaries in Aesthetic Domains: A Study of Buddhist Poetry (*Shakkyō-ka*) in the Late Heian and Early Kamakura Periods." Unpublished paper, 1990.

Miura, Isshū, and Ruth F. Sasaki. *Zen Dust.* New York: Harcourt, Brace & World, 1966.

Miyauchi Sotai 宮裡祖泰 et al. *Kokuyaku Zengaku taisei* 国訳禅学大成 (Collected Zen works in Japanese translation). Vol. 23. Tokyo: Nimatsudō Shoten, 1930.

Morita Shiryū 森田子龍, ed. *Bokubi* 墨美 (Beauty of calligraphy). No. 165. Kyoto: Bokubisha, 1967.

Morrell, Robert E. *Sand and Pebbles* (*Shasekishū*). Albany: State University of New York Press, 1985.

Morris, Ivan. *The Nobility of Failure: Tragic Heroes in the History of Japan.* New York: New American Library, 1975.

Nakada Yujirō 中田勇次郎, ed. *Shodō geijutsu* 書道芸術 (Calligraphic arts). Vol. 17. Tokyo: Chūō Kōronsha, 1975.

Nakatsuka Eijirō 中塚栄次郎, ed. *Shinkishū* 宸記集 (Imperial records [diary of Emperor Hanazono]). Vol. 2. Tokyo: Reisei Zenshū Hensankai, 1917.

Nanjo Banyū 南条文雄 et al. *Dai Nihon Bukkyō zensho* 大日本仏教全書 (Complete works of Japanese Buddhism). Vols. 102, 108, 109. Tokyo: Bussho Hangyōkai, 1917.

Ogisu Jundō 荻須純道. *Musō, Daitō* 夢窓・大燈 (Musō, Daitō). Rev. ed. Tokyo: Kōbundō Shobō, 1944.

————. *Nihon chūsei Zenshū-shi* 日本中世禅宗史 (History of medieval Japanese Zen). Tokyo: Mokujisha, 1965.

————. "Daitō" 大燈. In Nishitani Keiji 西谷啓治, ed., *Zen no rekishi: Nihon* 禅の歴史・日本 (History of Zen: Japan). *Kōza Zen*, vol. 4. Tokyo: Chikuma Shobō, 1967.

————, ed. *Zen to Nihon bunka no shōmondai* 禅と日本文化の諸問題 (Problems in Zen and Japanese culture). Kyoto: Heirakuji Shoten, 1969.

Ōkubo Dōshū 大久保道舟, ed. *Dōgen Zenji zenshū* 道元禅師全集 (Complete works of Zen Master Dōgen). 2 vols. Tokyo: Chikuma Shobō, 1969–1970.

Okuda Shōzō 奥田正造, ed. *Kōzen Daitō Kokushi nenpu* 興禅大燈国師年譜 (Biography of Kōzen Daitō Kokushi). Tokyo: Morie Shoten, 1933.

Ōta Zen 太田ぜん, ed. *Shiryō sanshū: Hanazono Tennō shinki* 史料纂集・花園天皇宸記 (Compilation of historical documents: diary of Emperor Hanazono). 3 vols. Tokyo: Heibunsha, 1982.

Pollack, David. *Zen Poems of the Five Mountains*. New York: Crossroad, 1985.

————. *The Fracture of Meaning: Japan's Synthesis of China from the Eighth Through the Eighteenth Centuries*. Princeton: Princeton University Press, 1986.

Raiba Takudō 采馬琢道, ed. *Zenshū seiten* 禅宗聖典 (Zen scriptures). Kyoto: Heirakuji Shoten, 1976.

Sanae Kensei 早苗憲生. "Yomogisa Bunkobon *Shōichi kanahōgo* no kenkyū: I" 蓬左文庫本「聖一假名法語」の研究 (Research on the *Vernacular Sermons of Shōichi* in the Yomogisa archives: I). *Zenbunka kenkyūjo kiyō* 6: 265–294 (May 1974).

Sanford, James H. *Zen-man Ikkyū*. Chico, Calif.: Scholars Press, 1981.

Sansom, George. *A History of Japan to 1334*. Tokyo: Charles E. Tuttle, 1979.

Sasaki, Ruth F., trans. *The Record of Lin-chi*. Kyoto: Institute for Zen Studies, 1975.

Sekida, Katsuki. *Two Zen Classics*. New York: Weatherhill, 1977.

Shibayama, Zenkei. *Zen Comments on the Mumonkan*. New York: The New American Library, 1975.

Shibayama Zenkei 柴山全慶, ed. *Gōko fugetsu shū* 江湖風月集 (Zen wind and moon [poetry] collection). Osaka: Sōgensha, 1975.

————, ed. *Zenrin kushū* 禅林句集 (Zen phrase anthology). Rev. ed. Kyoto: Kichūdō, 1980.

Shigematsu, Sōiku. *A Zen Forest*. New York: Weatherhill, 1981.

————. *A Zen Harvest*. San Francisco: North Point, 1988.

The Shorter Oxford English Dictionary. Vol. 1. Oxford: Clarendon Press, 1988.

Sōji 宗二, ed. *Hekigan kugi* 碧巌口義 (Spoken meaning of the *Blue Cliff Record*). 10 vols. Calligraphic ms., 1560.

Suzuki Daisetsu 鈴木大拙. "Nihon Zen shisōshi no ichidanmen" 日本禅思想史の一断面 (One step in the history of Japanese Zen thought). In *Suzuki*

Daisetsu zenshū 鈴木大拙全集 (Complete works of Suzuki Daisetsu). Vol. 4. Tokyo: Iwanami Shoten, 1968.

―――. *Suzuki Daisetsu zenshū* 鈴木大拙全集 (Complete works of Suzuki Daisetsu). Vol. 4. Tokyo: Iwanami Shoten, 1968.

Suzuki, D. T. (Suzuki Daisetsu) *Manual of Zen Buddhism*. Rev. ed. New York: Grove Press, 1960.

―――. *Japanese Spirituality*. Trans. Norman Waddell. Tokyo: Japan Ministry of Education, 1972.

―――. *Zen and Japanese Culture*. Princeton: Princeton University Press, 1973.

Suzuki, Shunryu. *Zen Mind, Beginner's Mind*. New York: Weatherhill, 1977.

Takakusu Junjirō 高楠順次郎 et al. *Taishō shinshū daizōkyō* 大正新修大蔵経 (Taishō era edition of the Buddhist canon). Vols. 8, 47, 48, 51, 80, 81. Tokyo: Daizō Shuppan, 1924–1932.

Takenuki Genshō 竹貫元勝. "Rinka ni okeru kyōdan keiei ni tsuite" 林下における教国経営について (Sectarian organization in the *rinka* group of Zen monasteries). *Bukkyōshigaku* 仏教史学 (Journal of the history of Buddhism) 15.2: 105–143 (October 1971).

Takeuchi Yoshinori, "The Philosophy of Nishida." In Frederick Franck, ed., *The Buddha Eye*. New York: Crossroad, 1982.

Tamamura Takeji 玉村竹二. *Musō Kokushi* 夢窓国師 (Musō Kokushi). Rev. ed. Kyoto: Heirakuji Shoten, 1977.

Tayama Hōnan 田山方南, ed. *Daitokuji* 大徳寺. *Hihō* 秘宝 (Treasures). Vol. 11. Tokyo: Kōdansha, 1968.

Tsuchiya Etsudō 土屋悦堂, ed. *Zenrin segoshū* 禅林世語集 (Anthology of Zen phrases in Japanese). Kyoto: Kichūdō, 1981.

Tsuji Zennosuke 辻善之助. *Buke jidai to Zensō* 武家時代と禅僧 (The warrior era and Zen monks). Tokyo: Sōgensha, 1932.

Varley, H. Paul. *Imperial Restoration in Medieval Japan*. New York: Columbia University Press, 1971.

―――. "Ashikaga Yoshimitsu and the World of Kitayama: Social Change and Shogunal Patronage in Early Muromachi Japan." In John Whitney Hall and Toyoda Takeshi, eds., *Japan in the Muromachi Age*. Berkeley: University of California Press, 1977.

―――, trans. *A Chronicle of Gods and Sovereigns*. New York: Columbia University Press, 1980.

Waddell, Norman, trans. "Wild Ivy (*Itsumadegusa*): The Spiritual Autobiography of Hakuin Ekaku (II). *The Eastern Buddhist* 16.1: 107–139 (Spring 1983).

Waddell, Norman, and Abe Masao, trans. "Dōgen's *Bendōwa*." *The Eastern Buddhist* 4.1: 124–158 (May 1971).

Watson, Burton. "Zen Poetry." In Kenneth Kraft, ed., *Zen: Tradition and Transition*. New York: Grove Press, 1988.

Webster's New International Dictionary. Springfield, Mass.: G. & C. Merriam, 1937.

Wright, Dale S. "Rethinking Transcendence: The Role of Language in Zen Experience." Unpublished paper, 1991.

Wu, John C. H. *The Golden Age of Zen*. Taipei: United Publishing Center, 1975.

Yamada Yoshio 山田孝雄 et al. *Konjaku monogatari shū* 今昔物語集 (Tales of times now past). *Nihon koten bungaku taikei* 日本古典文学大系 (Outline of Classical Japanese Literature). Vol. 4. Tokyo: Iwanami Shoten, 1962.

Yampolsky, Philip, trans. *The Platform Sutra of the Sixth Patriarch*. New York: Columbia University Press, 1967.

―――. "The Development of Japanese Zen." In Kenneth Kraft, ed., *Zen: Tradition and Transition*. New York: Grove Press, 1988.

Yanagida Seizan. "Japanese Zen and the Turning of the Seasons." Trans. Dennis Hirota. *Chanoyu Quarterly* 55: 13–31 (1988).

Yanagida Seizan 柳田聖山. *Rinzai no kafū* 臨済の家風. (Rinzai [Zen] styles). Tokyo: Chikuma Shobō, 1967.

―――. *Rinzai roku* 臨済録 (Record of Rinzai [Lin-chi]). *Butten kōza* 仏典講座 (Symposium on Buddhist texts). Vol. 30. Tokyo: Daizō Shuppan, 1972.

―――. *Ikkyū: Kyōunshū no sekai* 一休「狂雲集」の世界 (Ikkyū: World of the *Crazy Cloud Collection*). Kyoto: Jinbun Shoin, 1980.

―――. *Daruma* ダルマ (Bodhidharma). Tokyo: Kōdansha, 1981.

Yanagida Seizan and Katō Shōshun. *Hakuin* 白隠 (Hakuin). Kyoto: Kōdansha, 1979.

Yanagida Seizan and Umehara Takeshi 梅原猛. *Mu no tankyū* 無の探求 (In search of *mu*). Rev. ed. Tokyo: Kadokawa Shoten, 1980.

Yasuraoka Kōsaku 安良岡康作. "Kenkō no tonsei seikatsu to *Tsurezuregusa* no seiritsu" 兼好の遁世生活とつれづれ草の成立 (Kenkō's life as a recluse and the composition of *Essays in Idleness*). *Bungaku* 文学 (Literature) 26.9: 30–40 (September 1958).

Yokoyama Hideya 横山秀哉. *Zen no kenchiku* 禅の建築 (Zen architecture). Tokyo: Shōkokusha, 1967.

Yuho Yokoi, trans. *Regulations for Monastic Life by Eihei Dogen*. Tokyo: Sankibo Busshorin, 1973.

INDEX

About the Author

Kenneth Kraft is associate professor of Japanese religions at Lehigh University in Bethlehem, Pennsylvania. A graduate of Harvard University, he received his M.A. from the University of Michigan and his Ph.D. from Princeton University. He is the editor of two books, *Zen: Tradition and Transition* (1988) and *Inner Peace, World Peace: Essays on Buddhism and Nonviolence* (1992).

Production Notes

Composition and paging were done on the
Quadex Composing System and typesetting
on the Compugraphic 8400 by the design
and production staff of University of
Hawaii Press.

The text typeface is Baskerville and the
display typeface is Compugraphic Optima.

Offset presswork and binding were done by
The Maple-Vail Book Manufacturing Group.
Text paper is Writers RR Offset,
basis 50.